BOUNDARIES A

Boundaries and Allegiances

Problems of Justice and Responsibility in Liberal Thought

SAMUEL SCHEFFLER

OXFORD
UNIVERSITY PRESS

OXFORD

UNIVERSITY PRESS

Great Clarendon Street, Oxford OX2 6DP

Oxford University Press is a department of the University of Oxford.
It furthers the University's objective of excellence in research, scholarship,
and education by publishing worldwide in

Oxford New York

Auckland Bangkok Buenos Aires Cape Town Chennai
Dar es Salaam Delhi Hong Kong Istanbul Karachi Kolkata
Kuala Lumpur Madrid Melbourne Mexico City Mumbai Nairobi
São Paulo Shanghai Singapore Taipei Tokyo Toronto

Oxford is a registered trade mark of Oxford University Press
in the UK and in certain other countries

Published in the United States
by Oxford University Press Inc., New York

British Library Cataloguing in Publication Data

Data available

Library of Congress Cataloging in Publication Data
Scheffler, Samuel
Boundaries and allegiances: problems of justice and responsibility in liberal thought /
Samuel Scheffler.
p. cm.
Includes bibliographical references and index.
1. Liberalism.   2. Justice.   3. Responsibility.   4. Globalization.   I. Title.
JC574.S34 2001   320.51—dc21   00-064988
ISBN 0-19-924149-X (hbk)
ISBN 0-19-925767-1 (pbk)

1 3 5 7 9 10 8 6 4 2

Typeset by Graphicraft Ltd, Hong Kong
Printed in Great Britain by
TJ International, Padstow, Cornwall

For Adam and Gabe

CONTENTS

INTRODUCTION

The revival of English-language moral and political philosophy in the late 1960s and early 1970s took place against the backdrop of intense social conflict and rapid social change. The social and political controversies of that era were reflected in the topics that captured the attention of moral and political philosophers writing at the time. During a period of widespread protests against the Vietnam War, philosophers turned their attention to issues of civil disobedience, conscientious objection, and the morality of warfare. With sexual mores undergoing a radical transformation and feminism emerging as an increasingly important social force, philosophers produced a significant body of work on the ethics of abortion. As political activism increased among black Americans in the wake of the civil rights movement, philosophers started to address questions of affirmative action and preferential treatment. With the welfare state in the ascendancy throughout the western world, distributive justice became one of the central preoccupations of philosophical theorizing, especially after the publication of John Rawls's *A Theory of Justice*. And with the United States and the Soviet Union locked in a global ideological struggle, moral and political philosophers in the Anglo-American tradition debated the justice of capitalism and socialism, and displayed a renewed interest in Marx and Marxism.

The resurgence of interest in moral and political philosophy continued unabated through the end of the twentieth century. But by the last decade of the century, social and political conditions had changed dramatically in various respects, and those changes too were reflected in the writings of philosophers. With the end of the Cold War, the rise of nationalism and identity politics, and the increasing pressure—much of it technology-driven—toward greater globalization of the economy, some of the topics that had preoccupied philosophers in the preceding decades began to receive less attention, while new topics emerged to take their place. As the conflicts surrounding the war in Vietnam faded into memory, less work was done on civil disobedience and the morality of warfare. With the collapse of the Soviet Union, interest in Marx and Marxism waned, and fewer discussions were cast as contributions to the debate between capitalism and socialism. Instead, a great deal of work was devoted to exploring the foundations of liberal thought and debating the merits of rival versions of liberal theory. In addition, philosophers began investigating the suddenly pressing challenges to liberalism posed by questions of gender and by a variety of positions—such as nationalism, communitarianism, and multiculturalism—that emphasize the importance of particularistic allegiances and identifications. At the same time, philosophers' sensitivity to globalizing pressures was reflected in increased attention to issues of international justice, cosmopolitanism, and the 'law of peoples'.

Although philosophers in the analytic tradition sometimes exaggerate the intellectual autonomy of their subject, there is nothing either surprising or unwelcome about the tendency for work in moral and political philosophy to be influenced by the moral and political concerns of the larger culture. Of course, philosophy has its own methods and traditions of thought, and philosophical inquiry differs from other forms of intellectual investigation in significant ways. Nevertheless, philosophers belong to the broader culture and are, perforce, participants in the conversation of that culture. On the one hand, their work is bound to be influenced—in ways they are not always in a position to identify—by the problems and circumstances of the culture at large. On the other hand, their work is itself a contribution to that culture, and may have effects outside of philosophy that can also be difficult to identify. All of this is especially evident in the case of moral and political philosophy, and certainly work in these areas that was thoroughly insulated from the changing circumstances and predicaments of human societies would have little to recommend it.

This book is a collection of eleven essays, ten of which were written during the 1990s. The eleventh was written a few years earlier. Not surprisingly, all of the essays reflect characteristic philosophical preoccupations of the period in which they were written. They deal with a cluster of related issues and themes, and the continuities among them are sufficiently strong that it seemed to me to make sense to bring them together within the covers of a single volume. At the most abstract level, the main topic of this volume is the capacity of liberal thought, and of the moral traditions on which it draws, to accommodate a variety of challenges posed by the changing circumstances of the modern world. Almost all of the essays are concerned, in one way or another, with what might be thought of as questions about the distribution of responsibility. That is, they are concerned with questions about how, at a time when people's lives are structured by social arrangements and institutions of ever-increasing size, complexity, and scope, we can best conceive of the responsibilities of individual agents and the normative significance of individual commitments and allegiances. Some of the essays are primarily concerned with the role of individual desert in liberal theorizing about the justice of large social institutions. Others focus on the nature of people's special responsibilities to their families, communities, and societies, and assess the compatibility of such responsibilities with liberal ideas of justice and equality. Still others deal with the possibility of developing a liberal conception of justice that acknowledges the normative significance of social and global interdependencies, while reaffirming the values of personal life and the continuing importance of ideas of individual responsibility.

The first essay, 'Responsibility, Reactive Attitudes, and Liberalism in Philosophy and Politics', considers the relation between contemporary liberal theories and liberalism as a position in American political life. In American politics, the term 'liberalism' is associated with a cluster of ideas and policies that, taken together, represent only one strand of liberal thought more broadly construed. At the time when this essay was written, the Soviet Union was in the process of disintegrating, thus providing liberalism in the broader sense with what was widely perceived as a kind of political vindication. Yet liberalism in the narrower sense had not been faring well in the Ámerican political arena. The essay was written in 1991, toward the end of a twelve-year period during which the Republican party controlled the American presidency. During that period, many of the social and political programmes favored by American liberals were eliminated or scaled back, and the very word 'liberal' was treated by the Republicans as a term of derision. In Great Britain, where the relevant political parties and outlooks go by different labels, a similar ideological change nevertheless took place during roughly the same period. The essay observes that the conservative attack on the liberal position in American politics traded on a perception that the policies associated with that position tend to undermine traditional notions of individual responsibility. Although many defenders of those policies would argue that this perception is unfounded, the essay points out that the concept of desert has a limited role to play in contemporary versions of liberal theory and, in this respect at least, such theories themselves rely on a reduced conception of individual responsibility.

The essay goes on to argue that liberal theorists' scepticism about desert may derive partly from the influence of naturalism within contemporary thought, an influence that reflects the enormous intellectual prestige of modern science. Without claiming that such scepticism is unfounded, the essay nevertheless suggests that liberal theorists may underestimate the human significance of the attitudes that find expression through judgements of desert. To the extent that that is so, it argues, there is a tension between philosophical accounts of liberalism and some deeply entrenched ideas about responsibility. However this tension may be resolved at the level of philosophical reflection, the essay concludes that the political prospects of American liberalism may in part depend on the capacity of liberal politicians to identify themselves with conceptions of individual responsibility that differ in some important respects from the ones embodied in contemporary liberal theories. In light of this speculation, it is interesting to note that, when the Democratic party recaptured the American presidency in 1992, it did so after an election campaign in which it emphasized traditional notions of individual responsibility and played down its commitment to some of the policies that are said by conservatives to undermine responsibility.

Whereas the first essay suggests that contemporary naturalism poses a threat to some traditional ideas about responsibility, and that this threat creates difficulties for liberalism both in theory and in practice, the second essay, 'Individual Responsibility in a Global Age', considers a growing threat to a different aspect of our thinking about responsibility. Common-sense moral thought sees the duties of individual agents—what might be called their *normative responsibilities*—as limited in certain significant ways. Individuals are thought to be more responsible for what they do than for what they merely fail to prevent, and they are thought to have greater responsibilities toward some people than toward others. These restrictions serve, in effect, to limit the size of the individual agent's moral world. Although they may seem so basic to moral thought as scarcely to require comment, I argue in this essay that the seeming naturalness of these restrictions is supported by a complex phenomenology of agency, and by a largely implicit conception of human relations as consisting primarily in small-scale interactions among independent individual agents. Yet these aspects of our self-understanding are under growing pressure from a variety of global developments that have served both to highlight and to reinforce the extensive interdependencies of modern life.

Up to a point, these developments appear to support a more expansive conception of individual responsibility. This essay argues, however, that there are deep reasons for doubting whether a radically expansive conception of individual responsibility could ever replace the common-sense conception. The more significant effect of an emphasis on global interdependencies, it argues, may be to raise doubts about the very practice of treating the individual agent as the primary bearer of normative responsibility. Since there is no obvious alternative to that practice, however, such an emphasis may in the end pose a general threat to our deployment of the categories of normative responsibility. The essay also argues that the competing tendencies in our world toward greater political and economic integration, on the one hand, and greater communal identification and fragmentation, on the other, serve both to intensify and to reflect the conflict between more and less expansive conceptions of normative responsibility. In this way, these tendencies may be viewed as symptomatic of the instability in our current thinking about responsibility.

The third essay, 'Families, Nations, and Strangers', examines in greater detail one aspect of that instability, and emphasizes the way it is both reflected in and exacerbated by the conflicting tendencies toward global integration and communal identification. This essay discusses the status in moral thought of 'associative duties', which are duties that the members of significant social groups and the participants in close personal relationships are often thought to have toward one another. Associative duties occupy a central place in ordinary moral thought, but they remain controversial in various respects, and this essay explores two different objections to them. The voluntarist objection views associative duties as potentially burdensome, and says that they are legitimate only when they arise from the voluntary choices or actions of those to whom they are ascribed. The distributive objection, by contrast, sees them as providing additional benefits, in the form of increased claims to one another's assistance, to the participants in otherwise rewarding groups and relationships, and regards them as potentially unfair to outsiders and non-participants. The voluntarist objection is reflected in some common criticisms of 'ascriptive' or 'essentialist' claims of identity, and also in liberal objections to various forms of nationalism and communitarianism. The distributive objection features in a familiar justice-based critique of the morality of affluence; it questions the extent to which the members of affluent families, groups, and societies are justified in giving one another's interests priority over the interests of those who are less fortunate. Whereas the voluntarist objection is rooted in an ideal of freedom and autonomy, the distributive objection is rooted in a principle of equality. To the extent that we share these values, both objections may seem to us to have some force. Yet most of us also believe that our family relations and social affiliations can be a source of responsibilities that do not derive solely from choices we have made, and so associative duties continue to be seen as a central component of moral experience. The upshot, I argue in this essay, is that both associative duties and the values that generate objections to them exert some influence within our moral outlook. Accordingly, there is the potential for genuine conflict in our thinking about the extent of our responsibilities to different individuals and groups. In so far as the simultaneous tendencies toward greater global integration and greater communal identification raise questions about the boundaries and distribution of such responsibilities, they lend urgency to the controversies about associative duties.

The next three essays continue the discussion of associative duties (or 'special responsibilities', as I prefer to say in the later essays). In 'Liberalism, Nationalism, and Egalitarianism', I observe that, although liberalism in one form or another is the dominant position in contemporary political philosophy, liberal theories have lately been subject to vigorous criticism from both globalist and particularist perspectives. I note that these criticisms are closely related to the debates about associative duties discussed in the previous essay, and I argue that, by attending to those debates, we can see how the globalist and particularist criticisms point to two different tensions within liberal thought. The globalist criticism points to a tension within liberalism between a conviction that all people everywhere are of equal worth, and a conviction that the members of a society are obligated to give the interests of other members priority over the interests of non-members. The particularist criticism points to a tension in much liberal thought and practice between the idea that the free choices of individuals are the source of the privileges and responsibilities of citizenship, and the idea that the members of an individual society constitute a national group whose privileges and responsibilities are transmitted from one generation to the next as a matter of birthright. I go on to argue, however, that the existence of these tensions is not fatal to liberalism. Instead, the two tensions highlight liberalism's commitment to diverse values whose joint accommodation is genuinely problematic, but none of which can easily be abandoned. This commitment to diverse values does not mean, as some critics have suggested, that liberalism suffers from a kind of theoretical incoherence or, as other critics have suggested, that it is misguided to seek a reasoned accommodation among the values that liberals prize. Instead, the essay concludes that the attempt to work out such an accommodation is in part a practical rather than a theoretical task, requiring the modification of existing practices and institutional arrangements and the development of new ones. As such, it is a task of an entirely familiar kind, for the need to accommodate diverse values is endemic to human practical reasoning.

'The Conflict between Justice and Responsibility', the fifth essay, deals with the bearing of debates about special responsibilities on issues of global justice. People sometimes invoke their special responsibilities to their families, communities, and societies as a way of justifying their resistance to claims of global justice and demonstrating that such resistance is not motivated by mere selfishness. This essay addresses the question of whether the 'distributive objection' provides advocates of global justice with an effective way of rebutting these appeals to special responsibilities. After considering several possible rejoinders to the distributive objection, the essay concludes that the objection cannot serve as the basis for a repudiation of special responsibilities. However, the concerns underlying the distributive objection remain legitimate ones, and the real force of the objection is to suggest that the tension between our commitment to special responsibilities and our commitment to equality is more problematic than we sometimes like to suppose. In effect, then, the distributive objection calls attention to the need for better integration among our values. The essay concludes with a brief consideration of some of the obstacles, both practical and theoretical, that need to be overcome if a concern for global justice is to be reconciled with a commitment to the moral significance of personal attachments and group affiliations.

Although the third, fourth, and fifth essays discuss the content of special responsibilities, assess the force of two fundamental objections to them, review some standard ways of defending them, and insist on their central place in moral thought, those essays do not put forward a positive account of the basis for special responsibilities. Such an account is developed in the sixth essay, 'Relationships and Responsibilities', which defends the view that participation in groups and personal relationships sometimes gives rise to responsibilities that cannot be reduced to obligations deriving from promises or agreements, or from any other discrete interactions among the participants. This essay begins by arguing that to attach non-instrumental value to one's relationship with a particular person just is, in part, to see that person's needs, interests, and desires as providing one with reasons for action, reasons that one would not have had in the absence of the relationship. In this sense, to value one's relationships non-instrumentally is already to see them as sources of special responsibilities. Of course, to say that people see themselves as having such responsibilities is not yet to say that they actually do have them. The essay goes on to argue, however, that one's relationships to other people give rise to special responsibilities when they are relationships that one has reason to value. After developing this 'non-reductionist' position in greater detail, the essay returns to the voluntarist and distributive objections. It argues that non-reductionism need not be insensitive to the concerns underlying those objections, but that the non-reductionist view makes it evident why neither objection can support the complete repudiation of unreduced special responsibilities.

The seventh essay, 'Conceptions of Cosmopolitanism', discusses the revival of interest within contemporary political philosophy in the idea of cosmopolitanism. It distinguishes between cosmopolitanism about justice and cosmopolitanism about culture, and identifies moderate and extreme versions of each of these views. The distinction between the moderate and extreme versions depends in each case on how the normative status of particular interpersonal relationships and group affiliations is understood. Drawing on the defence of special responsibilities in the preceding essay, I argue here that extreme forms of cosmopolitanism are untenable, in so far as they deny that relationships and affiliations can ever provide independent reasons for action or generate special responsibilities to one's intimates and associates. Moderate cosmopolitanism, on the other hand, is much more plausible. Yet there are certain difficulties that confront even the moderate forms of cosmopolitanism about justice and culture. In discussing these difficulties, I expand on one of the themes of 'Liberalism, Nationalism, and Egalitarianism', and argue that the task of defending moderate cosmopolitanism should not be thought of as a narrowly philosophical undertaking. Instead, the vindication of moderate cosmopolitanism about either justice or culture will require the exercise of creativity and imagination in the development of new social practices and institutions.

In the eighth essay, 'The Appeal of Political Liberalism', I discuss John Rawls's attempt to provide liberal institutions with a justification that is tailored to the conditions of modern, pluralistic societies. This essay is linked to the ones that precede it by a shared concern with questions about the moral significance of individuals' diverse commitments and allegiances and, more specifically, with questions about the capacity of our moral and political traditions to accommodate those commitments and allegiances. Of course, Rawls is less concerned with the responsibilities deriving from group membership than he is with the significance of the diverse moral, religious, and philosophical commitments that characterize a modern, pluralistic democracy. Broadly speaking, however, the focus is still on the possibility of reconciling the values of justice and equality with individuals' diverse attachments and allegiances.

The ninth essay examines the relation between Rawls's theory of justice and utilitarianism. Although utilitarianism is Rawls's primary target of criticism in *A Theory of Justice*, the two theories also have three important features in common. Both theories have a 'systematic' and 'constructive' character; both treat common-sense notions of justice as having a derivative status and as subordinate to some more authoritative standard; and both conceive of distributive justice holistically, in the sense that they regard the justice of any assignment of benefits to a particular individual as dependent on the justice of the overall distribution of benefits and burdens in society. Taken together, these three features mean that both views are prepared to appeal to higher principle to provide a systematic justification for interpersonal trade-offs that may violate common-sense maxims of justice. This helps to explain why certain critics have seen Rawls as vulnerable to some of the same objections that he directs against utilitarianism. I argue that this is a mistake, but I also argue that their shared commitment to distributive holism places Rawls and the utilitarian in opposition to those who favour a more individualistic conception of justice that is less tolerant of interpersonal trade-offs. The conflict between holistic and individualistic conceptions of justice is closely related to the problem discussed in 'Individual Responsibility in a Global Age'. The growing interdependency of modern societies creates great pressure to think holistically about our values and norms, but doing so threatens to undermine the moral status of the individual. Rawls, who rejects the specific criterion that utilitarians use to assess interpersonal trade-offs, nevertheless does not resist the pressure to think holistically about distributive justice. Instead, he tries to provide a fair and humane way for liberalism to accommodate that pressure while at the same time maintaining its commitment to the inviolability of the individual. In this way, his theory of justice suggests a possible strategy for accommodating some of the conflicting normative tendencies that threaten to destabilize our thinking about justice and responsibility.

The tenth essay, 'Justice and Desert in Liberal Theory', explores the prospects for such a Rawlsian strategy of accommodation with specific reference to the issue of desert. This essay revisits the question, first broached in 'Responsibility, Reactive Attitudes, and Liberalism in Philosophy and Politics', of why contemporary liberal theorists, including Rawls, have been reluctant to assign an important role to desert in their theorizing about justice. The first essay speculated that the influence of naturalism might be one important source of this reluctance. Without repudiating that suggestion, the newer essay explores a different kind of motivation. This essay takes more seriously Rawls's insistence that his scepticism about the role of desert is confined to the case of distributive justice, and does not generalize to the issue of retributive justice. I observe in this essay that desert is an individualistic notion, in the sense that the basis for a claim of personal desert is always some characteristic of, or fact about, the deserving person. To the extent that arguments for holism about distributive justice are compelling, they may provide reasons for denying that desert, as an individualistic notion, has a fundamental role to play in an adequate theory of just distribution. Yet holistic considerations seem not to apply with comparable force to retributive justice. If that is right, then desert may have a more secure role to play in our thinking about the justice of punishment than in our thinking about economic justice.

This suggests a more general way of developing the strategy of accommodation mentioned above. The normative pressures created by the interdependencies of modern life may be accommodated by conceiving of distributive justice in holistic terms, while other values and norms that play an important role in common-sense thinking about normative responsibility continue to be understood in more individualistic or particularistic terms. Of course, this strategy makes sense only if it is plausible to suppose that distributive justice can indeed the understood as holistic in a way that other values and norms are not, and only if it also makes sense to suppose that holistic and individualistic values can coherently be integrated within a unified normative scheme. If the strategy is successful, however, it may help to resolve some of the normative conflicts created by our continued adherence to individualist values and particularist allegiances at a time of mounting globalist and holistic pressure. Indeed, this may be one way to understand the aspirations of egalitarian liberalism of the sort associated with Rawls and others. In any case, I hope to explore the prospects for such a strategy in future work.

The final essay, 'Morality through Thick and Thin', is a critical notice of Bernard Williams's book, *Ethics and the Limits of Philosophy*. It is the earliest of the essays in this volume, and I have included it because there seems to me to be a connection between the kind of challenge to modern moral ideas that Williams mounts in his book, and some of the issues I am concerned with throughout these essays. Williams's book, with its opposition to the justificatory and theoretical ambitions of 'the morality system' and its call for renewed attention to the ethical ideas of the ancient Greeks, is a leading—if not in all respects typical—example of one important tendency in the moral philosophy of the late twentieth century. The tendency in question is to reject systematic moral theorizing in favour of an emphasis on such matters as individual character, virtue, and judgement, which the systematic theories seem often to neglect. This anti-theoretical tendency represents one form of resistance to the pressure to reconceive our moral ideas in ever more systematic, holistic, and global terms. Although I sympathize with some aspects of Williams's critique of the 'morality system', and although I agree that modern moral theorizing has tended to neglect some important dimensions of human experience, I argue in this essay that the repudiation of modern moral ideas would deprive us of tools that are necessary if one is to engage in the kind of social criticism that Williams himself endorses. Rather than repudiating modern moral formulations, therefore, I believe we should try to modify them in such a way as to remedy their omissions and to acknowledge the importance of the values they have neglected. This is the same conviction that leads me in the other essays to explore the prospects for reconciling the diverse values of liberalism, and for accommodating the conflicting tendencies toward globalism and particularism, holism and individualism.

All eleven of the essays that are collected here have been published else-where, but each has been revised—some more than others—for inclusion in this volume. I have not made major changes of substance. My primary aim in revising has been to reduce overlap among the essays, while highlighting the continuities among them. I have also updated some references, made slight alterations in a few formulations, and introduced some minor stylistic modifications. Since the essays do deal with a common set of issues and themes, and since I wanted to preserve the capacity of each essay to be read on its own, some degree of repetition and overlap inevitably persists. There are, on the other hand, a few instances in which the later essays modify positions taken in the earlier essays, and I have not attempted to conceal these changes. The most significant changes concern my interpretation of Rawls's views on desert. On this question, the tenth essay revises, in a number of respects, the assessment offered in the first essay.

Apart from actual changes of position, of which there are only a few, there are certainly shifts of tone and emphasis. Sometimes, for example, I appear to be writing as a critic of liberal theory, while at other times I defend it. There is no inconsistency here, however. One of the ways of inhabiting an intellectual tradition is by worrying about its limitations and exploring the prospects for overcoming them. Both liberals and their critics seem sometimes to assume that allegiance to a tradition is an essentially conservative stance. There is something to this, of course, but unless the point is qualified it can distort our understanding both of liberalism and of tradition. Liberalism is itself a tradition of thought and practice; and one way of being a tradition-alist is by offering sympathetic criticism.

In the end, I hope that these essays succeed in articulating a reasonably coherent perspective on an important set of theoretical issues. At the risk of oversimplification, that perspective may be briefly summarized as follows. The interdependencies of modern life create pressure to think globally and holis-tically about moral norms. Contemporary liberal theories of justice are at least partly responsive to this pressure, although some globalist critics would argue that they do not go far enough. Yet particularistic allegiances and ideas of individual responsibility also occupy an important place in moral thought; no plausible moral outlook can deny their importance or aspire to dislodge them. The challenge for liberal theory, and for moral reflection more generally, is to find ways of accommodating global and holistic pressures with-out doing violence to the values of personal life or threatening our status as moral agents. In trying to meet this challenge, there are many different ways in which philosophy can be helpful, not least by clarifying the content of important values and norms and their place in our lives, and by under-mining the rigid dichotomies and artificial dualisms that sometimes inhibit attempts to accommodate a plurality of values. But there are also things that philosophy cannot do, and much depends on our creativity and imagination in the development of new and modified social practices and institutions.

I hope in future work to develop some of these themes more systematically. For now, this book may perhaps serve to illustrate how a philosophical perspective on moral and political issues can take gradual shape over a period of years through engagement with a set of ongoing historical developments.

1

Responsibility, Reactive Attitudes, and Liberalism in Philosophy and Politics*

History will record that, during the 1980s, liberalism came under sustained and politically devastating attack in the United States.[1] The bearing of this attack, if any, on contemporary liberal philosophical theories, such as those advanced by John Rawls and others, is not obvious. In part, this is because the relation between American political liberalism and contemporary philosophical liberalism is not a simple one.[2] On the one hand, nobody would wish seriously to suggest that the United States, during the period that began when Franklin Roosevelt became president and ended when Ronald Reagan did, was a well-ordered Rawlsian society, or that the social welfare programmes implemented during that period gave full expression to the difference principle.

* Originally published in *Philosophy & Public Affairs* 21/4 (Fall 1992): 299–323. Copyright © 1992 by Princeton University Press. Reprinted by permission. Earlier versions of this article were presented to audiences at the University of Arizona, the University of California at Davis, the University of California at Santa Barbara, the University of Washington, and the Boalt Hall School of Law at the University of California at Berkeley. I am grateful to all of these audiences for valuable discussion, which prompted numerous improvements. In addition, I received enormously helpful written comments, for which I am greatly indebted, from G. A. Cohen, Eric Rakowski, T. M. Scanlon, and the Editors of *Philosophy & Public Affairs*.

[1] Similar developments also occurred, to one degree or another, in some of the other western democracies, most notably Great Britain. But I will limit my discussion to the United States, which is where the philosophical debate about liberalism was most active during the period in question.

[2] In his later work Rawls distinguishes between 'political liberalism', which is said not to depend on any 'comprehensive moral doctrine', and 'comprehensive liberalism', which does so depend. His own view is said to be an instance of the former, while those of Kant and Mill are cited as examples of the latter. The distinction I am drawing is, as should be evident, a different one. I am concerned with the relations between liberalism as a position in American political life and liberalism as a view in contemporary political philosophy. In this sense, Rawls's view is an example of philosophical liberalism. I discuss political liberalism in Rawls's sense in 'The Appeal of Political Liberalism', Chapter Eight in this volume.

Yet, at the same time, Rawls's work is naturally understood as providing a theoretical justification for many of the sorts of programmes advocated by political liberals, and it would surely be a mistake to think of liberalism in the philosophical context as entirely unrelated to the liberal politics of the day. Thus it is reasonable to wonder about the philosophical relevance of the political repudiation of liberalism represented by the 'Reagan revolution'.

The conservatives who came to power during the 1980s are standardly interpreted as having tapped into two different sources of dissatisfaction with political liberalism. The first was primarily economic, and focused on liberal taxation and social welfare policies. The second was primarily social, and focused on liberal policies with respect to issues like abortion, pornography, and the role of religion in society. To the extent that social conservatives emphasized traditional values of family and community, their concerns had something in common with the opposition by communitarian philosophers to the purportedly excessive individualism of liberalism. At the same time, however, much of the dissatisfaction with political liberalism in the 1980s was due not to the belief that it was excessively individualistic but rather to the belief that it was, in an important respect, not individualistic enough. In saying this, I do not mean merely that liberalism was perceived as insufficiently individualistic in economic terms. It is certainly true, as everyone agrees and as I have said, that the overwhelming success of the political right was due to its capacity to appeal both to social conservatives and to economic conservatives. It is also true, and it has been widely noted, that the alliance between these two groups was sometimes an uneasy one, precisely because of the tension between the libertarian spirit of *laissez-faire* capitalism and the broadly communitarian tendency of much social conservatism. But when I say that liberalism came under attack partly because it was perceived as insufficiently individualistic, I am not just alluding to the conservative criticism of liberal economic policies. Rather, I mean that a more general conception of individual responsibility, a conception whose appeal cuts across political lines, was perceived as under threat both from liberal programmes of economic redistribution and from liberal policies on certain social issues. Both types of liberal position were perceived, in effect, as resting on a reduced conception of individual agency and responsibility. And so resistance to this diminished conception of responsibility helped to fuel opposition to both parts of the liberal agenda.

Of course, many liberals would vigorously deny that the programmes and policies they favour rely on a reduced conception of responsibility, as opposed to a proper understanding of the standard conception. These liberals might expect that support for their position could be found in contemporary liberal philosophical theories. I will argue in this essay, however, that the reason various liberal programmes may appear incompatible with ordinary thinking about responsibility is that they assign important benefits and burdens on the basis of considerations other than individual desert.[3] And, I will argue, it is noteworthy that none of the most prominent contemporary versions of philosophical liberalism assigns a significant role to desert at the level of fundamental principle. Moreover, contemporary philosophical defenses of liberalism appear to underestimate the importance of the human attitudes and emotions that find expression through our practices with respect to desert. If these claims are correct, then contemporary philosophical liberalism may provide little support for the view that liberal policies can be reconciled with ordinary notions of responsibility. Indeed, if these claims are correct, then there are deeply entrenched ideas about responsibility that have contributed to the political repudiation of liberalism, and that leading contemporary versions of philosophical liberalism simply do not accept. This suggests that, far from helping political liberals to rebut the charge of incompatibility with ordinary notions of responsibility, contemporary philosophical liberalism may itself be vulnerable to such a charge.

I

There are a variety of liberal political positions that have been perceived as incompatible with ordinary beliefs about the responsibility of an individual agent for his or her actions. For example, liberals have long been accused of responding to crime by advocating policies that emphasize the social causes of criminal behaviour while neglecting the responsibility of the individual who engages in such behaviour. In the area of criminal justice in particular, this emphasis is said to have manifested itself in interpretations of the insanity defense and related pleas that treat an excessively broad range of conditions and circumstances as nullifying an individual's responsibility for his or her criminal conduct. Liberalism has also been blamed, relatedly, for the growing tendency in our culture to reinterpret what were previously viewed as vices—excessive drinking or gambling, for example—as diseases or addictions, thus relocating them outside the ambit of personal responsibility. Liberal social welfare programmes, meanwhile, have been accused of undermining individual responsibility by making society bear the cost of meeting its poorest members' most urgent needs. This is said to provide the poor with strong incentives to avoid making efforts to support themselves, thus producing a permanent class of dependent citizens who view social welfare programmes as 'entitlements', and who see no need to take responsibility for improving their own material position. Finally, liberal affirmative action programmes

---

[3] For illuminating discussion of many issues concerning desert, see Joel Feinberg, 'Justice and Personal Desert', in his *Doing and Deserving* (Princeton, NJ: Princeton University Press, 1970), 55–94; and George Sher, *Desert* (Princeton, NJ: Princeton University Press, 1987).

have been perceived as implying a reduced conception of individual responsibility insofar as they award social positions and opportunities on the basis of membership in targeted social groups rather than on the basis of individual effort, merit, or achievement. Thus, on some of the most important and intensely controversial social issues of the day, the liberal position has met with resistance at least in part because of a perception that it rests on an attenuated conception of personal responsibility.

To avoid misunderstanding, let me emphasize that I am not endorsing the criticisms of liberalism that I have mentioned. I am merely calling attention to the range of liberal positions and policies that have been subject to political attack on the grounds of their supposed incompatibility with ordinary principles of personal responsibility. In so doing, I am trying to focus attention on an important question that arises for liberals about the form that their response to such criticisms should take. Should liberals dispute the charge that the policies they advocate are incompatible with the standard conception of personal responsibility, or should they instead concede that the alleged incompatibility is genuine, but argue that this reveals a flaw in the standard conception rather than in liberalism?

As a matter of political strategy, liberals may well be reluctant to present their position as resting on a reduced conception of responsibility. For any such conception would appear to run counter to the dominant ethos of American society. The extraordinary litigiousness of modern-day America has been widely commented upon. In combination with other features of the prevailing cultural climate, it has led some observers to conclude that Americans no longer believe in simple bad luck, but think instead that any misfortune that befalls a person must be somebody's fault. Offhand, this would not seem to be a promising climate in which to argue the virtues of a reduced conception of responsibility. Admittedly, it may be argued that much of the litigiousness of American society has been made possible by developments in tort law that have themselves been taken to illustrate the erosion of traditional standards of responsibility. Yet the erosion of those standards cannot plausibly be said to explain the prevalence of the underlying litigious impulse, still less the wider impulse to blame and find fault. It is true, as earlier noted, that there has been a growing tendency in our culture to extend the concept of *disease* to certain patterns of behaviour that were previously regarded as vices, thus narrowing the scope of individual responsibility in some areas. Yet, at the same time, countervailing tendencies have also developed, including, interestingly enough, a sharply increased level of moralizing about personal health itself: with the individual's habits of diet and exercise, for example, treated increasingly as appropriate objects of moral approval or disapproval. Thus, in short, although the perceived boundaries of individual responsibility are to some extent in flux, and although, as the political controversies we are discussing indicate, there is a widespread sense that traditional notions of responsibility are under attack and that their influence is eroding, there is no evidence that the impulse to employ the concepts and categories of responsibility is disappearing or even diminishing significantly in strength.

In view of these considerations, it would seem that the more promising political strategy for liberals would be to present the policies they advocate as compatible with traditional notions of responsibility. This would presumably mean arguing that any appearance of incompatibility is due to a failure properly to interpret the implications of those notions. The question, however, is whether this argument can be successfully made. In the case of each of the liberal policies I have mentioned, the appearance of incompatibility arises, as I have said, from the fact that the policy in question assigns important benefits or burdens on the basis of considerations other than those of individual desert. In order to reconcile these policies with ordinary notions of responsibility, what liberals would need to argue is not that we should, in general, be sceptics about desert, but rather that ordinary principles of desert, properly understood, do not have the policy implications in these cases that critics of liberalism suppose them to have. Many liberals would undoubtedly say that they are fully prepared to offer such arguments. As I shall attempt to show, however, it is a striking fact that, according to the dominant philosophical defenses of liberalism that are current today, desert has no role to play in the fundamental normative principles that apply to the basic social, political, and economic institutions of society. This suggests that political liberals can expect to receive little assistance from contemporary liberal philosophers as they attempt to demonstrate the compatibility of their agenda with ordinary notions of desert and responsibility. And this cannot but raise the question of whether there is any theoretically defensible interpretation of liberalism that would support such a demonstration.

Of course, philosophical defenses of liberalism continue to be offered, as they always have been, from a variety of importantly different perspectives. My claim, however, is that none of the major strands in contemporary liberal philosophy assigns a significant role to desert at the level of fundamental principle. This is most obvious in the case of the utilitarian strand. Although Rawlsian liberalism explicitly defines itself in opposition to utilitarianism, there is of course an important tradition of utilitarian support for liberal institutions that extends from Mill to the present day. Yet there is no form of utilitarianism that treats desert as a basic moral concept. Indeed, utilitarianism as it is most naturally interpreted presents a radical challenge to ordinary notions of responsibility. On the one hand, utilitarianism greatly widens the scope of individual responsibility, in so far as it treats the outcomes that one fails to prevent as no less important in determining the rightness or wrongness of one's actions than the outcomes that one directly brings about. On the other hand, the responsibility whose scope is thus widened is also quite shallow, on the utilitarian view, for assignments of responsibility carry no direct implications of blame or desert, and amount to little more in themselves than judgements about the optimality of acts. The shallowness of utilitarian responsibility is reflected in J. J. C. Smart's well-known comment that 'the notion of *the* responsibility [for an outcome] is a piece of metaphysical nonsense'.[4] This does not mean that utilitarians are incapable of recognizing that, in order to function efficiently, a social institution or cooperative scheme may need to assign distinct functions and roles to different individuals, thus producing a clear division of responsibility among the participants in that institution or scheme. Nor need utilitarians deny that there are often sound reasons for social institutions to distribute benefits and burdens of certain types in accordance with publicly acknowledged standards of individual merit or demerit, or that when they do so, individuals who meet the relevant criteria or standards may be said to deserve the benefit or burden in question. But here desert is understood as an institutional artefact rather than as one of the normative bases of institutional design.

For the purposes of my argument, it is an important fact that the most influential contemporary proponent of a purely institutional view of desert is not a utilitarian at all, but is rather Rawls himself. As is well known, Rawls maintains in *A Theory of Justice* that it is 'one of the fixed points of our considered judgments that no one deserves his place in the distribution of native endowments any more than one deserves one's initial starting point in society'.[5] He takes this uncontroversial judgment to imply that the better endowed also do not deserve the greater economic advantages that their endowments might enable them to amass under certain possible institutional arrangements. According to Rawls, the 'principles of justice that regulate the basic structure [of society] and specify the duties and obligations of individuals do not mention moral desert', or desert of any other kind for that matter.[6] Nevertheless, he says:

It is perfectly true that given a just system of cooperation as a scheme of public rules and the expectations set up by it, those who, with the prospect of improving their condition, have done what the system announces that it will reward are entitled to their advantages. In this sense the more fortunate have a claim to their better situation; their claims are legitimate expectations established by social institutions, and the community is obligated to meet them. But this sense of desert presupposes the existence of the cooperative scheme; it is irrelevant to the question . . . [of how] in the first place the scheme is to be designed.   (Rawls, *A Theory of Justice*, 103.)[7]

---

[4] J. J. C. Smart, 'An Outline of a System of Utilitarian Ethics', in J. J. C. Smart and Bernard Williams, *Utilitarianism: For and Against* (Cambridge: Cambridge University Press, 1973), 54.

[5] John Rawls, *A Theory of Justice* (Cambridge, MA: Harvard University Press, 1971), 104.

[6] Ibid., 311.

[7] Rawls suggests in passing (on 314–15) that reliance on a preinstitutional conception of desert *is* appropriate in the case of retributive justice, despite the fact that it is inappropriate in the case of distributive justice. As Michael Sandel argues in *Liberalism and the Limits of Justice* (Cambridge: Cambridge University Press, 1982, 89–92), it is very

On this way of understanding desert, the idea that social institutions should be designed in such a way as to ensure that people get what they deserve, makes about as much sense as the idea that universities were created so that professors would have somewhere to turn in their grades, or that baseball was invented in order to ensure that batters with three strikes would always be out.

The fact that Rawlsian and utilitarian liberals agree about the derivative status of desert suffices to establish this view as the prevailing liberal orthodoxy in philosophy. This does not mean, however, that it has attracted no opposition. The best-known criticism of Rawls's position on desert is the one developed by Robert Nozick in *Anarchy, State, and Utopia*.[8] Nozick is especially critical of the way Rawls moves from the premise that people do not deserve their 'natural assets' to the conclusion that they do not deserve the advantages that those assets may enable them to amass. 'It needn't be', Nozick writes, 'that the foundations underlying desert are themselves deserved, *all the way down*'.[9] Yet when Nozick develops his own conception of distributive justice, the concept of desert once again plays no role. Instead, he argues that individuals are 'entitled' to their natural assets whether or not they can be said to deserve them, and that they are also entitled, within limits, to the 'holdings' that those assets enable them to acquire.

difficult to see what basis Rawls has for making this distinction, since the considerations that lead him to reject preinstitutional desert in the case of distributive justice seem to apply with equal force to the case of retributive justice. And, as T. M. Scanlon observes, 'Rawls' theory of distributive justice' employs 'a general philosophical strategy' that is equally available in the retributive case: 'In approaching the problems of justifying both penal and economic institutions we begin with strong pretheoretical intuitions about the significance of choice: voluntary and intentional commission of a criminal act is a necessary condition of just punishment, and voluntary economic contribution can make an economic reward just and its denial unjust. One way to account for these intuitions is by appeal to a preinstitutional notion of desert: certain acts deserve punishment, certain contributions merit rewards, and institutions are just if they distribute benefits and burdens in accord with these forms of desert.

The strategy I am describing makes a point of avoiding any such appeal. The only notions of desert which it recognizes are internal to institutions and dependent upon a prior notion of justice: if institutions are just then people deserve the rewards and punishments which those institutions assign them. In the justification of institutions, the notion of desert is replaced by an independent notion of justice; in the justification of specific actions and outcomes it is replaced by the idea of legitimate (institutional) expectations.' ('The Significance of Choice', in *The Tanner Lectures on Human Values VIII*, ed. Sterling McMurrin. Salt Lake City, UT: University of Utah Press, 1988, 188)

Scanlon himself is generally sympathetic to the strategy he describes, and his own account of the 'significance of choice' also avoids any reliance on a preinstitutional notion of desert. Because Rawls's view of retributive justice is not developed at any length and is dubiously consistent with his account of distributive justice, I will not devote any further attention to it. I regard it as an insufficiently motivated departure from the general attitude toward desert that dominates his work. [I revise this assessment in 'Justice and Desert in Liberal Theory', Chapter Ten in this volume.]

[8] Robert Nozick, *Anarchy, State, and Utopia* (New York, NY: Basic Books, 1974).
[9] Ibid., 225.

Although Nozick's libertarian conception of justice is not a liberal position in the sense we are discussing, it does of course belong to the older tradition of Lockean liberalism, to which the version of liberalism that we are considering stands in a complex relationship both historically and conceptually. And if there is any position capable of laying claim to the term *liberal* that might be expected to assign an important role to the concept of desert, it is surely this type of Lockean libertarianism. It is therefore a remarkable fact that the most conspicuous contemporary proponent of such a position makes no more use of the notion of desert in elaborating his own view of distributive justice than do the Rawlsian and utilitarian positions he so severely criticizes. It is even more remarkable when one considers that these three positions—Nozick's, Rawls's, and the utilitarian's—represent three of the four viewpoints that, taken together, have dominated American political philosophy since the 1970s.

Nor do things look very different when we consider the fourth position: communitarianism. Readers of Michael Sandel's influential book *Liberalism and the Limits of Justice*[10] might be tempted to think otherwise. In that book, Sandel provides an extended critique of Rawlsian liberalism from a communitarian perspective, and he devotes considerable attention both to Rawls's treatment of desert and to Nozick's criticism of that treatment. The main thrust of Sandel's argument is that Rawls's treatment of desert is an outgrowth of his reliance on an unsatisfactory conception of the self: a conception that leaves the self 'too thin to be capable of desert'.[11] In Sandel's view, the Rawlsian self is a 'pure subject of possession', whose identity is fixed independently of the aims, attributes, and attachments that it happens to have.[12] Conceived of in this way, the self is said to lack any features by virtue of which it could be thought to deserve anything; it is a mere 'condition of agency standing beyond the objects of its possession'.[13] 'Claims of desert', by contrast, 'presuppose thickly-constituted selves', whose very identity is in part determined by their particular aims, attachments, and loyalties.[14]

Since Sandel thinks that we 'cannot coherently regard ourselves'[15] in the way that he believes Rawls requires us to do, but must instead regard ourselves as 'thickly-constituted', one might expect that he would then go on to assign a more important role to desert than Rawls does. Yet that is just what he does not do. In the course of a discussion of affirmative action, he considers the 'meritocratic' position 'that the individual possesses his attributes in some unproblematic sense and therefore deserves the benefits that flow from them, and that part of what it means for an institution or distributive scheme to be just is that it rewards individuals antecedently worthy of reward'.[16] Rather than endorsing these propositions, Sandel says that 'Rawls and Dworkin present powerful arguments against these assumptions

---

[10] Cited in note 7. [11] Sandel, *Liberalism and the Limits of Justice*, 178.
[12] Ibid., 85. [13] Ibid., 93. [14] Ibid., 178.
[15] Ibid., 65. [16] Ibid., 139.

which defenders of meritocracy would be hard-pressed to meet'.[17] And although Sandel reiterates his claim that the liberal vision provided by philosophers like Rawls and Dworkin nevertheless depends on unsatisfactory notions of community and the self, nowhere does he actually argue that a proper understanding of community and self would vindicate the conception of desert that Rawls and Dworkin reject.[18]

Not only, then, do the main lines of contemporary philosophical liberalism agree in avoiding any appeal to a preinstitutional conception of desert—any appeal, that is, to an independent standard of desert by reference to which the justice of institutional arrangements is to be measured—but, moreover, some of the most prominent critics of contemporary liberalism also shy away from such appeals. And they do so even when, like Sandel, they see the liberal rejection of preinstitutional desert as associated with an unsatisfactory conception of the self, and even when, like Nozick, they are clearly sympathetic to the idea of preinstitutional desert. How is this surprising degree of convergence to be explained? Doubtless there are a number of factors at work, no single one of which will suffice to explain the thinking of each and every philosopher. However, I believe that there is one factor that any adequate explanation of the general phenomenon will need to cite, and that is the influence of naturalism. The widespread reluctance among political philosophers to defend a robust notion of preinstitutional desert is due in part to the power in contemporary philosophy of the idea that human thought and action may be wholly subsumable within a broadly naturalistic view of the world. The reticence of these philosophers—their disinclination to draw on any preinstitutional notion of desert in their theorizing about justice—testifies in part to the prevalence of the often unstated conviction that a thoroughgoing naturalism leaves no room for a conception of individual agency substantial enough to sustain such a notion. This problem, the problem of the relation between naturalism and individual agency, is of course a descendant of the problem of determinism and free will. Or, more accurately perhaps, it is the variant of that problem that seems most urgent from a contemporary standpoint. Thus my suggestion is that the reluctance of many

---

[17] Ibid.

[18] Alasdair MacIntyre may be cited as a critic of liberalism who endorses a robust notion of desert and who does so within the context of a broadly communitarian framework. It is certainly true that MacIntyre calls attention to the absence in contemporary theories of justice, especially those of Rawls and Nozick, of any significant role for desert, and that he attaches great significance to this omission. However, it cannot be said that MacIntyre develops a rival theory of justice for modern societies that does assign a fundamental role to desert. He is more concerned to persuade us of how far-reaching a repudiation of modern political thought would be necessary in order to embrace such a conception. Indeed, he believes that the tradition of thought in which the concept of desert is most securely situated requires 'a rejection of the modern political order' altogether (*After Virtue*, 2d ed. Notre Dame, IN: University of Notre Dame Press, 1984, 237). His argument therefore provides not a counterexample to, but rather additional support for, my thesis about the extent of scepticism within contemporary political philosophy about the concept of desert.

contemporary political philosophers to rely on a preinstitutional notion of desert results in part from a widespread though often implicit scepticism about individual agency, a form of scepticism that is the contemporary descendant of scepticism about freedom of the will.

It might be thought an objection to this diagnosis that the same contemporary philosophers who avoid any reliance on desert nevertheless make heavy use of other moral notions, including notions of rights, justice, equality, and the like. As in the case of free will and determinism, however, the moral notions that seem most directly threatened by modern naturalistic outlooks are the notions of desert and responsibility. That is because the threat to morality posed by such outlooks proceeds via their threat to individual agency, and of all moral notions, the notions of desert and responsibility are the ones that depend most obviously and immediately on an understanding of what human agency involves. Thus if the internalization of a broadly naturalistic outlook were going to produce scepticism about any single aspect of morality, this would surely be the one. Of course, it might be argued that, in the end, naturalism supports scepticism about desert only if it also supports scepticism about moral thought more generally, so that it is ultimately inconsistent to forswear any reliance on desert while continuing to use other moral notions as before. Even if this is correct, however, it does not impugn the diagnosis I have offered. For, as I have said, desert and responsibility are the moral notions that are most conspicuously threatened by a thoroughgoing naturalism. So whether or not their position is ultimately consistent, it is not implausible that political philosophers whose justificatory ambitions give them every reason to resist scepticism about morality in general, but who have also absorbed a broadly naturalistic view of the place of human beings in the world, should register their uneasiness about the implications of naturalism through a reluctance to rely on any preinstitutional notion of desert.

II

If the diagnosis just offered is correct, then the project of reconciling the policies advocated by political liberals with traditional ideas about individual responsibility is one that contemporary philosophical liberals are poorly equipped to undertake. For they reject the preinstitutional notion of desert on which the traditional ideas rely, and, if I am right, they do so, at least in part, out of a sense that, given our best current understanding of how the world works, that preinstitutional notion can no longer be taken seriously. The defense of political liberalism would therefore appear to require either a liberal theory unlike those that dominate contemporary political philosophy or a frank repudiation of traditional ideas about responsibility, at least in so far as those ideas rely on a preinstitutional notion of desert. I have already argued that such a repudiation is unlikely to be popular politically. However, this invites a further question. If indeed the repudiation of traditional ideas about responsibility would be politically unpopular, is that owing to contingent features of the present political climate, or do those ideas have a deeper and more securely entrenched hold on our thought?

There is at least some reason to think that the latter may be the case. This can be seen most readily by considering the relation between the conception of desert advocated by contemporary philosophical liberals and some of the attitudes recommended by a familiar form of 'compatibilism' about free will and determinism. As against those who believe that the truth of determinism would leave no room for traditional notions of desert and responsibility, and would, therefore, undermine our existing practices of moral praise and blame, one standard version of compatibilism holds that even if determinism were true, such practices would continue to be justified by virtue of their social efficacy or utility. As P. F. Strawson has noted,[19] however, far from reassuring those 'pessimists' who see determinism as posing a threat to our practices of praise and blame, this compatibilist argument seems to them not to provide 'a sufficient basis, . . . or even the right *sort* of basis, for these practices as we understand them'.[20] For the argument represents the practices in question 'as instruments of policy, as methods of individual treatment and social control'.[21] And, Strawson says, pessimists react to this representation with both conceptual and emotional shock: conceptual shock, because the compatibilist construal omits an important feature of our actual concepts of praise and blame, and emotional shock, because this omission suggests that compatibilism, if accepted, would require a drastic change in human attitudes and personal relations. What the compatibilist construal leaves out is any acknowledgment of the fact that our actual practices of moral praise and blame, in addition to having social utility, serve to express a variety of feelings and attitudes, such as gratitude, resentment, and indignation, liability to which is essential to participation in most of the types of human relationship that we value most deeply.[22] Strawson refers to these emotions as 'reactive attitudes', because, he says, they are reactions to the attitudes and intentions of others, either toward ourselves or toward third parties. When we do not regard an individual as capable of participating in ordinary human relationships, because, for example, of some extreme psychological abnormality, then the reactive attitudes tend to be inhibited and replaced by an 'objective attitude'

---

[19] In 'Freedom and Resentment', *Proceedings and Addresses of the British Academy* 48 (1962): 1–25, reprinted in *Free Will*, ed. Gary Watson (Oxford: Oxford University Press, 1982), 59–80. References to Strawson's essay will be to the reprinting in Watson's volume.

[20] Ibid., 62.   [21] Ibid., 76.

[22] Feinberg makes some closely related points in 'Justice and Personal Desert' and in 'The Expressive Function of Punishment' (in his *Doing and Deserving*, 95–118), although he is not concerned in those essays with questions about freedom of the will.

in which the person is viewed, in a clinical spirit, as someone to be managed or treated or controlled. The compatibilist construal of our practices of moral praise and blame is unnerving because the exclusively instrumental role that it assigns to those practices would be appropriate only in a relationship in which the reactive attitudes were absent and a thoroughgoing objectivity of attitude prevailed. Thus the effect of that construal is to convince pessimists that determinism may threaten not only our existing practices of praise and blame but also the wide range of ordinary human relationships that could not exist if, as this version of compatibilism appears to require, the reactive attitudes were systematically suspended.

Strawson himself believes that, in the end, such pessimism is unwarranted, for the reactive attitudes as a whole neither need nor admit of any justification, and so no thesis of determinism could possibly give us a reason to suspend them, still less 'require' us to do so. If certain influential compatibilist formulations treat our practices of praise and blame in isolation from their connections to the reactive attitudes, that is just a defect in those formulations. It does not testify to any genuine incompatibility between determinism and the attitudes themselves.

Much as I admire Strawson's article, I find myself more persuaded by his diagnosis of what troubles pessimists about the form of compatibilism he discusses, than by his conclusion that pessimism is in the end unwarranted. My aim here, however, is not to argue against that conclusion. It is rather to call attention to the way in which the issues Strawson raises are relevant to debates about liberalism. What makes them relevant is the close connection between the compatibilist construal of praise and blame to which Strawson objects, and the purely institutional conception of desert favored by liberal philosophers. Strawson's compatibilist seeks to justify the practices whereby we hold people responsible or accountable for their actions by reference to the social utility of such practices. Liberal philosophers, meanwhile, regard the defensibility of the practices whereby we treat individuals who behave in certain ways as deserving certain rewards or penalties as entirely dependent on the prior defensibility of the social institutions that are said to give rise to those practices.[23] In each case, the assignment of benefits and burdens in accordance with a conception of merit or desert is seen as requiring justification by reference to something putatively more fundamental: either to the utility of such assignments or to their placement within a larger institutional framework that is thought of as independently justifiable. In neither case is a conception of merit or desert treated as morally fundamental or as an independent normative constraint on the design of social institutions.

It is true that liberal philosophers, or at least those liberal philosophers whose orientation is not utilitarian, need not conceive of our practices with respect

---

[23] As noted earlier, Rawls would apparently take this view only of our practices with respect to distributive justice, and not of our practices with respect to retributive justice. Other liberal philosophers would take the same view of both.

to merit and desert in the narrowly instrumental way that is characteristic of what Strawson calls 'the objective attitude'. In this respect, their position differs from the type of compatibilist position that Strawson criticizes. Yet it resembles that position in the ways that I have described, and this is sufficient to raise the question of whether it too is insufficiently sensitive to the role of the relevant practices in giving expression to our reactive attitudes. Admittedly, some liberal philosophers who reject the idea of preinstitutional desert in favor of the notion of legitimate institutional expectations would nevertheless agree that punishment, at least, has an important 'expressive function'.[24] Yet these philosophers need to show that the reactive attitudes whose expression through the institution of punishment they acknowledge, do not rest on just the sorts of assumptions about preinstitutional desert that they reject. Offhand, it would seem that if the punishment of a murderer or a rapist, say, serves to express the community's outrage and indignation, it does so by answering to the thought that the perpetrator *deserves* a severe penalty, where this does not mean merely that he has reason to expect one. Furthermore, the liberal philosophers I am discussing do not treat desert-based judgements about the assignment of social and economic benefits as serving to express significant interpersonal reactions at all. Yet it is clear that judgements to the effect that certain individuals do or do not deserve certain benefits have an important expressive function in many contexts. This might not present a problem for liberals if the reactive attitudes were sufficiently plastic that they were capable of finding full expression via whatever system of institutional expectations and entitlements happened to be in place. To the extent that those attitudes are less than fully flexible, however, any purely institutional conception of desert runs the risk of conflicting with them, and hence of presenting itself as incompatible with a web of fundamental interpersonal responses. Thus, if liberalism proposes to replace our ordinary notion of desert with the idea of legitimate institutional expectations, and if that proposal meets with political resistance, the possibility cannot be excluded that such resistance is responsive in part to an underlying tension between liberalism and the reactive attitudes, rather than stemming exclusively from contingent features of the prevailing political climate.

The upshot of the discussion to this point may be summarized as follows. Political liberalism has come under heavy attack in America owing in part to a perception that many of the programmes and policies advocated by liberals rest on a reduced conception of individual responsibility. Although some liberals might wish to reject this perception as erroneous, it is a striking fact that the dominant contemporary philosophical defenses of liberalism, by virtue of their reliance on a purely institutional notion of desert, do indeed advocate a reduced conception of responsibility. And in so doing, they may to some extent be underestimating the significance of the human attitudes

---

[24] An example is Scanlon in 'The Significance of Choice'.

and emotions that find expression through our practices with respect to desert and responsibility. If so, then two conclusions seem to follow. The first is that contemporary philosophical liberalism may be vulnerable to a criticism not unlike the one that has been directed at contemporary political liberalism. The second is that the prospects of political liberalism might best be served, not by additional arguments in favor of a purely institutional conception of desert, but rather by a demonstration that liberal programmes and policies do not in fact require such a conception.

As I have indicated, these conclusions could perhaps be avoided, at least in the case of liberal principles of distributive justice, if it could be shown that the reactive attitudes were sufficiently plastic as to render them fully compatible with an institutional system of economic expectations that was insensitive to any independent considerations of desert. It is unclear whether a convincing argument to this effect is available. To the best of my knowledge, the closest thing to such an argument that one finds in contemporary liberal theory is Rawls's argument for the stability of his conception of justice.[25] That argument turns on the claim that citizens in a well-ordered society regulated by Rawlsian principles would acquire a more effective sense of justice than would citizens in societies ordered by other conceptions of justice, most notably utilitarianism. In order to establish this claim, Rawls sketches an account of the development of the moral sentiments with the aim of demonstrating that an effective sense of justice would be the normal outcome of the processes of moral development in a Rawlsian society. Rawls's account emphasizes the intimate relation between the sense of justice and reactive attitudes like shame, guilt, and resentment, and he takes pains to argue that these attitudes would tend to develop in a well-ordered society in such a way that, in their mature form, they would naturally come to be regimented by the Rawlsian principles of justice. That is, people would feel guilty if they violated those principles, they would feel resentful of violations committed by others, and so on. Rawls takes the psychological plausibility of his account to depend on the idea that his principles of justice embody an ideal of reciprocity or mutuality, and it is therefore natural that he should contrast his account primarily with the moral psychology of utilitarianism. For the ideas of reciprocity and mutuality have no fundamental ethical significance for utilitarianism, and as a result utilitarian moral psychology seems forced to make implausibly heavy demands on the human capacity for sympathetic identification. In so doing, utilitarianism seems to underestimate the psychological constraints on the design of stable social and political institutions, and Rawls's account has great force by comparison. Yet Rawls never explicitly addresses the question whether his own repudiation of preinstitutional desert may not itself involve such an underestimation, albeit one of a less extreme sort. In other words, he never explicitly considers, and thus never

[25] In chapter 8 of *A Theory of Justice*.

convincingly rules out, the possibility, first, that our judgements about the proper distribution of benefits and burdens in society may, in addition to regimenting our reactive attitudes, serve as a vehicle for expressing those attitudes; and, second, that the attitudes in question may rest on an assumption that individuals are responsible agents in a sense that implies that their distributive shares ought to be influenced in certain ways by their behaviour.[26] Here it seems relevant to note that, whereas Strawson says that resentment and other reactive attitudes are 'essentially reactions to the quality of others' wills toward us',[27] resentment in political contexts—whether it arises on the left or on the right—is more often a reaction to what are perceived as the *undeserved advantages* of others, and not to the quality of their wills at all.

III

There is some irony in the fact that the difficulty to which I have been calling attention arises for nonutilitarian versions of contemporary liberal theory. For such theories tend to appeal to people who regard utilitarianism's aggregative character as rendering it incapable of providing a tolerably secure foundation for individual rights, and who regard its instrumental, goal-oriented structure as rendering it incapable of attaching sufficient weight, or the right kind of weight, to those features of human life and personal relations about which we care most. Many such people would view the failure of familiar forms of compatibilism to appreciate either the role of our practices of praise and blame in giving expression to our reactive attitudes or the role of the reactive attitudes in human interpersonal relations as an unsurprising consequence of the instrumental, utilitarian character of those compatibilist formulations. In this way, they would see the failings of such formulations as serving to illustrate the very sorts of considerations that make non-utilitarian versions of liberal theory look attractive. Hence the irony in the fact that those versions of liberalism may themselves be insufficiently sensitive to the significance of the reactive attitudes in relation to our notions of desert and responsibility.

Even if this is granted, of course, it may be thought to reveal nothing more important than the existence of an internal tension in the views of a

---

[26] In an unpublished manuscript—'Justice as Fairness: A Restatement' (Cambridge, MA, 1990), 58–64, Rawls says that he does not reject preinstitutional desert altogether; he merely denies that it can play any role in a 'political' conception of justice designed for a modern, pluralistic democracy, and believes that it must be replaced for the purposes of such a conception by the idea of legitimate expectations. This seems to me to represent a significant departure from the views expressed in *A Theory of Justice*, at, for example, 312–13. And, in any case, it leaves the question I have raised in the text unanswered.

[27] Strawson, 'Freedom and Resentment', 70.

certain group of people. However, I believe that the tension between philosophical liberalism and ordinary notions of desert and responsibility has wider
significance, for three main reasons. The first reason, which I have already
emphasized, is that the prospects of political liberalism may depend in part
on how this tension is resolved. This will be so, at any rate, at least in so far
as it is contemporary philosophical liberalism, with its disavowal of preinstitutional desert, that is seen as providing the theoretical foundation for the
positions and policies advocated by political liberals.

The second reason is that an appreciation of the tension between liberalism and desert helps to illuminate the intense philosophical controversy
surrounding liberalism's alleged 'neutrality' among competing 'conceptions
of the good'. Liberalism's claims to neutrality have always struck critics of
varying persuasions as involving a certain degree of bad faith. There are a
number of reasons for this, but one of the most important is that liberalism
seems to many of its critics to presuppose a conception of human life and
an understanding of the place of human beings in the world, that is itself in
conflict with many conceptions of the good. To these critics, the difficulty
is not that liberalism directly endorses some particular conception of the good
or directly condemns some other conception. The fundamental problem arises
much earlier, at the stage at which liberalism defines the 'individuals' among
whose conceptions of the good it purports to be neutral. To its critics, the
liberal framework itself seems to incorporate an understanding of what it
is to be a human individual that is highly contentious, and that leads
inevitably to the design of institutions and the creation of conditions that
are far more hospitable to some ways of life than to others. The argument I
have been developing in this essay reveals one of the bases for this criticism.
For, as I have said, the unwillingness of liberal philosophers to rely on any
preinstitutional conception of desert is due in part to their internalization of
a broadly naturalistic outlook, and to their sceptical understanding of how
robust a notion of individual agency is compatible with such an outlook.
Yet a purely naturalistic understanding of human life *is* contentious. The
modern world is deeply divided in its attempt to come to terms with the
power of naturalism, and one of the defining features of modern life is a deep
uneasiness about what place there may be for our selves and our values in
the world that science is in the process of discovering. It is clear, moreover,
that different conceptions of the good respond to this uneasiness in very different ways. Thus if liberalism does presuppose a naturalistically based scepticism about individual agency, it is hardly surprising that its claims to neutrality
among diverse conceptions of the good should seem suspect. Moreover,
although the political prospects of liberalism might be improved if liberal
policies could be defended by appeal to a more robust conception of agency
and responsibility, there would be no gain in neutrality if liberalism were
seen to rest upon such a conception. For as long as a purely naturalistic understanding of human life remains controversial—as long as the place of human

beings in the world of science is subject to debate—*no* conception of agency and responsibility can claim to be neutral among conceptions of the good. This may seem to imply that, in order to preserve its neutrality, liberalism should refrain from endorsing any conception of individual agency or responsibility. However, even if such abstinence were a conceptual possibility, as it almost certainly is not,[28] it would have the peculiar effect of reducing liberalism to silence on the very subject that was supposed to be its specialty, namely, the nature and moral importance of the individual human agent.

The third reason why the tension between philosophical liberalism and ordinary notions of desert and responsibility is significant is that it raises a philosophically and politically important question about the moral psychology of liberalism. I have already argued that the question of the plasticity of the reactive attitudes assumes great importance for liberal philosophers in view of their reliance on a purely institutional conception of desert. However, this is really but an instance of a more general challenge facing liberalism. The more general challenge is to allay the suspicion that the interpersonal attitudes that liberals value in the private sphere may be psychologically continuous with social and political attitudes whose implications are uncongenial to liberalism. The suggestion that our reactive attitudes may presuppose a preinstitutional notion of desert that is incompatible with liberal principles of justice represents one way in which this suspicion can arise. Another way in which it can arise is via the suggestion that the very same psychological proclivities that lead people to develop personal loyalties and attachments may also lead them to develop forms of group identification and allegiance that liberalism cannot easily accommodate. The suggestion, in other words, is that the psychology of friendship and close personal relations is also the psychology of communal solidarity and partiality. This suggestion receives support from communitarianism in the domain of theory, and from the rise of nationalism and multiculturalism in the domain of political practice. Indeed, it is at this point that the communitarian criticism of liberalism and the desert-based criticism begin to converge. For each sees liberalism as demanding, at the level of political interaction, an individual psychology of bland impartiality: a psychology that is thoroughly unrealistic, and that would be incapable, even if it *were* realistic, of sustaining the rich interpersonal relations that liberals are prepared to celebrate in the realm of private life.[29]

[28] The 'almost' is a mark of my respect for the 'method of avoidance' employed by Rawls in 'Justice as Fairness: Political Not Metaphysical' (*Philosophy & Public Affairs* 14 [1985]: 223–51) and subsequent writings. The 'certainly' is a measure of my scepticism about whether that method can successfully be extended to the issue at hand.

[29] In 'Foundations of Liberal Equality' in *The Tanner Lectures on Human Values XI*, ed. Grethe Peterson (Salt Lake City, UT: University of Utah Press, 1990) 3–119, esp. sec. 2, Ronald Dworkin addresses the apparent discontinuity between what he calls the 'personal' and 'political' perspectives in liberal thought.

IV

I should emphasize that my aim in this essay has not been to defend the preinstitutional notion of desert that is embedded in traditional conceptions of responsibility. Indeed, liberals—among whom I number myself—may well be right to be sceptical of this notion, and, hence, of the traditional conceptions that rely on it. My aim has merely been to call attention to the extent of such scepticism among liberals, and to its significance. Before concluding, however, let me address two objections to my argument that will long since have occurred to the reader. The first objection is that my characterization of contemporary liberal philosophy as having internalized a naturalistically based scepticism about individual agency and responsibility cannot possibly be correct, at least as applied to the liberalism of Rawls. For, especially in those writings that postdate *A Theory of Justice*, Rawls takes pains to emphasize the Kantian roots of his theory, and to highlight the role played in that theory by a conception of citizens as 'free and equal moral persons'. Moreover, he says it is a feature of that conception that citizens 'are regarded as taking responsibility for their ends and [that] this affects how their various claims are assessed'.[30] Thus it may seem clearly inaccurate to represent Rawls as relying on an attenuated conception of agency and responsibility.

In response, however, I would make two points. First, the doctrine of 'responsibility for ends', as Rawls presents it, does not involve any preinstitutional conception of desert, nor is it intended as an independent constraint on the design of just institutions. Instead, it simply amounts to the claim that

given just background institutions and the provision for all of a fair index of primary goods (as required by the principles of justice), citizens are capable of adjusting their aims and ambitions in the light of what they can reasonably expect and of restricting their claims in matters of justice to certain kinds of things. They recognize that the weight of their claims is not given by the strength or intensity of their wants and desires, even when they are rational. (John Rawls, 'Kantian Constructivism in Moral Theory: The Dewey Lectures 1980', *Journal of Philosophy* 77 (1980): 545.)[31]

Rawls's argument in this passage is that people have the capacity to adjust their aims and aspirations in light of their institutional expectations, provided that the institutions in question are just. The purpose of this argument is to explain why a reliance on primary goods as an index of well-being is not inappropriate, despite the fact that someone with unusually expensive tastes and preferences may derive less satisfaction from a given bundle of those goods

---

[30] Rawls, 'Justice as Fairness: Political Not Metaphysical', 243.

[31] See also Rawls's 'Fairness to Goodness', *Philosophical Review* 84 (1975): 551–4; 'A Kantian Conception of Equality', *Cambridge Review* 96 (1975): 96–7; 'Social Unity and Primary Goods', in *Utilitarianism and Beyond*, ed. Amartya Sen and Bernard Williams (Cambridge: Cambridge University Press, 1982), 167–70; and 'Justice as Fairness: Political Not Metaphysical', 243–4.

than someone with more modest tastes and preferences. Rawls's claim is that just institutions need make no special provision for expensive preferences, not because individuals are responsible in some preinstitutional sense for their own preferences, but rather because people living in a just society have the capacity to adjust their preferences in light of the resources they can expect to have at their command. To be sure, this capacity may itself be preinstitutional in some sense. However, there is an important difference between the claim that people possess preinstitutional capacities that would enable them to adapt to a certain institutional assignment of responsibility and the claim that the assignment of responsibility is itself preinstitutional. Thus, whatever one thinks of Rawls's argument, there is, as far as I can see, nothing in it that has any tendency to vindicate traditional notions of responsibility or desert.[32]

A similar conclusion applies, incidentally, to Ronald Dworkin's treatment of expensive tastes. Dworkin appears at one point to express sympathy for the position that people do not *deserve* compensation for expensive tastes, or at least for those expensive tastes that they have deliberately cultivated. However, it quickly emerges that, for Dworkin, the claim that some individual does not deserve compensation for his expensive tastes may be legitimate only in so far as it is based on a judgement that the individual in question has already received what has independently been identified as his fair share of social resources.[33] For Dworkin, in other words, there is no prior standard of desert that determines what counts as a fair share or as a just institutional arrangement. Thus Dworkin does not appeal to a preinstitutional conception of desert any more than do the other liberal theorists we have discussed.[34]

[32] For a discussion of Rawls's argument that I take to support this conclusion, see Scanlon, 'The Significance of Choice', 197–201. See also Scanlon's 'Preference and Urgency', *Journal of Philosophy* 72 (1975): 655–69. G. A. Cohen would apparently disagree with my reading of Rawls, for he says, in commenting on a passage similar to the one I have quoted in the text, that Rawls's 'picture of the individual as responsibly guiding his own taste formation is hard to reconcile with . . . the skepticism which he expresses about extra reward for extra benefit' ('On the Currency of Egalitarian Justice', *Ethics* 99 [1989]: 914). If, as I believe, Rawls's doctrine of responsibility for ends does not rely on a preinstitutional conception of desert or responsibility, then it need not conflict with his refusal to reward effort *per se*.

[33] Ronald Dworkin, 'What Is Equality? Part 1: Equality of Welfare', *Philosophy & Public Affairs* 10/3 (Summer 1981): 237–40.

[34] G. A. Cohen argues that we should 'distinguish among expensive tastes according to whether or not their bearer can reasonably be held responsible for them' ('On the Currency of Egalitarian Justice', 923). He also argues that although Dworkin's solution to the problem of expensive tastes rests explicitly on a distinction between preferences and resources, nevertheless Dworkin's position owes what plausibility it has to the fact that the notions of choice and responsibility lie in the background of his discussion, 'doing a good deal of unacknowledged work' (ibid., 928). Indeed, Cohen concludes that, despite his reliance on the preferences/resources distinction, 'Dworkin has, in effect, performed for egalitarianism the considerable service of incorporating within it the most powerful idea in the arsenal of the anti-egalitarian right: the idea of choice and responsibility. But that supreme effect of his contribution needs to be rendered more explicit' (ibid., 933). In my view, Dworkin's avoidance of preinstitu-

Returning to Rawls, the other point I want to make is simply that, although his broadly Kantian conception of the person may well be incompatible with the attenuated notion of individual agency to which I have referred, explicit endorsement of the former is compatible with tacit reliance on the latter. In so far as Rawls's unwillingness to accept preinstitutional desert gives rise to a reduced conception of individual responsibility, any tension between such a conception and Rawls's Kantian ideal of the person must be viewed as a tension internal to his theory. Moreover, a tension of this sort seems likely to afflict any form of liberalism that defers at crucial points to the authority of a naturalistic outlook, while seeking simultaneously to situate itself within the philosophical tradition of Kant.

The second objection that I wish very briefly to address may be put as follows. If, as I have argued, there is a surprising degree of agreement among contemporary philosophical liberals and their critics about the advisability of avoiding any appeal to preinstitutional desert, then why should it be a special problem for political liberalism if it too avoids any such appeal? The answer is that although liberalism's most prominent philosophical critics may be reluctant to appeal to preinstitutional desert, its most prominent political critics certainly are not. On the contrary, conservative politicians do not hesitate to invoke traditional notions of desert and responsibility in attacking liberal positions. Thus if political liberalism does require the rejection of preinstitutional desert, then although it will be in tune with the prevailing philosophical consensus, that may not suffice to prevent its political isolation. Indeed, if one takes the view that our reactive attitudes require a preinstitutional conception of desert that is incompatible with a broadly naturalistic outlook, then, to the extent that political liberalism reflects the prevailing philosophical consensus, pessimism about the philosophical implications of naturalism may translate into pessimism about the political prospects of liberalism.

tional desert, especially when combined with his explicit reliance on the preferences/resources distinction, casts serious doubt on the idea that he has incorporated the same conception of responsibility relied on by the 'anti-egalitarian right'. Of course, this is compatible with Cohen's claim that, 'insofar as [Dworkin] succeeds in making his cut [between preferences and resources] plausible, it is by obscuring . . . the differences between it' and a distinction that emphasizes the importance of responsibility (ibid., 922).

2

Individual Responsibility in a Global Age*

Introduction

Europe has been undergoing a process of political transformation whose outcome cannot be predicted with confidence, in part because the process is being driven by two powerful but conflicting tendencies. The first is the movement toward greater economic and political union among the countries of Western Europe. The second is the pressure, in the aftermath of the collapse of the Soviet Union, for the countries of Eastern Europe to fragment along ethnic and communal lines.

However these conflicting tendencies may be resolved in practice, they pose a theoretical problem for contemporary liberalism, and for many other political philosophies as well. The problem arises because contemporary liberalism —like many other political philosophies—tends to treat the *individual society* as the appropriate unit of justification, while tacitly assuming a one-to-one correspondence between individual societies and sovereign states. Thus, the dominant focus of liberal thought is on the question of how the political institutions of an individual society are to be justified, and it is taken for granted that the society in question, although undoubtedly comprising a population that is highly diverse in various respects, will nevertheless be organized as a single nation-state.[1] In addition, it tends to be assumed that any adequate justification of such a society's institutions will be one that is addressed exclusively to the citizens of that society, and that the justice or injustice of the society will depend entirely on the way in which it adjudicates among the interests of its own citizens.[2] Questions of global justice are considered under

* Originally published in *Social Philosophy and Policy* 12 (1995): 219–36. Copyright © 1995 Social Philosophy and Policy Foundation. Reprinted by permission.
[1] One liberal who does *not* take the nation-state for granted, but who recognizes that most liberals do, is Will Kymlicka in *Liberalism, Community, and Culture* (Oxford: Clarendon Press, 1989).
[2] As Yael Tamir observes in *Liberal Nationalism* (Princeton, NJ: Princeton University Press, 1993), 10: '[M]any national elements, although unacknowledged, have been fused into liberal thought.... For example, the liberal conception of distributive justice is

the heading of 'international' justice, if indeed they are considered at all; like international law, international justice is thought of as an area of specialized concern that is most naturally addressed once a body of principles for the more fundamental case of the individual nation-state is in hand. Thus, for example, John Rawls describes himself as working with 'the notion of a self-contained national community'.[3] His primary aim, he says, is to develop principles 'for the basic structure of society conceived for the time being as a closed system isolated from other societies'.[4] 'The significance of this special case', he adds, 'is obvious and needs no explanation'.[5] In Rawls's view, investigation of 'the principles of justice for the law of nations' may appropriately be postponed until after principles for a single society have been derived.[6]

As recent events in Europe demonstrate, this set of assumptions may be brought under pressure from two different directions at once. On the one hand, the growing economic and technological interdependence of the countries of the world, which has helped to produce the drive toward greater union in Western Europe, makes it natural to wonder whether one can in fact produce an adequate justification for the institutions of a single society by treating it as 'a closed system isolated from other societies'. Perhaps societies are so economically interdependent that the justice of the basic structure of any one of them essentially depends on the nature of its political and economic relations to the others. Or, more radically, some may wonder whether, in the conditions of the modern world, the political and economic institutions for which the strongest justification can be found will be those

particularistic and applies only within well-defined, relatively closed social frameworks, which favor members over nonmembers.' For a historical account of changes in the way the concept of a 'nation' has been understood, see E. J. Hobsbawm, *Nations and Nationalism since 1780*, 2nd ed. (Cambridge: Cambridge University Press, 1992).

[3] John Rawls, *A Theory of Justice* (Cambridge, MA: Harvard University Press, 1971), 457.

[4] Ibid., 8.   [5] Ibid.

[6] Ibid., 457. In *Political Liberalism* (New York, NY: Columbia University Press, 1993: 272n), Rawls writes: '[A]s a first approximation, the problem of social justice concerns the basic structure as a closed background system. To start with the society of nations would seem merely to push one step further back the task of finding a theory of background justice. At some level there must exist a closed background system, and it is this subject for which we want a theory. We are better prepared to take up this problem for a society (illustrated by nations) conceived as a more or less self-sufficient scheme of social cooperation and as possessing a more or less complete culture. If we are successful in the case of a society, we can try to extend and to adjust our initial theory as further inquiry requires.'

In his essay on 'The Law of Peoples', *Critical Inquiry*, 20 (1993): 36–68, and in his book of the same title (Harvard University Press, 1999), Rawls makes good on his suggestion that the topic of international justice should be addressed once a theory of justice for a single society has been developed. In chapter 6 of his *Realizing Rawls* (Ithaca, NY: Cornell University Press, 1989), however, Thomas Pogge argues that we should 'abandon Rawls's primary emphasis on domestic institutions in favor of globalizing his entire conception of justice' (240). For a similar suggestion, see Charles Beitz, *Political Theory and International Relations* (Princeton, NJ: Princeton University Press, 1979), Part 3.

of the individual society or state at all, as opposed to some more inclusive form of organization.[7]

On the other hand, although a focus on the political institutions of a single society may seem, from some vantage points, excessively narrow, events in Eastern Europe—and, indeed, in many other places as well—serve forcefully to remind us that there are also perspectives from which such a focus may seem too broad, for it may seem to underestimate both the extent and the political significance of the cultural diversity that exists within most actual societies. Certainly the expectation that each society will be organized as a *nation-state*—as opposed, say, to a multi-nation state—is open to serious question, given the evident power of shared identifications based on factors like religion, ethnicity, language, and cultural history, and given the heterogeneity of the populations of most existing states. Such an expectation may seem to rest on an inflated estimate of the significance of shared citizenship in relation to communal bonds of other kinds.

Thus, although it continues to be widely assumed both that the individual society is the appropriate unit of political justification and that such societies will be organized as nation-states, these assumptions are under political and intellectual pressure from two different directions. Caught between powerful universalistic and equally powerful particularistic tendencies, they define a widely held intermediate position which seems increasingly to require defense. To the extent that a political philosophy simply takes this position for granted, it begs some important theoretical questions to which recent events have lent considerable urgency.

This problem is especially acute for contractarian versions of contemporary liberalism, because of their explicit focus on the individual society as the relevant unit of justification and their tacit reliance on the category of the nation-state; but the problem also arises for other versions of liberalism, and for various other political philosophies as well. There is, however, one theory for which it would appear to be less of a problem, and that is consequentialism.[8] In general, social and communal ties have no direct justificatory significance for consequentialism, and the bond of shared citizenship is no

---

[7] In 'The Law of Peoples', Rawls writes: 'I follow Kant's lead in *Perpetual Peace* in thinking that a world government—by which I mean a unified political regime with the legal powers normally exercised by central governments—would either be a global despotism or else a fragile empire torn by frequent civil strife as various regions and peoples try to gain their political autonomy.' (46)

Thomas Nagel takes a similar position in *Equality and Partiality* (New York, NY: Oxford University Press, 1991), ch. 15. For a defense of the Kantian idea of a 'pacific union' of liberal states as the most plausible route to world peace, see the two-part article by Michael Doyle, 'Kant, Liberal Legacies, and Foreign Affairs', *Philosophy & Public Affairs*, 12 (1983): 205–35 and 323–53. See also Jeremy Waldron, 'Special Ties and Natural Duties', *Philosophy & Public Affairs*, 22 (1993): 3–30.

[8] Consequentialism, as I understand it, is a view that first gives some principle for ranking overall states of affairs from best to worst from an impersonal standpoint, and then says that the right act or policy or institutional arrangement in any given situation is the one that will produce the highest-ranked state of affairs that is available.

exception. Consequentialists hold that social and political institutions ought to be arranged in such a way as to produce the best overall outcomes, and they take the interests of *all* human beings to count equally in determining which outcomes are best. Thus, on the face of it, consequentialism would appear much better equipped than some other views to accommodate the universalistic tendencies in modern political life, and much less vulnerable to any charge that it takes the category of the nation-state for granted.

Indeed, consequentialists can manage to treat the individual society as a unit with special justificatory significance only by 'arguing back' to this more conventional position from their own radically universalistic and apparently revisionary starting point: by arguing, in other words, that the interests of all human beings will best be served by a division of labour in which the human population is organized into different societies, each of which has its own political institutions that are specially concerned with the welfare of that society. In much the same way, consequentialism can attach justificatory significance to familial bonds only by arguing that the interests of all humanity will best be served if individuals devote special attention to the members of their own families. In principle, the method of 'arguing back' provides consequentialism with a schematic strategy for attaching political significance not only to the individual society but to less-than-universal social groups of any size. However, it can hardly be said that this makes consequentialism directly responsive to particularist or communitarian concerns. On the contrary, what the method of arguing back provides is clearly a strategy for the indirect accommodation of particularist concerns, and one that the consequentialist is entitled to deploy only in circumstances where it is reasonable to assume that universalistic aims will, in fact, best be achieved through particularist structures. Even in these circumstances, moreover, the consequentialist remains committed to denying what the particularist is most concerned to affirm—namely, the unmediated moral significance of those special ties which bind members of a community to each other, but which, in so doing, also serve to set them apart from people outside the community.

In this essay, I will not be directly concerned with the question of whether the individual society is in fact the appropriate unit of justification in political philosophy, nor will I offer any argument about the proper status within political philosophy of the category of the nation-state.[9] Instead, I will be concerned with the universalistic and particularistic pressures that give these questions their present urgency, and, more specifically, with the way in which these conflicting pressures may be viewed in part as expressing conflicting conceptions of responsibility. My aim is to explore this conflict about responsibility and, in particular, to argue that its current political manifestations are in part the outgrowth of a variety of developments in the modern world that have combined to make some fundamental features of our thinking about responsibility look increasingly problematic.

---

[9] For some interesting suggestions, see Tamir, *Liberal Nationalism*, ch. 7.

Two Conceptions of Normative Responsibility

Different normative ethical theories may be seen as articulating different conceptions of individual responsibility. That is, such theories offer different interpretations of what it is the responsibility of the individual agent to do and to avoid doing. We may say that they offer different conceptions of the individual's *normative responsibility*. Within common-sense moral thought, two doctrines about normative responsibility play a central role. One is the doctrine that individuals have a special responsibility for what they themselves do, as opposed to what they merely fail to prevent. This doctrine is sometimes expressed in the principle that negative duties are stricter than positive duties, where this means, roughly, that it is more important to avoid doing certain sorts of things *to* people than it is to prevent unwelcome occurrences from befalling them or to provide them with positive benefits. The principle that negative duties are stricter than positive duties itself has two sides. The first consists in the idea that the negative duties ordinarily take priority over the positive in cases of conflict. Thus, for example, I may not ordinarily harm one innocent person even in order to prevent harm from befalling two other innocent people, because my negative duty not to harm the one is stronger than my positive duty to aid the two. The second side of the principle that negative duties are stricter than positive duties consists in the idea that the former constitute a greater constraint on one's pursuit of one's own goals, projects, and commitments. For example, I may not be permitted to harm an innocent person in order to advance my career aims, for to do so would violate my duty not to harm. Yet I may be permitted to advance my career aims in other ways, even if by so doing I will miss out on an opportunity to prevent a comparably serious harm from befalling a comparably innocent person.

The other common-sense doctrine is that one has distinctive responsibilities—or 'special obligations'—toward members of one's own family and others to whom one stands in certain significant sorts of relationships. It is true, as Sidgwick emphasized, that there is disagreement within common-sense morality about the specific types of relationships that give rise to special obligations.[10] Although close family relationships are undoubtedly the least controversial example, there is less consensus about relationships of other kinds. Nevertheless, the importance of special obligations in common-sense moral thought seems undeniable. By any measure, they serve to define a large portion of the territory of morality as it is ordinarily understood. The willingness

[10] See Henry Sidgwick, *The Methods of Ethics*, 7th ed. (London: Macmillan and Company, Ltd., 1907), Book III, chs. IV and XI. Sidgwick also emphasizes the absence of any consensus about the extent of many of these obligations. The point is not merely that the extent of the obligation depends on the type of special relationship involved, but that with respect to any single type of relationship, it is often difficult to say how far the obligations of the participants are thought to extend.

to make sacrifices for one's family, one's community, one's friends, and one's comrades is seen as one of the marks of a good or virtuous person, and the demands of morality, as ordinarily interpreted, have less to do with abstractions like the overall good than with the specific web of roles and relationships that serve to situate a person in social space.

Because of the significance that it attaches to the distinction between doing and failing to prevent, and to the category of special obligations, the common-sense conception of responsibility may be described as a *restrictive* conception. For the common-sense doctrines that make use of these ideas serve not only to delineate but also to limit the individual's normative responsibilities. Admittedly, there is room within common-sense morality for significant disagreement about the precise content of people's positive and negative duties, and also about the precise degree by which the strength of the latter exceeds that of the former. On any plausible interpretation, however, the principle that negative duties are stricter than positive duties serves to limit normative responsibility in such a way that individuals may, provided they avoid certain types of proscribed behaviour, exercise considerable discretion in the way they choose to lead their lives and to allocate their resources. Similarly, the doctrine that one has special obligations toward certain classes of individuals has, as a corollary, the principle that one's responsibilities toward other people are more limited.

As has often been pointed out, part of the radicalism of consequentialism lies in the challenge it presents to ordinary notions of normative responsibility.[11] To appreciate the radical character of this challenge we have only to observe that consequentialism rejects both of the common-sense doctrines I have mentioned. Thus, in the case of the first doctrine, whereas common-sense morality regards individuals as having special responsibility for what they themselves do, consequentialism treats the outcomes that one fails to prevent as no less important in determining the rightness or wrongness of one's actions than those that one directly brings about. This greatly widens the scope of one's normative responsibility, in so far as it implies that one's positive duties are as strict as one's negative duties—so that, for example, one's duty to alleviate suffering that one has had no hand in causing is as great as one's duty to avoid inflicting pain oneself. This in turn has two further implications, corresponding to the two sides of the common-sense principle that negative duties are stricter than positive duties. The first implication is that one may be required to harm or even to kill an innocent person if that is the only way to prevent still greater harm or death. The second implication is that the permissibility of any activity or pursuit, however innocent it may appear, must always depend on the unavailability of any alternative that would produce greater net benefit overall. Thus, on this conception, those who spend

[11] See, for example, Bernard Williams, 'A Critique of Utilitarianism', in J. J. C. Smart and Bernard Williams, *Utilitarianism: For and Against* (Cambridge: Cambridge University Press, 1973), 77–150.

money on relative luxuries like movies, restaurant meals, or consumer electronics, when the same money could instead be used to prevent suffering and death, are doing something that is the moral equivalent of killing innocent people. Indeed, in order for it to be legitimate, on this conception, to devote energy and attention to one's most fundamental projects and aspirations, it is not enough that those projects and aspirations should be innocent or benign in and of themselves. Rather, it must be the case that nothing else one could possibly do would produce greater net benefit for humanity as a whole. It scarcely seems necessary to point out how dramatically these tenets serve to widen the scope of individual responsibility, or how sharply they conflict with most people's common-sense moral understanding.

Consequentialism also rejects the second of the two common-sense doctrines I have mentioned. Whereas common-sense morality holds that one has distinctive responsibilities toward family members and others to whom one stands in certain special sorts of relationships, consequentialism maintains that the interests of all people, family members and strangers alike, count equally in determining what one ought to do. Thus, for example, if one can either provide a benefit for one's own child or a slightly greater benefit for a stranger's child, then, other things being equal, one ought to provide the benefit for the stranger's child. Here again, the effect of the consequentialist position is greatly to widen the scope of the individual's normative responsibility. And, in view of the prominence of special obligations in ordinary moral thought, consequentialism's refusal to recognize such obligations provides further testimony to the radicalism of its conception of responsibility.

Of course, although consequentialism neither assigns intrinsic moral significance to the distinction between doing and failing to prevent, nor recognizes special obligations as a fundamental moral category, some consequentialists may wish to 'argue back' to restrictions on individual responsibility that mimic those embraced by the common-sense conception. However, common-sense morality takes the restrictions to operate at the level of fundamental principle, and it is this that consequentialism denies. At the foundational level, in other words, consequentialism remains resolutely *non-restrictive*. Thus, the conflict between the consequentialist and common-sense conceptions may be viewed as a conflict about the legitimacy of restrictiveness in the assignment of normative responsibility.

Global Trends and Individual Responsibility

The restrictions imposed by the ordinary conception of responsibility serve, in effect, to limit the size of the agent's moral world. To the extent that such restrictions are part of moral common-sense, these limits seem natural to us. However, this sense of naturalness does not exist in a vacuum. It is supported by a widespread though largely implicit conception of human social relations as consisting primarily in small-scale interactions, with clearly demarcated lines of causation, among independent individual agents. It is also supported by a complex phenomenology of agency: that is, by a characteristic way of experiencing ourselves as agents with causal powers. Within this phenomenology, acts have primacy over omissions, near effects have primacy over remote effects, and individual effects have primacy over group effects. Let me comment briefly on each of these three phenomenological features.

The primacy of acts over omissions means that whereas our acts are ordinarily experienced by us as acts, we experience our omissions as omissions only in special contexts. Among these are contexts in which we believe an omission to fly in the face of some specific obligation or norm: as, for example, when I remain silent as the blind person strolls toward the edge of the cliff, or when I neglect to feed my child or to return my suicidal patient's telephone calls, or when I fail to provide you with a promised loan at the appointed time. In each of these cases, my belief that I have an obligation to act in a certain way may lead me to experience my failure to do so *as* an omission or failure to act. With respect to my acts themselves, however, no comparable background conviction is required. I experience my acts as acts whether or not they violate any norms or expectations.

The primacy of near effects over remote effects means that we tend to experience our causal influence as inversely related to spatial and temporal distance. Of course, we know that we can do things that will have effects in distant lands and remote times, and sometimes these effects matter greatly to us. The phenomenology of agency, however, is such that our influence on our local surroundings in the present and the near future tends, as we say, to seem more real to us. This is both because the relevant causal connections are ordinarily easier to discern in these circumstances and because we are more likely to witness the effects of our acts firsthand.

The primacy of individual effects over group effects means that when an outcome is the joint result of the actions of a number of people, including ourselves, we tend to see our own agency as implicated to a much lesser extent than we do when we take an effect to have resulted solely from our own actions. Again, this does not mean that we never feel any causal responsibility for outcomes produced jointly by our actions in conjunction with the actions of other people. However, it does mean that outcomes we perceive as resulting solely from our own actions tend to loom much larger for us, and that it is often easier for us to overlook our causal contributions to those outcomes that are the joint result of the actions of many people.[12]

---

[12] This is especially true in cases where the outcome in question results from the actions of an extremely large number of people, each of whom makes only a tiny contribution to the production of that outcome. For a discussion of the moral significance of such cases, see Part 1 of Derek Parfit's *Reasons and Persons* (Oxford: Clarendon Press, 1984), esp. ch. 3. For criticism of Parfit, see Michael Otsuka, 'The Paradox of Group Beneficence', *Philosophy & Public Affairs*, 20 (1991): 132–49.

As I have said, the limits placed by common-sense morality on individual normative responsibility seem natural to us, but this sense of naturalness does not exist in a vacuum. I have been suggesting that it arises instead within a context that is defined in part by a certain conception of social relations, and by certain familiar features of the phenomenology of agency. At the same time, a variety of developments in the modern world have conspired to place that conception of social relations, as well as the image of ourselves that is implicit in the phenomenology of agency, under enormous pressure. These developments include, most notably, the remarkable advances in science and technology in recent decades; the continuing revolutions in travel, commun-ications, and information processing; the increased economic and political interdependence among the countries of the world; and the enormous growth in world population.

These developments have made it more difficult than ever to sustain the conception of human social relations as consisting primarily in small-scale interactions among single individuals. The earth has become an increasingly crowded place. The lives of its inhabitants are structured to an unprecedented degree by large, impersonal institutions and bureaucracies. The interactions of these institutions across national borders have profound effects on the lives of people worldwide, and serve to link the fates of people in different parts of the world in multiple ways. Thus, the quality of life for people in any one part of the world is, to a large extent, a function of a network of institutional arrangements that supports a very different quality of life for people in other parts of the world. And important political and economic developments in one area of the globe often have rapid and dramatic effects on people in other areas, effects that are frequently intensified by the speed with which information about them is communicated. Moreover, in consequence of the growth of population and the development of new technologies, human behaviour now has effects on the natural environment that are unprecedented in scale. These environmental effects distribute themselves in complicated ways within and across national boundaries—often with profound consequences, in turn, for the lives of widely dispersed individuals and communities. In addition, they raise urgent questions about the impact of contemporary behaviour on the lives and circumstances of future generations of people. In this context, the image of human social life as defined primarily by small-scale personal relations among independent individual agents begins to seem like a significant distortion.

Similar remarks apply to the conception of human action that is suggested by the phenomenology of agency. Phenomenologically speaking, our actions loom larger than our omissions; near effects loom larger than remote ones; and outcomes produced individually loom larger than those produced jointly. Yet, in light of the developments I have mentioned, the phenomenology of agency seems like an increasingly poor guide to the dimensions of human action that are socially significant. For surely, any serious accounting of the most urgent problems now facing the human race, as well as any serious proposals for their solution, will need to refer both to what people have done and to what they have not done—as individuals, in groups, and through social institutions—with consequences both near and far. Whether we are seeking to identify the reasons for global warming, or for the threat to the survival of the Amazonian rain forests, or for the vast disparities in wealth and life expectancy among rich and poor nations, we will need to move beyond the phenomenology of agency if we are to understand the role of human beings in generating these problems.

Thus, although the restrictive conception of responsibility that is embodied in common-sense moral thought may indeed seem natural to us, reflection on the sources of this sense of naturalness should lead us to wonder whether it really counts in favour of the common-sense view. And these doubts will only be reinforced if we find ourselves tempted by the suggestion that 'common-sense' morality is in fact a quite specific cultural product: a product, moreover, that has its deepest roots in those relatively affluent societies that have the most to gain from the widespread internalization of a doctrine that limits their responsibility to assist the members of less fortunate societies.

It is, of course, a premise of this essay that the common-sense conception of responsibility is controversial despite its seeming naturalness. The prominence of consequentialism is one obvious manifestation of this controversy at the theoretical level. More generally, however, I think it is fair to say that there has been, within the culture at large, a decline in confidence in the common-sense conception, even among many people who basically accept it. If indeed the culture's confidence in the common-sense conception has been shaken, this is surely due, at least in part, to the developments I have mentioned. The communications revolution that is itself one of those developments has meant that information about *all* of the developments has been disseminated widely and insistently. To the extent that those developments cast doubt on ways of understanding ourselves and our social world that are congenial to the common-sense conception, it is not surprising that the widespread awareness of them should serve to erode our confidence in that conception.

As I have suggested, the persistence of consequentialism is one symptom at the theoretical level of the decline in confidence in the common-sense conception. It is not the only such symptom, however. Another one, which I have discussed elsewhere,[13] is the reluctance of contemporary liberal philosophers, as well as some of their most prominent critics, to appeal to any preinstitutional notion of desert of the kind that is often associated with the common-sense conception of responsibility. This reluctance is related to a more general tendency, which is clearly illustrated by the modern revolution

---

[13] See my 'Responsibility, Reactive Attitudes, and Liberalism in Philosophy and Politics', Chapter One in this volume.

in tort law, to conceive of responsibility as something that it is the job of social and political institutions to assign or to allocate to individuals on grounds that make institutional sense. Although this broad tendency is one that is quite hospitable to consequentialism, it need not take a distinctively conse-quentialist form, since the grounds on which responsibility is to be allocated need not be understood in narrowly consequentialist terms.

Although confidence in the common-sense conception of responsibility may have declined, however, it would be rash to predict the imminent demise of that conception or its imminent replacement by a thoroughly non-restrictive conception of individual responsibility. In order to have any hope of super-seding the common-sense conception—any hope, that is, of taking over the place that it now occupies within common-sense moral thought—a non-restrictive conception of responsibility would need, at a minimum, to be capable of being internalized and of coming to function as a guide to every-day thought and action. Yet, despite the decline in our culture's confidence in the common-sense conception, and despite the increasingly sophisticated articulation of alternative theoretical approaches to at least some questions of responsibility, it is by no means clear that any thoroughly non-restrictive conception of responsibility could meet these conditions. This is not because moral common sense is immutable; as I have already indicated, what it seems plausible to us to refer to as common-sense morality is undoubtedly a highly specific cultural product in certain respects. It is one thing to acknowledge this, however, and quite another thing to produce a viable conception of indi-vidual responsibility that does not employ any category like the category of special obligations, or any distinction like the distinction between negative and positive duties.

There are two reasons for this. The first has to do with the depth of the hold that such ideas have on us. Thus, for example, the sheer human import-ance of interpersonal bonds and relationships of various kinds makes it difficult to imagine the widespread internalization of a conception of responsibility that does not leave substantial room for special responsibilities arising out of such relationships. The sheer phenomenological force of the distinction between acts and omissions makes it similarly difficult to imagine the widespread internalization of a conception of responsibility that treats them entirely symmetrically. This helps to explain why, despite the fact that consequentialism considered in the abstract offers a radically expansive con-ception of individual responsibility, defenders of the view so often find themselves 'arguing back' to a more conventional position that does make room—albeit derivatively—for the analogues of special obligations and the distinction between negative and positive duties.

The second reason is more complicated. The developments that tend to erode our confidence in the common-sense conception, and to encourage us to look for a less restrictive alternative, have these effects because they make a global perspective on the lives and conduct of individual agents seem morally more salient than the narrower perspective that we are more accustomed to taking. But while these developments do indeed make the idea of a less restrictive conception of responsibility seem more plausible, they do not themselves present us with any clearly defined conception of this kind. An emphasis on the significance for human affairs of various large-scale global developments and dynamics—economic, political, technological, and environmental—does not translate in any obvious way into a determinate picture of how ordinary individuals should conduct their lives. After all, the individual agent *qua* individual agent will typically have only the most limited opportunities to influence these global dynamics, and, indeed, cannot in general be assumed to have any but the sketchiest and most speculative notions about the specific global implications of his or her personal behaviour. Here again, the example of consequentialism is instructive. Taken at face value, the consequentialist conception of responsibility is highly expansionist and thoroughly non-restrictive. It requires individuals always to act in such a way as to produce the optimal state of the world from an impersonal standpoint. In so doing, however, it seems to many people to make wildly excessive demands on the capacity of agents to amass information about the global impact of the different courses of action available to them. Faced with this objection, the most common consequentialist response is to treat it as another reason for arguing back to a more conventional demarcation of individual responsibility, thus abandoning the attempt to provide a non-restrictive conception of responsibility, except at the foundational level. This is, of course, just an instance of consequentialism's well-known normative schizophrenia: its tendency to alternate between presenting itself as a radically revisionist morality, on the one hand, and as a possibly surprising but basically conservative account of the foundations of ordinary moral thought, on the other. This very schizophrenia testifies to the difficulty of producing a credible alternative to a restrictive conception of individual responsibility.

Thus, to repeat, if we come to see the global perspective as morally salient, the immediate effect is not to present us with a developed alternative conception of individual normative responsibility. Instead, the global perspective highlights the importance of various large-scale causal processes and patterns of activity that the individual agent cannot in general control, but within which individual behaviour is nevertheless subsumed in ways that the individual is, at any given time, unlikely to be in a position fully to appreciate. The claim that individual behaviour is 'subsumed' within such patterns and processes is not, of course, meant to deny that individual human beings are the fundamental units of agency. Instead, the claim comprises two theses. The first is simply that it is not uncommon for an important outcome to be the product of a large number of acts performed by many different people, few if any of whom actually intend to produce the outcome in question. The second thesis is that many of the options and choices with which people are presented throughout their lives, although experienced by them as entirely natural, are nevertheless structured to a considerable extent by institutional arrangements of enormous complexity. By structuring individual choices in the way that they do, these arrangements serve, in effect, to harness and chan- nel human actions: to recruit them as contributions to larger processes that typically have little to do with people's reasons for performing those actions, but which often have profound and far-reaching effects. Frequently, more- over, the individual agents involved, far from intending to participate in the production of these effects, are scarcely even aware that they have done so. Their vision is obscured by the seeming naturalness of the choices presented to them, by the independent character of their own reasons for acting as they do, by the complexity of the larger processes to which their actions contribute, by the often minute contribution to those processes made by any single action considered individually, and by the phenomenological priority of individual over group effects. Thus it is that much of the daily behaviour we take for granted is linked in complicated but often poorly appreciated ways to broader global dynamics of the greatest importance.[14]

In view of these considerations, the most immediate effect of coming to see the global perspective as morally salient may be, not to present us with a developed, non-restrictive conception of normative responsibility, but rather to generate doubts about our practice of treating the individual agent as the primary locus of such responsibility. For although the larger processes within which individual behaviour is subsumed frequently have effects of enor- mous moral significance, the individual agent's relation to these effects is clearly not what one finds in paradigm cases of individual responsibility. The effects to which principles of individual responsibility are paradigmatically respon- sive are those produced solely or primarily by the individual's own actions.[15] Among the salient features of the phenomenon of subsumption, however, are the limited contribution each agent makes to the larger processes in ques- tion; the limited control each agent has over those processes; the pervasive- ness of the processes and the attendant difficulty of abstaining in any wholesale way from participation in them; the extraordinary difficulty of obtain- ing consistently reliable information about the processes and their effects;

[14] Consider, in this connection, Onora [Nell] O'Neill's claim that '[m]odern economic causal chains are so complex that only those who are economically isolated and self- sufficient could know' that they are 'not part of any system of activities causing unjustifiable deaths' ('Lifeboat Earth', *Philosophy & Public Affairs*, 4 (1975): 286).

[15] Consider, in this connection, the following remarks by H. L. A. Hart and Tony Honoré in *Causation in the Law*, 2nd ed. (Oxford: Clarendon Press, 1985), lxxx: 'The idea that individuals are primarily responsible for the harm which their actions are sufficient to produce without the intervention of others or of extraordinary natural events is important, not merely to law and morality, but to the preservation of some- thing else of great moment in human life. This is the individual's sense of himself as a separate person whose character is manifested in such actions. Individuals come to understand themselves as distinct persons, to whatever extent they do, and to acquire a sense of self-respect largely by reflection on those changes in the world about them which their actions are sufficient to bring about without the intervention of others and which are therefore attributable to them separately.'

and the equally formidable difficulty of ascertaining the different contributions that would be made to such processes by each of the various options
available to the agent at any given time. Thus, although these processes often
have effects of such great moral significance that there is an evident need to
bring them under the normative control of a viable system of responsibility,
the structure of the individual's relations to the processes makes it doubtful
whether we have available any principles of individual conduct that are capable of accomplishing this aim. What we appear to lack, in other words, is a
set of clear, action-guiding, and psychologically feasible principles which would
enable individuals to orient themselves in relation to the larger processes,
and general conformity to which would serve to regulate those processes
and their effects in a morally satisfactory way. In view of the moral importance both of the processes and of their effects, the absence of such principles raises an obvious question about the adequacy of a system of normative
responsibility that treats the individual agent as the primary bearer of such
responsibility.[16]

In brief, then, the second reason for doubting the imminent replacement
of the common-sense conception of responsibility by a thoroughly non-
restrictive conception is this: the same global developments that make a more
expansive conception of individual normative responsibility seem initially
more plausible also raise doubts about the very practice of treating individuals
as the primary bearers of such responsibility. Since it is by no means clear
what the alternative to that practice might be, however, these developments
also pose a more general threat to our deployment of the categories of normative responsibility.

If the argument I have been advancing is correct, our practices with
respect to normative responsibility face a significant threat. The problem arises
out of a perspective on human action that seems increasingly to be forced upon
us by a variety of developments in modern life. Up to a point, these developments appear to undermine the common-sense conception of normative
responsibility, for they make the limits on individual responsibility imposed
by that conception seem anachronistic and difficult to defend. Rather than
providing straightforward support for an alternative, non-restrictive conception of responsibility, however, these same developments tend instead to
raise a more fundamental question about the availability of a suitable locus

---

[16] Compare Thomas Pogge in *Realizing Rawls*, 8–9: 'The effects of my conduct rever-
berate throughout the world, intermingling with the effects of the conduct of billions
of other human beings. . . . Thus, many morally salient features of the situations of
human beings (persistent starvation in northeastern Brazil, civil war in El Salvador,
famine in India) arise from the confluence of the often very remote effects of the conduct of vast numbers of human beings. We as individuals have no hope of coping
with such complexity and interdependence if we take the existing ground rules for
granted and merely ask "How should I act?" . . . We can cope only by attending to the
scheme of ground rules which shapes the way persons act and co-determines how their
actions, together, affect the lives of others.'

of normative responsibility in an increasingly important range of cases. Thus, the net effect of these developments may be, not to encourage the substitution of a non-restrictive conception of responsibility for more restrictive ideas, but rather to leave our thinking about responsibility in some disarray.

Conclusion

I began this essay by taking note of the pressure toward universalism, and the conflicting pressure toward particularism, in modern political life, and by suggesting that these conflicting pressures serve in part to express conflicting conceptions of normative responsibility. It is now possible to clarify and to elaborate on this suggestion. The universalistic pressure—the pressure toward greater social and political integration—is an outgrowth of the very same developments that have made a more expansive conception of responsibility seem more plausible. Moreover, in so far as the tendency of such pressure is to suggest a diminished justificatory role for national and communal ties, and a reduced reliance on the distinction between acts and omissions in favour of a more inclusive concern for the enhancement of human well-being, it may itself be viewed as a manifestation of support for a more expansive conception. At the same time, the pressure toward universalism has met with great resistance, and recent years have witnessed an often ferocious resurgence of particularist loyalties. These complex developments should not be oversimplified, but they serve in part to remind us of the powerful hold that more restrictive notions of responsibility have on people. Indeed, if the argument of this essay is correct, there is a serious question about the extent to which an entirely non-restrictive conception of responsibility could ever fully dislodge such notions. The question arises not only because of the hold that restrictive ideas have on us, but also because the challenge to those ideas is fueled by the growing authority, or apparent authority, of a perspective whose strongest tendency may not be to support a non-restrictive conception, but rather to pose a more general threat to our thinking about normative responsibility.

It should not be surprising that we are faced with such a threat at this time. Recent decades have brought what one historian has called some of 'the most rapid and profound upheavals of human life in recorded history'.[17] Few important areas of life have been untouched by those upheavals, and there is little reason to suppose that our thinking about responsibility, which developed in the context of a radically different social world, is one of them. On the contrary, there is abundant evidence that our ideas about responsibility are in flux. The conflicting tendencies toward global integration and ethnic

---

[17] Hobsbawm, *Nations and Nationalism since 1780*, 174.

fragmentation constitute one symptom of this phenomenon on the political level. As I have tried to suggest in this essay, however, the underlying problem is a broader one, and we are unlikely to find a solution to the political problem without attaining greater stability in our thinking about normative responsibility more generally. What remains to be seen, then, is whether we can emerge from this period of normative confusion with a defensible and psychologically feasible conception of responsibility which can help to structure our social relations during the enormous additional upheavals that undoubtedly await us. In the meantime, we live in a world that seems increasingly divided, and dangerously so, between an ascendant high-tech global culture and a persistent web of fierce particularist loyalties.

3

*Families, Nations, and Strangers**

Anyone surveying the political life of our planet at this historical moment is bound to be struck by the prominence of two powerful but conflicting tendencies. The first of these is the tendency toward greater economic, technological, and political integration: a tendency that has been fueled in a variety of ways by the extraordinary progress of modern science. The second is the tendency toward greater communal identification and differentiation, a tendency that is evident in the recent resurgence of nationalism as a political force, in the rise of the idea of multiculturalism, and in the seemingly endless series of ethnic and communal conflicts to which recent years have been witness.

Among the many issues raised by these conflicting global and particularist tendencies are a variety of questions about responsibility. Most obviously, perhaps, there is the question of how we are to understand our own responsibilities to diverse categories of people: to our families and friends, to the people in our neighbourhoods and communities, to the members of other groups with which we are affiliated, and, of course, to those vast numbers of people who are strangers to us, and with whom our only significant social bond, if it can be called that, is that we are all members of the human race. This question is hardly a new one, and various cultures have, at various times, had reasonably settled ways of answering it. However, our own thinking about questions of responsibility seems to me to be in a very unstable condition, and the conflicting tendencies toward integration and differentiation that I have mentioned may be seen both as symptomatic of this condition and as serving to exacerbate it.

The common-sense morality of our culture holds that each of us has certain responsibilities toward other people simply as such—to avoid various forms of mistreatment, for example, and also to provide limited forms of assistance in certain contexts. At the same time, common-sense morality holds that there

* Originally published as The Lindley Lecture (Department of Philosophy, University of Kansas, 1995). Reprinted by permission. I am indebted to David Gill and Eric Rakowski for valuable comments on an earlier version of this essay.

are additional and often much greater responsibilities that the members of significant social groups and the participants in close personal relationships have to each other.[1] It is these additional responsibilities, which may be called 'associative duties', that I wish to discuss in this essay.[2] Some philosophers have expressed scepticism about whether associative duties constitute genuine duties at all, except perhaps in so far as they can be assimilated to duties of other kinds. Other philosophers have seen associative duties as absolutely central to moral life, and have seen scepticism about them as the outgrowth of an excessive, theory-driven universalism. My aim in this essay is neither to dispute nor to defend the claim that associative duties constitute genuine duties. Instead, I wish to explore the nature of these duties as they are ordinarily understood, to emphasize their importance within common-sense moral thought, to consider some possible explanations of their basis or rationale, and to indicate why, despite their centrality, they seem in some ways puzzling or problematic from a standpoint internal to our common-sense moral outlook itself. If I am right, then the conflicting tendencies on the political level toward integration and differentiation are mirrored within our moral thought by conflicting views about the boundaries of our responsibilities.

I

According to a familiar distinction, *general duties* are duties that we have to people as such, whereas *special duties* are duties that we have only to those particular people with whom we have had certain significant sorts of interactions or to whom we stand in certain significant sorts of relations.[3] Given this distinction, associative duties are of course a class of special duties. Other widely recognized classes of duties that are special in this sense include *contractual duties*—by which I mean duties arising out of promises, contracts,

---

[1] Recent discussions of these responsibilities include: Ronald Dworkin, *Law's Empire* (Cambridge, MA: Harvard University Press, 1986), 195–216; Alan Gewirth, 'Ethical Universalism and Particularism', *Journal of Philosophy* 85 (1988): 283–302; Robert Goodin, *Protecting the Vulnerable* (Chicago, IL: University of Chicago Press, 1985); Alasdair MacIntyre, 'Is Patriotism a Virtue?', The Lindley Lecture (University of Kansas, 1984); Andrew Oldenquist, 'Loyalties', *Journal of Philosophy* 79 (1982): 173–93; Christina Hoff Sommers, 'Filial Morality', *Journal of Philosophy* 83 (1986): 439–56.

[2] The term 'associative duties' is adapted from Dworkin, who uses the term 'associative obligations' instead. Although philosophers often use the terms 'duty' and 'obligation', interchangeably, to refer to moral requirements of any kind, the term 'obligation' is also used, more narrowly, to refer to moral requirements deriving from promises or agreements, or from other voluntary acts. For reasons that will soon become clear, it seems to me important to avoid using terminology that might appear to imply that the responsibilities I am concerned with are best understood in voluntaristic terms. Hence my preference for the word 'duty' in this context.

[3] See H. L. A. Hart, 'Are There Any Natural Rights?', *Philosophical Review* 64 (1955): 175–91; W. D. Ross, *The Right and the Good* (Oxford: Clarendon Press, 1930), 27.

and agreements, *reparative duties*—or duties to people one has wronged or harmed or mistreated,[4] and *duties of gratitude*—or duties to one's benefactors.

There are many different kinds of groups and relationships participation in which has at least sometimes been seen as giving rise to associative duties. Obviously, individuals are usually thought to have such duties to the members of their immediate families. In addition, however, people have been said to have associative duties to their friends, neighbours, and more distant relatives; to members of the same community, nation, or clan; to colleagues, co-workers and fellow union members; to classmates, compatriots, and comrades; to members of the same religious or racial or ethnic group; and even to members of the same team, gang, or club.[5]

There is no obvious feature that all of the relationships just mentioned have in common. Some of those relationships are ordinarily entered into voluntarily, but others of them cannot be. Many of the relationships on the list can be terminated voluntarily, but, again, others of them cannot be. In some cases, the people to whom one is said to have associative duties are people who have come to depend or rely on one in certain ways, but this is not so in all cases. Some of the relationships mentioned involve people who are engaged in some common co-operative enterprise, but others do not. And while some of the relationships can only arise among people who know each other well, in other cases the participants need never have met or had any sort of interaction. The apparent diversity of these relationships presents a *prima facie* difficulty for any view that proposes to assimilate associative duties to some putatively clearer or more fundamental category of duties: to contractual duties, for example, or to duties of gratitude. While any given proposal of this kind may have a measure of plausibility in some cases, it will be difficult for any such proposal to accommodate the full range of groups and relationships, participation in which has been thought to give rise to associative duties.

Of course, although the vast majority of people believe themselves to have a variety of associative duties, many people are, at the same time, unsympathetic to some of the perfectly sincere claims of duty made by others. For example, some people who are in no doubt about their associative duties to their friends or to the members of their own families are nevertheless unreceptive or even hostile to the idea that members of the same national or

---

[4] For a recent discussion of such duties, see Shelly Kagan, 'Causation and Responsibility', *American Philosophical Quarterly* 25 (1988): 293–302.

[5] The special duties of doctors to their patients, lawyers to their clients, and teachers to their students are sometimes grouped together with those mentioned in the text, although it may seem misleading to think of such duties as arising from shared membership in a group or participation in a personal relationship. Michael Hardimon distinguishes between associative duties and what he calls 'role obligations', but he includes within the second of these categories many duties, such as the duties of family members to each other, that clearly do count as associative duties in my sense. See M. Hardimon, 'Role Obligations', *Journal of Philosophy* 91 (1994): 333–63.

ethnic or religious group have special, associative duties to each other. Thus, although many different kinds of groups and relationships have been seen as generating associative duties, there is only limited consensus about when such duties do in fact arise.

The best explanation of this diversity and disagreement is that virtually any kind of group or personal relationship that has significance for the people it unites may be seen by them as giving rise to associative duties. This would explain the otherwise heterogeneous assortment of groups and relationships that have been seen as generating such duties. It would also explain why many people who believe that they themselves have associative duties of various kinds are nevertheless resistant to some of the deeply-felt claims of duty made by others. For, if we disapprove of certain sorts of groups and relationships, or of the tendency to invest participation in those groups and relationships with significance, then we may be reluctant to regard such participation as generating associative duties. If we disapprove of gangs, or of unions, or of religion, then we may be unreceptive to the suggestion that members of the same gang or union or religious group have special moral duties to each other. If, on the other hand, we attach great importance to our own membership in a group of a certain kind, then not only are we apt to see ourselves as having duties to the other members of the group, we may also be inclined to suppose that membership in a group of this kind always gives rise to such duties, and we may disapprove of group members who fail to acknowledge their duties as we see them.

II

In addition to the diversity of associative duties and the limited consensus about when they arise, there is also considerable unclarity, within common-sense moral thought, about the content of such duties.[6] One thing that *is* clear is that this may vary depending on the nature of the group or relationship that gives rise to the duty. An athlete may have associative duties both to her teammates and to her family, say, but nobody supposes that the content of these duties will be exactly the same in the two cases. Even with respect to a particular type of group or relationship, however, the precise content of the participants' duties is often difficult to specify. In general, philosophers who discuss associative duties tend to characterize them as duties to provide positive benefits for one's associates (as I shall refer to them), duties that go beyond whatever positive duties we may already have toward people in general. It is understood, in these discussions, that the content of the additional

---

[6] These points are all emphasized by Sidgwick in *The Methods of Ethics* [7th edn.] (London: Macmillan and Company, 1907), Book III, Chapters IV and XI.

benefits to be provided may vary depending on the nature of the group or relationship in question. However, it seems generally to be assumed that associative duties do not involve any addition to or strengthening of our negative duties—our duties not to harm or mistreat people. This assumption is compatible, of course, with a recognition that the same relationships that give rise to associative duties can also create special opportunities for mistreatment, and can, indeed, make possible specially intimate forms of mistreatment. Thus, even if one does not regard such relationships as giving rise to additional negative duties, one may nevertheless see them as creating new opportunities for the violation of those negative duties that we already have.

This consideration notwithstanding, it oversimplifies matters to think of associative duties solely as positive duties that go beyond our positive duties to people in general. To see this, we may first observe that this characterization itself is normally taken to mean not only that one's positive duties to one's associates are more extensive than one's positive duties to other people, but also that they are stronger. This 'greater strength', in turn, comprises more than one feature. First, it means that one's positive duties to one's associates are less easily nullified or overridden than one's positive duties to others by considerations of cost to oneself. Thus, for example, although I may be expected to bear some costs in order to provide assistance to a stranger, I may be expected to bear greater costs in order to provide comparable assistance to my brother or my child. Second, it means that one's positive duties to one's associates often take precedence over one's positive duties to others in cases where the two conflict. Thus, for example, if both my brother and a stranger need the same sort of assistance, but I can provide this assistance only to one of them, then I may be required to help my brother, even if I would have been required to help the stranger had he been the only person needing my assistance. Indeed, I may sometimes be required to help my brother even if his need is less urgent than the stranger's. Third, the idea of greater strength may also mean, although this is more controversial, that the threshold at which a positive duty can override a negative duty is sometimes lower if the positive duty is to an associate, than it would be if the positive duty were to a stranger. For example, it may be thought that circumstances can arise in which I would be required or at least permitted to harm some person, or to violate his property rights, in order to provide a badly needed benefit for my brother or my child, even though it would be wrong for me to do the same thing in order to provide a comparable benefit for a stranger.

Note, however, that those who make this last supposition may equally well suppose that the threshold at which a positive duty can override a negative duty is sometimes *higher* if the *negative* duty is, say, to a family member, than it would be if the negative duty were to a stranger. For example, it may be thought that circumstances can arise in which it would be permissible for me to inflict a lesser harm on one stranger in order to prevent a much greater harm to another stranger, even though it would be wrong for me to do the same thing if the person on whom I would have to inflict the lesser harm were my own brother or child. This example shows that, on some interpretations at least, it is a mistake to think of associative duties as exclusively positive in character. For the example illustrates one way in which our negative duties to our associates may be thought stronger than our negative duties to others. And, as in the case of positive duties, this greater strength may be thought to manifest itself in other ways as well. Thus, it may be thought that one's negative duties to one's associates are less easily nullified or overridden than one's negative duties to others by considerations of cost to oneself. For example, although I may be expected to bear some costs in order to avoid harming a stranger, I may be expected to bear greater costs in order to avoid harming my brother or my child in the same way. Similarly, it may be thought that one's negative duties to one's associates take a certain precedence over one's negative duties to others in cases where the two conflict. So, for example, if one is driving a runaway trolley as it approaches a fork in the track, and one must either steer it onto the branch on which one's brother is trapped or onto the branch on which a stranger is trapped, then, on this view, one ought to do the latter.

In view of these reflections, what we can say is the following. Within common-sense moral thought, the precise content of associative duties is often unclear. It may vary depending on the nature of the relationship giving rise to the duty, and, even with respect to a single type of relationship, the duties of the participants are often difficult to delineate with precision. Speaking very generally, associative duties require one to give the interests of one's associates priority of various kinds over the interests of other people. First, one must provide positive benefits for one's associates which one need not provide for other people at all, and which one may not provide for others in preference to one's associates. Indeed, providing such benefits for one's associates takes priority over the provision to non-associates of any benefit that one lacks a duty to provide. In addition, however, when conflicts among one's positive and/or negative duties arise, duties owed to one's associates take precedence of various sorts over duties to other people, although some of these forms of precedence are more controversial than others. In general, for most types of relationships there is no detailed consensus either about the extent of the positive benefits one must provide or about the degree of precedence that associative duties take.

III

Despite the absence of greater consensus either about the content of associative duties or about which kinds of groups and relationships give rise to them, the importance of such duties in common-sense moral thought is clear.

Indeed, associative duties supply much of the substance of morality as it is interpreted by most people. Nevertheless, two influential objections have been raised against the idea of an associative duty as we have been understanding it. The first of these, which we may call *the voluntarist objection*, is, in effect, an objection on behalf of the individual who is supposed to be bound by such duties. The voluntarist objection asserts that mere membership in a group or participation in a relationship cannot by itself give rise to any duties at all. Although it is true that we sometimes have special responsibilities to our associates, we have such responsibilities, according to this objection, only in so far as we have voluntarily incurred them. In other words, mere participation in a relationship or membership in a group is not sufficient to generate any special responsibilities whatsoever. Instead, one's special responsibilities must always arise from some voluntary act on one's part: if not from one's explicit acceptance of those responsibilities, then perhaps from one's voluntary entry into the group or relationship in question—or if not from one's voluntary entry into the group or relationship in question, then perhaps from one's voluntary acceptance of the benefits of participation in that group or relationship.[7] But, the voluntarist insists, one cannot simply *find oneself* with such responsibilities without having done anything at all to acquire them.

The voluntarist objection has been one major impetus for an *assimilationist* treatment of associative duties. The assimilationist, as I have already indicated in passing, regards associative duties as being genuine duties only in so far as they can be assimilated to other, putatively less problematic types of duties.[8] The voluntarist version of this position treats associative duties as legitimate only in so far as they can be assimilated to contractual duties broadly understood. I have already expressed doubts about the possibility of what might be called *wholesale monistic assimilation*: that is, about the possibility of assimilating the full range of perceived associative duties to any other single type of duty. In view of the diversity of groups and relationships that have been seen as giving rise to such duties, any attempt at wholesale monistic assimilation is bound to seem Procrustean. However, this does not mean that monistic assimilationism as a general strategy is mistaken, only that, in its more plausible deployments, it will not offer any wholesale endorsement of

---

[7] On the voluntary acceptance of benefits as a source of special responsibilities, see Hart, 'Are There Any Natural Rights?'; John Rawls, *A Theory of Justice* (Cambridge, MA: Harvard University Press, 1971), 111–14, 342–50, 376–7. For criticism, see Dworkin, *Law's Empire*, 193–5; Robert Nozick, *Anarchy, State, and Utopia* (New York, NY: Basic Books, 1974), 90–5; A. John Simmons, *Moral Principles and Political Obligations* (Princeton, NJ: Princeton University Press, 1979), Chapter V.

[8] Utilitarian accounts of associative duties, while not most naturally described as assimilationist in quite this sense, share with assimilationist treatments the feature of not taking associative duties to constitute a fundamental moral category. For examples, see Sidgwick, *The Methods of Ethics*, Book IV (especially Chapter III, section 3); R. M. Hare, *Moral Thinking* (Oxford: Clarendon Press, 1981), 135–40.

the full range of associative duties that have been recognized within common-sense moral thought, but will tend instead to be revisionist in character. For it will validate only those supposed duties that it can plausibly assimilate, and this will inevitably mean rejecting certain others. Indeed, in so far as associative duties are seen within ordinary moral thought as constituting a fundamental class of duties in their own right, monistic assimilationism, in its more plausible deployments, will be doubly revisionist. For it will fail to recognize some putative duties as being duties at all, and it will reject the common-sense understanding of those duties that it does regard as genuine.

These points may be illustrated with reference to the voluntarist version of monistic assimilationism. It is clear, to begin with, that people are often seen as having associative duties by virtue of their participation in some group or relationship, even though their entry into the group or relationship in question was not accompanied by any explicit acceptance of those duties as such. In addition, we have already observed that some of the relationships that are thought to generate associative duties cannot be entered into voluntarily, while others cannot be ended voluntarily. In fact, some of the paradigmatic duty-generating relationships can neither be entered into nor exited from voluntarily. The relations of children to their parents, and siblings to each other, are the most obvious examples. In other cases, groups that have been seen as generating associative duties can sometimes be joined voluntarily, but the more typical pattern is for members to be socialized into the group gradually in the course of their development, so that they come to see themselves as part of the group without any consciousness of ever having made a decision to join it, and without any sense that there was ever a time in their lives when they were not part of it. So it is, often, with membership in a community or in a national or religious group. Even when relationships are indeed entered into voluntarily, moreover, this general description may mask considerable diversity; thus, for example, entering into a friendship is a very different process from joining a club,[9] and becoming a parent is very different from moving into a new neighbourhood.

It is this complex and diverse set of facts that drives the proponents of many versions of voluntaristic assimilationism to argue that a range of relationships that do not fit the voluntaristic model narrowly construed may nevertheless be represented as contractual in an extended sense, and hence as duty-generating, because they involve the voluntary acceptance of benefits. At the same time, however, any relationships that cannot be represented as contractual even in this extended sense must be regarded, according to these versions of assimilationism, as incapable of generating genuine duties at all. To the extent that this excludes some commonly recognized duties, and to the extent that people do not ordinarily see their voluntary acceptance of benefits as the source

---

[9] As Dworkin points out in *Law's Empire*, 197.

of their associative duties, these versions of assimilationism are prepared to be revisionist. As I have suggested, this illustrates the revisionist tendency of monistic assimilationism more generally.[10]

An alternative to monistic assimilationism is pluralistic assimilationism. Rather than asserting that associative duties are genuine duties only in so far as they can be assimilated to duties of some one other type, the pluralistic position seeks to assimilate different classes of associative duties to putatively less problematic duties of several different types. As compared with monistic assimilationism, the pluralistic position appears, in the abstract, to hold out the promise of reduced revisionism without increased Procrusteanism. In order to make good on this promise, however, the pluralist must first identify several different types of duties, all of which are clearer and better grounded than the unassimilated associative duties themselves. For those with voluntarist leanings, in particular, this may be difficult to do, since the voluntarist's reason for objecting to associative duties would seem equally to be a reason for objecting to any special duties that cannot be construed on a broadly contractual model.

As I have said, the voluntarist objection to associative duties is, in effect, an objection on behalf of the individual who is supposed to be bound by such duties. Associative duties, if conceived of as ascribable to individuals in the absence of any relevant consensual act, would, according to the voluntarist, constitute an unreasonable constraint on the individuals in question. As I have also said, however, there is another influential objection to associative duties. This objection, which we may call *the distributive objection*, is, in effect, an objection on behalf of those individuals who are not participants in the groups and relationships that are thought to give rise to associative duties. The distributive objection sees such duties, not as imposing unreasonable burdens on the participants in special relationships, but rather as supplying them with benefits that may be unreasonable. This objection may be developed as follows.

Associative duties require individuals to give priority of various kinds to the interests of their associates. These requirements, however, work to the disadvantage of other people. Suppose, for example, that there are three individuals, A, B, and C, none of whom has any special tie or relationship to any of the others. Each has only general duties toward the others, which is to say that each's duties toward the others are distributed equally. Indeed, a perfectly egalitarian distribution of duty obtains among the three individuals, since none of the three has any special claim on the services of any of the others. Now, however, suppose that A and B, acting independently of each other, become members of some group of a kind that is ordinarily thought

---

[10] Robert Goodin's attempt, in *Protecting the Vulnerable*, to assimilate special duties as a whole to duties deriving from special need, seems to me similarly illustrative of this tendency.

to give rise to associative duties. And suppose that C is not a member of this group, which we may call the *In Group*. If, as a result of their membership in the In Group, A and B come to have associative duties to each other, then the egalitarian distribution of duty that previously prevailed no longer obtains. Instead, A and B are now required to give each other's interests priority over the interests of C in a wide range of contexts. Thus, each of them now has stronger claims, on the other than C has on either of them. This means that, for each of them, C's interests have been demoted in relative importance. Indeed, C's claims on each of them may now be weaker, not only than his claims on them were before, and not only than their claims on each other are now, but also than their claims on him are now. For, we may suppose, C has no associates to whose interests he is required to give priority over the interests of A and B. Thus, the reduction in the strength of his claims on A and B may not be matched by a comparable reduction in the strength of their claims on him; the reduction of strength may be, in this way, asymmetrical. In any case, the overall distribution of duty that now prevails seems both inegalitarian and decidedly unfavourable to C.

But, the distributive objection asks, why should the fact that A and B have become members of the In Group have these effects? Why should their membership in the In Group work to C's disadvantage in this way? We may suppose that both A and B attach considerable significance to their membership, that both experience their participation in the In Group as very rewarding, and, indeed, that each of them sees membership in the Group as an important aspect of his identity. None of these suppositions seems capable of explaining why their membership should, as a matter of morality, work to C's disadvantage in the way that it does if it generates associative duties. Indeed, the distributive objection continues, far from explaining this, these suppositions seem rather to make the need for such an explanation more acute. For if A and B derive great value from their membership in the In Group, then they already have an advantage that C lacks. The effect of associative duties is to build a second advantage on top of this first one. If, in other words, A and B have associative duties to each other, then, in addition to enjoying the rewards of Group membership, which C lacks, A and B also get the benefit of having stronger claims on each other's services than C has. Why should this be? Why should the fact that A and B are in a position to enjoy the first sort of advantage give rise to a moral requirement that they should also get the second, and that C, who has already lost out with respect to the former, should now lose out with respect to the latter?

This way of formulating the distributive objection suggests that the objection can also be directed against the voluntarist who seeks to assimilate associative duties to contractual duties. For, even if associative duties are seen as arising from the voluntary acceptance by group members of the rewards of membership, the distributive objection will still challenge the idea that morality requires those who have secured such rewards to have their good fortune compounded through a favourable redistribution of duty, while those who never acquired the original rewards are further disfavoured by that same redistribution.

More generally, to the extent that members of the In Group have significantly greater resources than non-members independently of any redistribution of duty, the objection to such a redistribution will only be intensified, whether or not the greater resources that Group members have are actually a consequence of their membership. Thus, for example, if A and B are much wealthier than C, either because this has always been so or because membership in the In Group has conferred wealth upon them, the idea that morality requires them also to receive the advantage of having increased claims to each other's services will, according to the distributive objection, be all the more clearly open to question. And this will remain so even if C and other people of modest means join together to establish a duty-generating group of their own. For proponents of the objection will still charge that, by requiring those who are wealthier to give each other's interests priority over the interests of those who are poorer, associative duties unjustifiably reinforce the inequality in resources between the two groups.

In short, the distributive objection sees associative duties as providing additional advantages to people who have already benefited from participation in rewarding groups and relationships, and it views this as unjustifiable whenever the provision of these additional advantages works to the detriment of people who are needier, whether they are needier because they are not themselves participants in rewarding groups and relationships or because they have significantly fewer resources of other kinds.

Many people will feel that the distributive objection has its greatest force when it is directed at those associative duties that are sometimes said to obtain at the political level, among members of the same community or society or nation.[11] At this level, the idea that associative duties provide a mandate for those who are already rich in resources to turn their attention inward, and largely to ignore suffering and deprivation in the rest of the world, is likely to have considerable resonance for many people. However, once associative duties are seen as problematic at the political level, it is unclear why they shouldn't also seem problematic at the level of smaller-scale personal relationships. For associative duties also provide a mandate for relatively affluent families, say, to turn *their* attention inward, and to lavish resources upon each other while largely ignoring the needs of the less fortunate. Indeed, by

[11] The idea that there are associative duties at this level has a long history, and it is an explicit or implicit theme of contemporary 'communitarian' writers. See, for example, Michael Sandel, *Liberalism and the Limits of Justice* (Cambridge: Cambridge University Press, 1982), 179. In recent years, some liberal theorists have also endorsed the idea. See, in addition to Dworkin's discussion in *Law's Empire*, Yael Tamir, *Liberal Nationalism* (Princeton, NJ: Princeton University Press, 1993), 99–102, 130–9. Also relevant is Neil MacCormick, 'Nation and Nationalism', in his *Legal Right and Social Democracy: Essays in Legal and Social Philosophy* (Oxford: Clarendon Press, 1982), 247–64.

emphasizing the costs to others of those patterns of partiality to one's intimates that are ordinarily seen as defining the abstract structure of 'personal
life', the distributive objection represents one way of challenging the very
distinction between the personal and the political.

IV

The formulation of the distributive objection that we have been discussing
describes associative duties as providing additional advantages for people who
have already secured the advantage of participation in rewarding groups and
relationships. One response to the objection might be to deny that the two
types of advantage are separable in the way that this formulation suggests.
It is a mistake, or so it may be said, to suppose that *first* a rewarding relationship is established between two people, or among the members of a group,
and *then* a question arises about how, if at all, this relationship affects the
duties of the participants. Instead, it may be argued, an implicit commitment
by the participants to give priority to each other's interests in various contexts is a precondition for the existence of a rewarding relationship. And, the
argument may continue, it is such commitments that give rise to associative
duties. Thus, it may be said, people cannot derive rewards from their participation in special relationships without acquiring associative duties, and any
advantages they may provide, in the process.

Proponents of the distributive objection may reply that if people have a
strong interest in obtaining the rewards deriving from participation in special relationships, and if they cannot obtain those rewards without acquiring associative duties in the process, then all that follows is that people
have a strong interest in acquiring such duties—a conclusion that does not
rebut the distributive objection but rather concedes one of its main claims.
However, defenders of associative duties may respond that people's interest
in obtaining the rewards of special relationships is so strong that morality
cannot possibly fail to accommodate it. Those rewards are among the greatest goods that human beings can enjoy, and morality must surely permit
people to make the kinds of commitments on which the rewards depend.
Accordingly, it may be said, associative duties should be seen as arising out
of commitments that people permissibly make to each other.

This amounts to a two-stage defence of associative duties. The first stage
appeals to people's strong interest in participating in rewarding social relationships to secure the permissibility of making the commitments on which
such relationships are said to depend. The second stage identifies those commitments as the actual source of people's associative duties. Thus, according
to this defence, one does not acquire associative duties simply by virtue of
standing in a special relationship to some person or by virtue of belonging

to some special group. Instead, one acquires such duties when one makes a commitment to one's associates, either explicitly or implicitly, that includes an undertaking to give priority to their interests in various contexts.

The first thing to notice about this defence is the extent of the concessions that it makes to the voluntarist objection in the course of trying to ward off the distributive objection. By denying that either the mere fact of group membership or the mere existence of a special relationship can give a person associative duties, and by insisting that one cannot acquire such duties without making some commitment oneself, this defence brings associative duties entrely under the control of the will. Indeed, its identification of commitment as the relevant duty-generating factor appears to relegate this defence to a form of voluntaristic assimilationism, and a highly revisionist one at that. For, to take an obvious example, we do not ordinarily suppose that parents have special duties to their children only if they have made a commitment to give priority to the children's interests.

At the same time, this defence of associative duties is unlikely to defuse the distributive objection. For that objection does not deny that people have a strong interest in participating in various groups and relationships, and hence in committing themselves to give priority to their associates. On the contrary, the distributive objection is quite sensitive to the way in which such commitments serve the interests of the participants in special relationships. However, it argues that the participants are not the only people whose interests are affected when such commitments are made; those who are not participants also have interests at stake, and their interests are apt to be especially strong when they already have fewer resources than the participants do. Accordingly, the distributive objection insists that, at the very least, the permissibility of undertaking to give priority to the interests of one's associates must be seen as sharply constrained by consideration of the effects on others of one's doing so. The proposed defence of associative duties does not really engage with this position, and so seems incapable of undermining it.

In addition, those who are sympathetic to the distributive objection may point out that although this defence says that associative duties arise out of people's permissible commitments, it does not actually explain how this happens. It appeals to people's interest in participating in interpersonal relationships to explain the permissibility of the commitments, but it provides no explanation of why the commitments give rise to duties. Of course, if people's strong interest in participating in interpersonal relationships makes it permissible for them to undertake to give priority to their associates, then the same consideration may also make it permissible for them actually to give priority to their associates. However, the idea of associative duties is not that one is permitted but rather that one is required to give such priority, and it is this further idea that requires explanation. Moreover, those sympathetic to the distributive objection may say, no appeal to the interests of those who make the commitments is capable of providing such an explanation. For the fact that people have legitimate self-interested reasons for making and acting on certain commitments does not explain why they have a duty to honour those commitments even if doing so works to the significant disadvantage of third parties. After all, we do not in general think that, if one has a legitimate interest in acting in some way that does not benefit others, then one is morally required not to benefit them. Thus, proponents of the distributive objection may argue, some other strategy is needed for explaining why commitments give rise to duties, rather than mere permissions, to favour one's associates. One obvious strategy would appeal not to the interests of those who make the commitments but rather to the interests of those who receive them. However, proponents of the distributive objection will insist that, in assessing the normative implications of interpersonal commitments, both these sets of interests must be balanced against the interests of those who will lose out if the commitments are indeed honoured.

Thus, to recapitulate, it may be argued that associative duties are generated by commitments which people must make to each other if they are to establish rewarding relationships, and which morality permits them to make for that reason. However, this 'defence' of associative duties is tantamount to a form of voluntaristic assimilationism. At the same time, it is unlikely to satisfy proponents of the distributive objection, who may press two points in response. First, they may argue that the permissibility of committing oneself to give priority to one's associates is constrained by the effects of those commitments on other people. Second, they may insist that some additional explanation is required of how permissible commitments give rise to associative duties. No appeal to the interests of those who make the commitments can provide such an explanation, they may argue, and any appeal to the interests of those who receive the commitments must be balanced by a consideration of the interests of those who do not receive them.

The question of how permissible commitments give rise to duties has, of course, been extensively discussed in the special case of promising. Although even the most thoroughgoing voluntarist is unlikely to argue that all genuine associative duties arise from actual promises, certain features of the promising example may appear to be of more general relevance. The standard function of promises, it is often said, is to facilitate social co-operation by providing promisees with a special kind of assurance. Making a promise provides such assurance because, in promising, one communicates an intention to incur an obligation by that very act of communication. In other words, one expresses one's intention to *make it the case* by virtue of that very expression of intention that one has a special kind of reason for acting as one says one will act. Without assurances of this kind, it is asserted, co-operative undertakings would often be difficult or even impossible to establish and sustain. Now it might be argued, by analogy to this case, that the commitments that give rise to associative duties make rewarding relationships possible precisely because they are seen by the participants in such relationships as generating special, duty-based reasons for giving priority to each other's interests. This perception, it might be argued, enables these commitments to provide a kind of assurance without which rewarding relationships would be difficult or impossible to establish and sustain. Accordingly, it might be suggested, the reason why these commitments give rise to associative duties is that the perception of them as giving rise to such duties is what enables them to make rewarding relationships possible.

Proponents of the distributive objection are likely to offer at least two replies to this argument. The first is that the participants in special relationships often have, and are seen as having, strong reasons apart from any perceived associative duties for giving priority to each other's interests. These reasons may derive, for example, from their love for each other, or from some shared identification or interest. Often it is reasons of this kind that motivate interpersonal commitments, and, it may be said, the recognition of such reasons is often sufficient to sustain rewarding relationships without any additional assurance provided by a shared perception of duty. The second reply is that even if a perception that interpersonal commitments give rise to duties is what enables such commitments to facilitate special relationships, this by itself does not show that these commitments really do give rise to duties. The promising case, it may be said, is similar, for the mere fact that one communicates an intention to incur an obligation does not itself explain how this brings it about that one actually does incur an obligation. Just what the explanation may be remains a matter of controversy, but many accounts appeal, in the end, either to the interests of promisors in being able to bind themselves, or to the interests of promisees in being able to rely on promises that are made to them, or to a general social interest in the existence of a stable practice of promising. And, proponents of the distributive objection may say, if any of these accounts is taken as the model for associative duties, then the case for such duties will once again rest, ultimately, on a kind of interest that needs to be balanced against the interests of those who are not participants in the putatively duty-generating groups and relationships.[12]

Thus it remains the case that the defense of associative duties that we have been discussing is apt to be challenged by proponents of the distributive objection despite the extensive concessions that it makes to the voluntarist

[12] For an account of the duty to keep one's promises that emphasizes the interests of promisors, see Joseph Raz, *The Morality of Freedom* (Oxford: Clarendon Press, 1986): 173–6. For accounts that emphasize the interests of promisees, see Neil MacCormick, 'Voluntary Obligations and Normative Powers I', *Proceedings of the Aristotelian Society*, Suppl. Vol. 46 (1972): 59–78; Thomas Scanlon, 'Promises and Practices', *Philosophy & Public Affairs* 19 (1990): 199–226. For criticism of MacCormick, see Joseph Raz, 'Voluntary Obligations and Normative Powers II', *Proceedings of the Aristotelian Society*, Suppl. Vol. 46 (1972): 79–101. Other important contemporary discussions include Rawls, *A Theory of Justice*, 344–50; Raz, 'Promises and Obligations', in *Law, Morality, and Society: Essays in Honour of H. L. A. Hart*, ed. P. M. S. Hacker and Joseph Raz (Oxford: Clarendon Press, 1977); John Searle, *Speech Acts* (Cambridge: Cambridge University Press, 1969), Chapters 3 and 8.

objection. This confirms our earlier observation that the distributive objection may be directed against associative duties, not only when they are conceived of as constituting a fundamental category in their own right, but also when they are construed along voluntaristic lines. It is worth reflecting on why this is so. We have already observed that whereas the voluntarist objection to un-assimilated associative duties is, in effect, an objection on behalf of those who are supposed to be bound by such duties, the distributive objection is, in effect, an objection on behalf of those to whom such duties are supposed *not* to be owed. This contrast may be further developed. The voluntarist objection is sensitive to the potentially burdensome character of social life, to the costs that must be incurred and the sacrifices that must be made in order for a human relationship to be sustained. The voluntarist, sensitive to these costs, argues that agents should not be required to bear them against their wills. Since this is precisely what unassimilated associative duties may require, such duties are themselves perceived as unreasonably burdensome, and are rejected accordingly. The distributive objection, however, is sensitive to the enormous rewards of social life, to the unparalleled capacity of interpersonal relations to enrich human existence. In consequence, it sees the opportunity to assist one's associates, and so to contribute to the flourishing of one's social relationships, as a great luxury. Accordingly, when it is suggested that one may be required to provide such assistance even if doing so works to the detriment of those who are already needier, the distributive objection per-ceives this as conferring a great benefit on oneself and one's associates: a benefit that is so great, in fact, as to amount to an unfair advantage. So far as this perception is concerned, moreover, it makes no difference whether such require-ments are thought of as arising from some voluntary act on the part of the agent or not. Either way, they are seen as unfairly benefiting the agent and his or her associates. Since associative duties are requirements of precisely this kind, the distributive objection views them as problematic whether or not they are construed as susceptible to voluntaristic assimilation.

Clearly, both objections capture part of the truth about human relation-ships. For such relationships can of course be both burdensome and reward-ing. They make great demands, but they are a source of incomparable satisfactions. They may call for great sacrifices, yet there are some sacrifices that it is a luxury to be able to make. And just as both objections capture part of the truth about human relationships, so too both capture part of the truth about associative duties. For, in so far as such duties would impose burdens upon us without our consent, they constitute genuine constraints. Yet, in so far as they would have us cultivate rewarding ties even when there are more urgent needs to be met, they also confer genuine advantages. Like our social lives themselves, the associative duties that are so often thought to accompany them may be demanding and enriching at once. The voluntarist objection focuses on the demands, and judges these to be unreasonable in so far as they are imposed without our agreement. The distributive objection focuses on the advantages, and judges these to be unreasonable in so far as they work to the detriment of those who are needier.

And, yet, there is a tenacious strand of ordinary moral opinion that dismisses both objections, and continues to see associative duties as central components of moral experience. In so doing, it recognizes some claims upon us whose source lies neither in our own choices nor in the needs of others, but rather in the complex and constantly evolving constellation of social and historical relations into which we enter the moment we are born. For we are, after all, born to parents we did not choose at a time we did not choose; and we land in some region we did not choose of a social world we did not choose. And, from the moment of our birth and sometimes sooner, claims are made on us and for us and to us. We are claimed by families and clans, by nations and states, by races and religions, by cultures and communities and classes—all clamouring to confer privileges and responsibilities upon us, and to initiate us into their histories and their traditions, their sorrows and their joys, their passions and their hatreds, their wisdom and their follies. And if, in due course, we inject our own wills into this mix—straining against some ties and embracing others, sometimes severing old bonds and sometimes acquiring new ones—the verdict of common moral opinion seems to be that we can never simply wipe the slate clean. Our specific historical and social identities, as they develop and evolve over time, continue to call forth claims with which we must reckon: claims that cannot without distortion be construed as contractual in character, and which are not reduced to silence by general considerations of need.

At the same time, the voluntarist and distributive objections are not themselves alien to ordinary moral opinion, for both of them are rooted in values that are also securely entrenched within modern moral thought. The voluntarist objection grows out of an ideal of freedom and autonomy which is one of the hallmarks of a liberal society and which has a central place in our evaluative outlook. The distributive objection is rooted in a principle of equality which is also a fundamental tenet of modern moral thought, and which asserts that all people, however varied their relations to us may happen to be, are nevertheless of equal value and importance. The problem, then, is not that these objections to associative duties are alien to us. On the contrary, the problem is that both associative duties and the values that generate objections to them exert genuine authority within our moral thought, so that what might otherwise be a mere clash of philosophical positions is instead a deep conflict within contemporary moral life.

V

This brings us back to the point from which we began. As we seek to orient ourselves in relation to the conflicting tendencies toward global integration and communal differentiation that I mentioned at the outset of this essay, no resource would be more helpful than a settled conception of our responsibilities toward others. Unfortunately, however, this is a resource we can suppose ourselves to possess only if we are prepared to repudiate some of the values we hold dearest. For, in the end, those values pull us in genuinely different directions on questions of responsibility. We prize our freedom to choose, and thus to control the extent of our duties to others. Yet we are committed to the equality of persons, and are sensitive to claims of need that do not themselves spring from choices we have made. Moreover, most of us recognize a region of moral space that is occupied by claims deriving neither from our own choices nor from the needs of others, but rather from our membership in particular groups and our participation in particular relationships. So it is little wonder, then, that we tend to flounder as we confront a world in which the boundaries of responsibility are increasingly contested. We are swayed by the sophisticated, cosmopolitan rhetoric of global integration, and we are genuinely moved by scenes of starvation and disease in faraway lands, but, at the same time, we resist those ideas of global justice that might broaden the scope of our own responsibility and threaten our standard of living. We recoil in horror from the bloody ethnic conflicts of which television has made us all spectators, but we celebrate diversity and difference and are suspicious of the idea of a common culture. We decry the fragmentation of our societies, but we seek above all else to protect and promote the interests of those who are dearest to us. We insist on our status as autonomous agents and on the centrality of our freedom to choose, but increasingly we see ourselves as victims and blame others for our misfortunes, as if to indicate how little we see our own choices as counting for in a world of complex interdependencies, massive institutional structures, and breathtaking new technologies. In all of these ways and more, we reveal that we have lost any sure sense of our responsibilities toward others and their responsibilities toward us. The idea of associative duties, important as it continues to be to us, can by itself provide no solution to this problem. Instead, the quest for a satisfactory conception of associative duties is but one part of a much larger task: the task of trying to identify a conception of responsibility we can live with in a world where the distribution of responsibility has become one of the most divisive questions of all.

4

Liberalism, Nationalism, and Egalitarianism *

Liberalism in one form or another is the dominant position in contemporary political philosophy. Despite this, or perhaps because of it, liberalism continues to attract criticism of many different kinds. Some critics believe that liberalism underestimates the human and political significance that attaches to membership in a nation, or in a cultural or communal group, and that it therefore misjudges the significance of the national and cultural diversity that is a feature of so many modern societies. These critics view liberalism as insufficiently particularist in its orientation. At the same time, there are other critics who believe that liberalism as standardly formulated places too little emphasis on questions of global or international political morality, and that it focuses too much of its attention on the individual society, which is assumed to be organized as an independent country or state, and which is treated as a self-sufficient co-operative enterprise. These critics view liberalism as insufficiently globalist in its orientation.

The philosophical disagreements among liberals and their globalist and particularist critics range over many issues. One of these issues, and the one that I wish to address in this essay, concerns the question of responsibility or, more precisely, the question of how various kinds of social ties affect the responsibilities that people have to each other. Disagreements about this issue may be thought of as disagreements about the boundaries of our responsibilities. Particularist critics charge that by focusing on the individual society, which it takes to be organized as a political unit, liberalism neglects the special responsibilities that arise from membership in a nation or community, where nations and communities are defined in cultural rather than political terms. Globalist critics, on the other hand, charge that liberalism overemphasizes the individual's responsibilities to his *own* society, and underestimates the extent of

* Originally published in *The Morality of Nationalism*, ed. Robert McKim and Jeff McMahan (Oxford University Press, 1997), 191–208. An earlier version of this essay was presented as the 1994–95 John Dewey Memorial Lecture at the University of Vermont, and I benefited from the helpful discussion on that occasion. I am also indebted to Michael Green, Christopher Kutz, and Jeff McMahan for valuable comments, criticisms, and suggestions.

his duties to people in other societies. Although globalists allow that there may be practical or instrumental reasons why one should take special responsibility for the members of one's own society, they insist that it is a mistake to exaggerate the extent of this responsibility or to treat it as a matter of fundamental principle. Thus, whereas particularists criticize liberals for neglecting the responsibilities associated with membership in a national or communal group, globalists argue that liberals' emphasis on the individual society is itself too particularistic.

The political importance of these disagreements is clear. Both particularist and globalist ideas have become increasingly influential in contemporary politics, and one of the most important tasks for contemporary liberal theory is to address the twin challenges posed by particularist and globalist thinking.[1]

As I have said, I will be concerned in this essay with questions about the boundaries of our responsibilities. I will argue that the particularist and globalist criticisms of liberalism point to two different tensions within liberal thought: first, a tension between an explicit voluntarism and an implicit nationalism and, second, a tension between a commitment to moral egalitarianism and a commitment to some form of particularism about political responsibility. In the final section of the essay, I will assess the significance for liberalism of these two tensions.

I

The disagreements about responsibility that I have mentioned are closely related to debates within normative ethics about the status of 'associative duties'. These are the special duties that the members of significant social groups and the participants in close personal relationships are thought to have to one another. Associative duties occupy a central position in common-sense moral thought. It is normally taken for granted that one has special responsibilities to one's associates—that is, to one's family and friends and to the members of other significant groups to which one belongs. In general, these duties or responsibilities require us to give the interests of our associates various forms of priority over the interests of non-associates. Sometimes this will mean incurring greater costs for the sake of our associates than we would be expected to incur for the sake of others; and sometimes it will mean assigning the interests of our associates precedence over the interests of others in cases of conflict.[2] Although there is only a partial consensus about which types

---

[1] For pertinent discussion, see the debate between Martha Nussbaum and twenty-nine commentators on the subject of 'Patriotism or Cosmopolitanism?', *Boston Review* 19 (October/November 1994): 3–34. See also Nussbaum *et al.*, *For Love of Country: Debating the Limits of Patriotism* (Boston, MA: Beacon Press, 1996).

[2] For more detailed discussion of the content of associative duties, see section 3 of my 'Families, Nations, and Strangers', Chapter Three in this volume.

of groups and relationships give rise to such duties, most people take it for granted that they have at least some responsibilities of this sort. Thus, in so far as the particularist criticism of liberalism amounts to the claim that we have associative duties to the members of national or communal groups to which we belong, it invokes a normative category that represents an important dimension of common-sense moral thought.

Despite their common-sense moral credentials, however, associative duties are philosophically controversial. Much of the controversy derives from what I have elsewhere called the *voluntarist objection*.[3] This objection does not deny that we often have special duties to people who are related to us in certain ways and to the members of various groups with which we are affiliated, but it insists that such duties or responsibilities must always arise from our own voluntary acts. Different voluntarists disagree about which voluntary acts are duty-generating. Some require that we explicitly accept the responsibilities in question. Others require only that we voluntarily enter into the putatively duty-generating group or relationship. Still others think that our voluntary acceptance of the benefits of participation in such a group or relationship suffices. All voluntarists agree, however, that some voluntary act is necessary. Associative duties, they insist, cannot be ascribed to us without our having done anything at all to acquire them. Thus, voluntarists typically recognize such duties as valid only in so far as they can be assimilated to contractual duties broadly construed or to voluntarily incurred duties of other kinds. What voluntarists deny, in other words, is that associative duties constitute an independent class of duties, which can be incurred simply by virtue of standing in relationships of certain sorts to other people.

Associative duties constitute assignments of responsibility that can in some respects be quite burdensome for those who bear them, and the voluntarist objection reflects a sense that such responsibilities cannot be imposed on people without their consent or, at any rate, without their suitably voluntary performance of some act about which they have a genuine choice. On the face of it, this objection seems a natural outgrowth of a more general concern with the freedom and autonomy of the individual agent. As such, of course, it resonates with central values of liberalism, and, indeed, one standard liberal objection to nationalism and communitarianism simply recapitulates the voluntarist objection to unassimilated associative duties. To the liberal, the idea that one's responsibilities may be determined by social ties over which one has no control is regressive and atavistic; it is a hallmark of systems of social caste and hierarchy, and it represents an unacceptable constraint on the freedom of the individual. Moreover, in so far as it invites the thought that one's privileges may also be determined by social ties over which one has no control, it seems to many liberals to pave the way for the

---

[3] For additional discussion of the voluntarist objection, see Chapter Three in this volume, sections 3 and 4.

most invidious forms of discrimination and differential treatment. Thus, to many liberals, the repudiation of this idea represents the triumph of freedom over constraint: the liberation of the individual chooser from the stultifying and divisive claims of blood and historical inheritance. Accordingly, liberal theories tend officially to disavow associative duties. In so far as such theories are concerned with the responsibilities of individual citizens, the responsibilities in question are usually categorized as 'political obligations', which are conceived of as consensually generated obligations to uphold the laws and institutions of one's society.

Most of us who have grown up in liberal societies have internalized liberal values to a considerable extent and have a strong allegiance to them. Yet as we have seen, the idea of associative duties also has deep roots within common-sense moral thought. Thus there is a tension within the common-sense morality of our culture: a tension between a powerful strand of voluntaristic conviction and a continuing commitment to the moral relevance of various types of interpersonal bonds whose susceptibility to voluntaristic assimilation is, at the very least, open to question.

The existence of this tension is not, perhaps, very surprising. What may be more surprising is that this same tension is also reflected within liberalism itself, and that many liberal theories that explicitly reject associative duties seem tacitly to rely on them, or at least to incorporate elements that serve to mimic such duties in important respects. To see this, we may begin by reminding ourselves of a point upon which globalists insist—namely, that despite being subject to particularist criticism, liberalism itself has an important particularist dimension. Clearly, for example, liberal accounts of political obligation have a particularist character, inasmuch as such obligations are not supposed to be owed to the world at large or to other people in general. Instead, political obligations are thought of as special obligations that are owed either to the other members of one's own society or to its political officials or institutions, who are in turn conceived of as specially responsible for protecting and promoting the interests of the members of that society. Thus, whether or not political obligations are thought of as owed directly to one's fellow citizens, they are, in any case, special obligations whose ultimate beneficiaries are one's fellow citizens.

Of course, the mere fact that liberal political obligations are particularistic in this way does not call into question their voluntarist basis. However, there are other particularist features of liberalism whose compatibility with voluntarist ideas is more doubtful. When liberals address questions of justice, for example, it is 'social justice' with which they are typically concerned—that is, the justice of a single society or its major institutions. Even more striking is the liberal view of membership or of how one comes to acquire citizenship in the liberal state. Although a thoroughgoing voluntarism would presumably dictate that liberal citizenship should be purely a matter of individual choice, and although that idea is enshrined in the liberal tradition via the myth of the social contract, liberal theorists have, in general, had little to say about how membership is determined, and actual liberal societies attach far more weight to birth than to choice in assigning citizenship and its associated privileges and obligations. In addition, although liberal theorists focus explicitly on the question of how the political institutions of an individual society are to be justified, they also tend, either explicitly or implicitly, to assume that each society will be organized not merely as a state but as a 'nation-state'. This means that the citizens of each state are thought of as constituting a national group with a common culture.[4]

The net result of this cluster of positions and practices is to call into question the liberal rejection of associative duties, for although liberalism officially eschews such duties, the citizens of the liberal state are standardly represented, both in theory and in practice, as constituting a national group whose members have particularistic responsibilities toward each other, either directly or as a result of their duties to shared political institutions. Moreover, liberal citizens are commonly seen as passing these responsibilities on to their children, along with the various perquisites of membership, as a matter of birthright. Thus, as Yael Tamir has emphasized,[5] there is a tension within the liberal position between an explicit voluntarism and an implicit nationalism— a largely unacknowledged tendency to invest national ties with a kind of moral and political significance that cannot be accounted for in purely voluntaristic terms.

II

In recent years, some liberal theorists have begun to distance themselves from the traditional liberal reliance on a thoroughly voluntaristic notion of political obligation. Some of these theorists, such as Ronald Dworkin and Yael Tamir, have actually suggested that political obligations should be reconstrued as associative duties.[6] In so doing, these theorists have renounced or substantially modified the voluntaristic objection to such duties. Other liberal theorists, such as John Rawls and Jeremy Waldron, have appealed instead to a 'natural duty of justice' to account for the political responsibilities of the individual citizen.[7] As Rawls characterizes it, '[t]his duty requires us to

[4] See, for example, John Rawls, *A Theory of Justice* (Cambridge, MA: Harvard University Press, 1971), p. 457, and *Political Liberalism* (New York, NY: Columbia University Press, 1993), 272n.

[5] See Yael Tamir, *Liberal Nationalism* (Princeton, NJ: Princeton University Press, 1993), esp. ch. 6. In the final three paragraphs of this section I have relied heavily on Tamir's discussion.

[6] See Ronald Dworkin, *Law's Empire* (Cambridge, MA: Harvard University Press, 1986), 195–216; Tamir, *Liberal Nationalism*, chs. 5, 6.

[7] See Rawls, *A Theory of Justice*, secs. 18–19, 51–2; Jeremy Waldron, 'Special Ties and Natural Duties', *Philosophy & Public Affairs* 22 (1993): 3–30.

support and comply with just institutions that exist and apply to us'.[8] The natural duty of justice is said to be ascribable to all individuals and not to depend on their consent or any other voluntary act.

A. John Simmons has argued that the appeal to a natural duty of justice cannot serve the purposes of liberal theory because it cannot explain why a citizen has a special responsibility to the institutions of his particular society—as opposed to a general responsibility to support just institutions everywhere.[9] More precisely, Simmons claims that this 'particularity requirement' cannot be satisfied by the appeal to a natural duty of justice unless the natural duty of justice turns out to be indistinguishable from voluntaristic political obligation. Of course, the natural duty as Rawls characterizes it is formally compatible with the particularity requirement, for it says that we are bound only to those just institutions that 'apply to us'. However, Simmons asks how this notion of 'application' is to be understood. Only if it is a morally significant notion will the fact that a just institution applies to us be capable of explaining why we have special responsibilities toward that institution that we do not have toward other just institutions. There are, Simmons suggests, two broadly different ways of understanding the notion of application. In one sense, an institution might be said to apply to me just by virtue of 'my birth and growth in a territory within which the institution's rules are enforced'.[10] However, Simmons argues that application in this sense is not a morally significant notion because 'my birth is not an act I perform, or something for which I am responsible'.[11] In another sense, an institution may be said to apply to me by virtue of my having '*done* things'[12] that tie me to it, such as consenting to be governed by its rules or accepting benefits from it. Simmons argues that '[o]nly in cases of application in [this] "strong" sense, those that involve an individual's consent, say, or his *acceptance* of significant benefits, does "application" begin to look morally important'.[13] Obviously, however, consent and the acceptance of benefits are just the sorts of acts to which voluntaristic accounts of political obligation appeal. Thus, Simmons concludes, the only way in which the natural duty of justice can satisfy the particularity requirement is by relying on a notion of application that renders this supposed natural duty indistinguishable from voluntaristically-generated political obligation.

On one level, Simmons's argument seems to beg the question, for he appears simply to assume that only something that one has done could give one a morally significant tie to a particular institution. This is itself a voluntaristic assumption, which guarantees that the appeal to natural duty will seem untenable except in so far as it fails to offer any real alternative to voluntarist political obligation. It seems open to a defender of natural duty to reject this

---

[8] Rawls, *A Theory of Justice*, 115.
[9] A. John Simmons, *Moral Principles and Political Obligations* (Princeton, NJ: Princeton University Press, 1979), ch. 6.
[10] Ibid., 149–50.   [11] Ibid., 150.   [12] Ibid.   [13] Ibid., 150–1.

assumption and argue that there are certain relations between individuals and just institutions that can be morally significant even if they don't arise from anything that the individuals have done. For example, it might be said that citizenship is such a relationship and that the fact that one is a citizen of a just society can give one a special responsibility to support the institutions of that society even if one became a citizen at birth and not as a result of anything that one did.

Note, however, that such an argument would have one effect that seems at variance with the intentions of those who appeal to a natural duty to support just institutions, which is that it would make this duty seem more like an associative duty. For, whereas the ground of the natural duty seemed initially to lie in the justice of the just institution, this argument suggests that the individual's relation to the institution also plays a crucial role in generating the duty. And, of course, the notion that participation in certain sorts of relationships can give rise to special responsibilities is what lies behind the idea of associative duties. Admittedly, associative duties as I have characterized them are owed to specific individuals, whereas Rawls says that natural duties are owed 'to persons generally',[14] so that, even on the interpretation we are considering, a difference between the two types of duty would remain. Nevertheless, the two would also have an important feature in common, and one that would make it more difficult for liberals who appeal to natural duty to deny the possibility of unassimilated associative duties. Indeed, one moral of Simmons's argument, it seems to me, is that the voluntarist objection to associative duties can also be directed against the natural duty to support just institutions if the natural duty is defended in the way that I have suggested.

Thus the effect of such a defence is, for better or worse, to push the 'particularized' natural duty of justice in the direction of an associative duty. However, the preceding remarks also raise an additional question about the internal coherence of the natural duty so interpreted. According to that interpretation, the duty appears to be the product of two factors that tend in different directions. The first factor is justice itself, whose tendency is to suggest a non-particularized duty to support just institutions generally. The second factor, which is the particularizing factor, is the individual's relationship to a specific set of institutions. What may seem unclear, however, is why this second, particularizing tendency should take precedence over the putatively universal claims of justice. In other words, if justice really does generate non-particularized reasons, how does the scope of those reasons get reduced by the individual's relation to a particular set of institutions? Rather than meshing smoothly to generate a single, particularized duty, the two factors may seem to represent conflicting values that cannot easily be harmonized. Thus the natural duty of justice may look like an unstable attempt to integrate

---

[14] Rawls, *A Theory of Justice*, 115.

opposing moral values, and as such it may seem an unattractive alternative to voluntaristic political obligation.[15]

However, I want to argue that the apparent instability of the natural duty to support just institutions is symptomatic of a broader problem that afflicts any form of liberalism that seeks to reconcile egalitarian values with a particularistic account of our political responsibilities. By a particularistic account of our political responsibilities I mean any account that claims we have fundamentally different responsibilities to the citizens or institutions of our own society than we have to the rest of the world. If I am correct, the problem of reconciling such an account with egalitarian values marks a second important tension within liberal theory.

III

One way to bring this second tension into focus is by taking note of a second objection to associative duties, an objection that I have referred to elsewhere as *the distributive objection*.[16] Whereas the voluntarist objection reflects a concern with the freedom and autonomy of the individual agent, and is likely to be pressed by liberals, the distributive objection is strongly egalitarian in spirit, and is likely to be pressed by globalists. As we have seen, the voluntarist objection is concerned with the potentially burdensome character of associative duties for those who bear them. By contrast, the distributive objection sees the same duties as capable of conferring important benefits on their bearers and important disadvantages on others. More specifically, the distributive objection claims that one effect of associative duties is to provide people who have already had the good fortune to be included in rewarding groups and relationships with extra benefits, in the form of increased claims to one another's assistance. In other words, if the participants

---

[15] In defending the natural duty of justice against Simmons's criticism, Jeremy Waldron argues that such duties can be particularized because principles of justice can be limited in their application and because a person can have a special duty to an institution that administers such a 'range-limited' principle. This may be so if the person is an 'insider' with respect to that institution—that is, 'if it is part of the point of that institution to do justice to some claim of his among all the claims with which it deals' ('Special Ties and Natural Duties', 16). However, Waldron also suggests that range limitations are justified only on a 'provisional' or 'pro tem' basis (15). If those who are not insiders with respect to a given range-limited principle interfere with the administration of such a principle because they wish to promote a principle of wider application, such as 'a principle of global redistribution', there may be 'no moral basis for condemning' this interference (17n). But then, on Waldron's interpretation, the natural duty of justice hardly seems to represent a stable way of integrating universalist and particularist considerations, for it presents no fundamental barrier to a thoroughgoing globalism.

[16] See section 3 of 'Families, Nations, and Strangers', Chapter Three in this volume.

in rewarding relationships have associative duties, then they must give higher priority to one another's claims than they would otherwise have been expected to do. But, by the same token, they must also give lower priority to the claims of non-participants. Thus, if participation in rewarding groups and relationships does indeed give rise to associative duties, then, according to the distributive objection, non-participants lose out twice: in addition to missing out on the other rewards of participation, their claims on the participants for assistance become weaker.

The distributive objection challenges the fairness of associative duties so understood. It asserts that claims to assistance from others constitute a kind of normative resource, and that the effect of associative duties is to bring about an inegalitarian distribution of that resource. The objection does not claim that this distribution is unfair in itself, but rather that it becomes unfair when it serves to reinforce inequalities in the distribution of resources of other kinds. An assignment of associative duties may, in the manner already suggested, build on and reinforce inequalities in the distribution of humanly rewarding relationships. More importantly for present purposes, however, it may also reinforce material inequalities, for if the participants in the relevant groups and relationships are richer than other people, then associative duties will require them to give one another's interests priority over the interests of those who are poorer. The distributive objection argues that this is unfair, and that associative duties cannot be justified when they work to the disadvantage of those are already worse off. Nor, according to the distributive objection, can the problem be avoided by assimilating associative duties to contractual duties rather than construing them as an independent class of duties in their own right. Even if they are thought of as voluntaristically generated, the objection asserts, associative duties will remain open to challenge on distributive grounds. Or, more accurately perhaps, they will remain open to challenge on distributive grounds unless those who are not members of the putatively duty-generating groups and relationships are given the opportunity to join and voluntarily decline to do so. In the absence of such opportunities, the objection concludes, the claim that the duties of membership arise from voluntary acts does not suffice to establish their distributive fairness.

If we return now to the discussion of liberalism, we can see that the distributive objection may be directed by globalists against those versions of liberal theory that postulate the existence either of associative duties or of voluntaristic political obligations. For, at the political level, the distributive objection challenges the idea that the members of an individual society have special duties to each other that they do not have to other people, and as we have seen, it does not matter, for the purposes of this objection, whether the duties in question are construed voluntaristically or not. Either way, these supposed duties are seen as providing an unjustifiable mandate for the members of affluent societies to lavish resources on each other while largely ignoring the suffering and deprivation of people in much poorer societies.

However widespread this pattern of behaviour may, in fact, be and however natural it may seem, the idea that such conduct is not merely morally permissible, but morally required, strikes proponents of the distributive objection as a transparently self-serving conceit.

The fact that the distributive objection is liable to be directed both against versions of liberalism that rely on associative duties and against versions that rely on voluntaristic political obligations, suggests that the tension internal to the 'particularized' natural duty of justice is symptomatic of a much broader tension within liberal theory. Recall that the particularized natural duty seemed like a possibly unstable attempt to integrate a universalistic notion of justice with a particularistic conception of our political responsibilities. The distributive objection suggests that a similar problem faces liberal theories that rely on associative duties or voluntaristic political obligations. These theories, too, offer particularized conceptions of political responsibility, and as the distributive objection shows, these theories, too, are subject to challenge from the standpoint of a universalistic, egalitarian set of values.

Now it may be argued that the distributive objection represents an external challenge to these theories; it does not show that they are characterized by any internal tension. By contrast, it may be said, the difficulty with the particularized natural duty of justice was not that it was subject to external challenge but rather that the two elements that were supposed to generate it seemed in conflict with each other. Thus, it may be argued, those versions of liberalism that rely on the natural duty of justice are problematic in a way that the other versions are not. This is misleading, however, for the distributive objection implicitly appeals to an egalitarian premise upon which virtually all contemporary liberal theories insist—namely, that all persons have equal moral worth and that no person's interests are of greater intrinsic moral importance than any other person's. The distributive objection claims that associative duties, whether interpreted voluntaristically or not, are incompatible with a recognition of the equal moral importance of each person's interests. Whether or not this objection is correct, it counts as an internal objection to those versions of liberalism that rely on such duties, for it argues from a premise that is an important tenet of liberalism itself. Understood in this way, the objection points to a tension between moral egalitarianism and a particularistic understanding of our political responsibilities that is present in virtually all contemporary versions of liberalism, and is the same tension that is reflected in the particularized natural duty of justice. It is true that the particularized natural duty is itself supposed to be the product of universalistic and particularistic considerations, so that the tension between those considerations is internal not merely to theories that rely on the natural duty but also to that duty itself. Although the same cannot be said about theories that rely on associative duties or voluntaristic political obligations, this does not mean that the tension within those theories is any shallower or less problematic, only that it is less conspicuous.

IV

I said at the outset of this essay that the particularist and globalist criticisms of liberalism point to two different tensions within liberal thought. The particularist criticism, as we have now seen, points to a tension between an explicit voluntarism and an implicit nationalism that is characteristic of much of liberal theory and practice. The globalist criticism points to a tension between a commitment to moral egalitarianism and a commitment to particularism about political responsibility that is also quite typical of contemporary liberal thought. Significantly, the way that we identified these two tensions was by attending to two different objections that have been leveled against associative duties—the duties to which nationalist and other particularist critics of liberalism appeal. The voluntarist objection, as we saw, is one that is typically offered by liberals themselves, although the inability of those same liberals to avoid relying on something like associative duties at certain points in their own accounts was revelatory of the first tension within liberalism. The distributive objection, meanwhile, is one that is typically offered by globalists, and since it can be directed against associative duties whether or not those duties are construed in voluntaristic terms, it presents a challenge both to liberals and to their particularist critics. This objection reveals a tension within liberal theory because it appeals to a premise on which liberals themselves insist. The role of these two objections to associative duties in revealing the tensions within liberal thought suggests that both tensions stem from a kind of liberal ambivalence about the moral and political significance of people's social affiliations and allegiances. There is ambivalence, reflected in the first tension, about whether and in what way these affiliations and allegiances must be voluntary in order to have such significance, and there is ambivalence, reflected in the second tension, about how a recognition of their significance can be reconciled and integrated with a commitment to the equal worth of persons.

It may seem clear that the existence of these tensions constitutes a flaw in liberal theory. Yet up to a certain point, at least, it can also be viewed as a virtue, inasmuch as the tensions within liberal theory bespeak a sensitivity to three important values whose joint accommodation is genuinely problematic. Along with the familiar liberal value of autonomy, there is the value of moral equality, as expressed in the idea that all people are of equal worth and that their interests are of equal importance, and the value of loyalty, as expressed in the idea that particular interpersonal relations and social ties are a source of special normative considerations.[17] The tensions within liberal theory, I am suggesting, reflect its sensitivity to these three different values, all of which matter to us, but which are also genuinely in tension with each other. This suggestion may be challenged, of course, and in a number of different ways.

---

[17] For a book-length discussion of loyalty, see George Fletcher, *Loyalty* (New York, NY: Oxford University Press, 1993).

First, it may be doubted whether all three of these values really do matter to us. Second, it may be doubted whether liberalism really is sensitive to all of them. Third, it may be doubted whether the values really are in tension with each other.

I will say nothing about the first of these challenges. However, I do want to take up one version of the second challenge and one version of the third. The second challenge denies that liberalism is, in fact, sensitive to all three of the values I have mentioned. The version of this challenge that I will consider is implicit in an influential argument by Alasdair MacIntyre.[18] MacIntyre draws a contrast between 'liberal morality' and 'the morality of patriotism'. Liberal morality, he says, is 'a morality of universal, impersonal and impartial principles'; the morality of patriotism, by contrast, is 'a morality of particularist ties and solidarities'.[19] These two moralities, he says, are 'deeply'[20] and 'systematically'[21] incompatible. In other words, what I have represented as a tension within liberal theory MacIntyre represents as a contrast between two distinct and incompatible moral outlooks. MacIntyre says that there are different versions of liberal morality, including Kantian, utilitarian, and contractarian versions, but that all of these versions have a common core that renders them incompatible with the morality of patriotism. For example, MacIntyre argues, if each of two communities needs the use of the same natural resource in order to survive and flourish, then 'the standpoint of impersonal morality requires an allocation of goods such that each individual person counts for one and no more than one, while the patriotic standpoint requires that I strive to further the interests of my community and you strive to further those of yours'.[22] In effect, MacIntyre's argument is that a moral outlook is sensitive to the value of loyalty only if it holds that individuals have special duties to give priority to the interests of their own communities; that liberalism rejects such duties because of its commitment to moral egalitarianism; and, hence, that liberalism is insensitive to the value of loyalty.

However, this argument is unpersuasive because it fails to acknowledge or engage the particularist dimension of liberalism, especially liberal particularism about political responsibility. More generally, it overlooks the fact that most liberals who endorse the idea of moral equality, as a claim about the equal worth or value of persons, nevertheless deny that this idea fully determines the content of the principles governing the conduct of individual agents. Notwithstanding MacIntyre's claims about the common core of 'liberal morality', this is a familiar point of disagreement between utilitarians and other consequentialists, on the one hand, and various non-consequentialists, including Kantians and contractarians, on the other. Consequentialists argue that the right act in any given situation is the one that will produce the best overall outcome, as judged from an impersonal standpoint that gives equal

[18] See Alasdair MacIntyre, 'Is Patriotism a Virtue?', Lindley Lecture, University of Kansas, 1984.
[19] Ibid., 19.   [20] Ibid., 18.   [21] Ibid., 5.   [22] Ibid., 6.

weight to the interests of everyone. By contrast, however, most liberals accept what are sometimes called 'agent-relative' principles, which make the rightness of acts at least partly independent of considerations of overall value.[23] Those liberals who accept agent-relative principles do not deny that people are of equal value or importance. However, they do believe that facts that have special significance for an individual agent can sometimes have special weight in determining what that agent may permissibly do, despite the fact that the agent is no more valuable or important than anyone else.[24] This general conviction has been explicitly applied to the case of associative duties by Tamir, who denies that such duties are 'grounded in the idea that what is mine is more valuable than what is yours'.[25] She adds: 'When I claim that charity begins at home I do not intend to imply that the poor of my town are better but merely that . . . I have a greater obligation toward them than to strangers because they are members of *my* community. . . . [Such] claims do not . . . imply an objective hierarchy among different forms of life.'[26] Not all liberals accept associative duties, of course, but the vast majority accept some kind of particularism about responsibility, and they would surely agree with Tamir that such particularism is not excluded by a commitment to the equal worth of persons.

These observations, however, invite a version of the third challenge. For they seem to suggest that there may be, in the end, no tension at all between moral egalitarianism and particularism about responsibility and hence, presumably, no tension between the underlying values of moral equality and of loyalty. This is not so, however. It is one thing to point out that most liberals do, in fact, accept both moral egalitarianism and a significantly particularistic account of responsibility, but it is another thing actually to demonstrate the compatibility of these two features of liberal thought. And many liberals, it seems to me, underestimate the difficulty of doing this. Tamir's defense of associative duties is a case in point. Along with other contemporary liberal writers, such as Will Kymlicka, Neil MacCormick, and Joseph Raz,[27]

---

[23] As this suggests, the relation between liberalism and consequentialism is in some ways a problematic one. I have examined the contrast between consequentialism and agent-relative morality in *The Rejection of Consequentialism*, rev. ed. (Oxford: Clarendon, 1994).

[24] I have discussed this point at greater length in *Human Morality* (New York, NY: Oxford University Press, 1992), ch. 6.

[25] Tamir, *Liberal Nationalism*, 100.   [26] Ibid., 100–1.

[27] See Will Kymlicka, *Liberalism, Community, and Culture* (Oxford: Clarendon, 1989); Neil MacCormick, 'Nation and Nationalism', in *Legal Right and Social Democracy: Essays in Legal and Social Philosophy* (Oxford: Clarendon, 1982): 247–64; Joseph Raz and Avishai Margalit, 'National Self-Determination', and Joseph Raz, 'Multiculturalism: A Liberal Perspective', in Raz's *Ethics in the Public Domain* (Oxford: Clarendon, 1994): 110–30, 155–76. See also Avishai Margalit and Moshe Halbertal, 'Liberalism and the Right to Culture', *Social Research* 61 (1994): 491–510. It is significant, I think, that all of these writers are concerned primarily with the question of how liberalism can accommodate the claims of communities to recognition, legal protection, and self-determination. They have little or nothing to say about the duties of community members to each other.

as well as earlier liberal thinkers like John Dewey,[28] she makes a strong case for the importance in people's lives of group affiliations of one sort or another. However, we must remember that associative duties do not merely permit the assignment of priority to the interests of one's associates; they require it. And as the distributive objection reminds us, it is not obvious how the importance to a person of his group affiliations translates into a requirement that he favour the members of his group. Tamir says that associative duties are 'not grounded on consent, reciprocity, or gratitude, but rather on a feeling of belonging and connectedness'.[29] However, the step from such a feeling to a requirement that one favour the interests of those to whom one feels connected remains problematic. In order to reconcile associative duties and moral egalitarianism, we need an answer to the following question: if all people are of equal value and importance, then what is it about my relation to my associates that makes it not merely permissible but obligatory for me to give their interests priority over the interests of other people? Many attempts at reconciliation fail to confront this question squarely and instead move back and forth between claims about the duty to give priority to one's associates and claims about the permissibility of doing so. It remains to be seen whether the question can be given a satisfactory answer. Certainly the fact that I feel connected to my associates seems, on the face of it, like a more promising ground for a permission to favour them than for a requirement to do so.[30]

Moreover, even if the question could be given a satisfactory answer, that would not mean that there was no longer any tension between the underlying values of loyalty and moral equality. On the contrary, there are at least two types of tension between those values that would not be eliminated by a satisfactory justification of associative duties. First, the values are *mutually constraining* in the sense that each, if accepted, places limits on the ways in which the other may legitimately be realized or advanced. Second, the values are *practically competitive* in the sense that institutions and practices that serve to recognize or foster one of them sometimes undermine or erode the realization of the other. If the distributive objection can be given a satisfactory answer, then we may conclude that associative duties help to define the relation of mutual constraint between the two values. We may not, however, conclude that the values are no longer in tension.

In summary, we have taken note of two tensions within liberal theory: the tension between an explicit voluntarism and an implicit nationalism, and the tension between a commitment to moral egalitarianism and a commitment

---

[28] See John Dewey, *The Public and Its Problems* (New York, NY: Henry Holt, 1927), 143–84, 211–19.

[29] Tamir, *Liberal Nationalism*, 137.

[30] For discussion of an argument that seeks first to establish the permissibility of favouring one's associates and then to move from this permission to associative duties, see 'Families, Nations, and Strangers', Chapter Three in this volume, section 4.

to particularism about political responsibility. These theoretical tensions reflect ambivalence about the moral and political significance of people's social affiliations and allegiances: about the extent to which and the respects in which the affiliations must be voluntary in order to have such significance and about how a recognition of their significance can be integrated with a commitment to the equal worth of persons. This very ambivalence, I have argued, indicates that liberalism is sensitive to three different values: the values of autonomy, loyalty, and moral equality. If these values are themselves in tension with one another, then theoretical tensions like the ones within liberalism may be the inevitable result of trying to accommodate, within normative political thought, all of the values we wish to have realized in our social world. Unless we are prepared to deny the significance of one or more of those values, our political outlook may never be entirely free of such tensions. This is, on the one hand, no cause for despair; neither tensions among our values nor tensions within our political outlook need be unlivable. More important, perhaps, it is no cause for complacency; it does not mean that liberals can simply ignore globalist and particularist criticism. While the fact that our values are in tension means that there will inevitably be tensions within any political outlook that seeks to accommodate those values, it does not mean that all forms of accommodation are equally satisfactory. Thus the inevitability of such tensions does not tell us that their manifestation within liberal theory is unproblematic. What is does suggest, I think, is that in so far as their manifestation within liberal theory *is* problematic, the problem is not that liberalism is threatened with the kind of theoretical incoherence that might disqualify it as an acceptable system of thought but that liberalism may not yet have found the most satisfactory way of accommodating an unruly set of values, none of which we are willing simply to abandon.

This characterization of the problem is significant. It is sometimes said that liberal societies are heirs to a heterogeneous set of values of varying historical provenance, only some of which are distinctively liberal in character. In consequence, it is suggested, such societies display an incoherent attachment to inconsistent moral outlooks. MacIntyre himself makes this suggestion.[31] But modern societies are hardly the first societies to build on diverse historical antecedents, nor need a mixed historical pedigree lead to incoherence. Liberalism is a living tradition of thought and practice, and the values it seeks to accommodate are the values that now make sense to people inside that tradition. The challenge for liberals is to see what kind of mutual accommodation among those values is possible.

This is not, in my view, a purely theoretical problem, or rather, it is not a problem that admits of a purely theoretical solution. For although liberal theorists do aim to produce an accommodation at the level of normative political thought, much of the point of this enterprise would be lost if the

---

[31] MacIntyre, 'Is Patriotism a Virtue?', 19–20.

accommodation stood no significant chance of being socially instantiated. This means that the success of the liberal project—like most projects in normative political theory—is hostage to actual patterns of historical change that alter the empirical conditions within which social institutions must operate. If, for example, during a certain period of time, liberal theorists take it for granted that most societies have reasonably homogeneous populations, and if, subsequently, economic and technological changes produce a level of mobility and migration that renders that assumption empirically untenable, then a scheme of normative thought that once seemed adequate for many purposes may no longer seem adequate. In general, an institutional configuration that represents a reasonable way of balancing a diverse group of values under one set of conditions may cease to do so under other conditions. And a practice or assumption that does not offend against a given value in some circumstances may do it considerable violence in others. Our own circumstances, at present, include a very rapid rate of change in many important areas of human life. Under these conditions, it becomes even more difficult than it would otherwise be to identify feasible social and political arrangements that can do an adequate job of accommodating all of the values that liberals prize, and there is no guarantee that attempts to produce such an accommodation will meet with success.

At the same time, however, we need not assume in advance that such an accommodation is impossible. Nor need we defer to those critics who see any attempt to arrive at a reasoned accommodation among liberal values as just another vestige of a discredited Enlightenment enterprise.[32] Some writers give the impression that unless we accept an excessively ambitious conception of reason or an implausibly reductionist conception of value, we must regard every choice involving diverse considerations as a tragic dilemma that admits of no rational resolution. But most of us do not think this way about the choices that we face in our daily lives, and there is no more reason why it should be true at the level of political theory. Indeed, although tragedy abounds in our world, one of the most striking things about the heterogeneity of human ends is the extent of our success in dealing with it. It remains to be seen how well liberalism can adapt to the conditions of the modern, or postmodern, world. However, the task for liberal practical reason remains what it has always been: to determine the extent to which the diverse values that liberals care about can be jointly accommodated within the constraints fixed by the prevailing historical circumstances.

[32] See, for example, John Gray, 'Agonistic Liberalism', *Social Philosophy and Policy* 12 (1995): 111–35.

5

*The Conflict between Justice and Responsibility**

Introduction: Global Justice and Special Responsibilities

Claims of global justice encounter considerable resistance among the members of affluent societies, whose way of life and standard of living they appear to threaten. If the resistance to these claims were motivated by nothing but simple self-interest, it would pose no moral or philosophical puzzle, despite its obvious practical, political significance. In fact, however, such resistance is often couched in normative terms and defended by appeal to familiar moral ideas. It is argued, for example, that we have special responsibilities to the members of our own families, communities, and societies and that these responsibilities are both weightier and more extensive than our responsibilities to other people. Accordingly, the argument continues, it is not only permissible but obligatory for us to give the interests of our associates—the people with whom we have significant interpersonal ties—priority over the interests of non-associates. We would be remiss if we failed to do this. It may be conceded, of course, that the required priority is not unlimited and that the interests of non-associates cannot be completely disregarded. Within certain broad limits, however, we are duty bound to give priority to the interests of our associates when deciding how to allocate our time, energy, and resources.

To those who take the idea of global justice seriously, these claims of special responsibility can seem like transparently self-serving rationalizations whose primary function is to make the limited generosity of the wealthy look like a matter of high principle and to encourage complacency about the shocking disparities between rich and poor nations. Yet, at the same time, the idea that we have special responsibilities to our families, friends, and communities —to those with whom we have significant interpersonal ties—is taken for granted by most people, and not only in affluent societies. To be sure, there

* Originally published in *NOMOS XLI: Global Justice*, ed. Ian Shapiro and Lea Brilmayer (New York, NY: New York University Press, 1999), NY: New York, 86–106. Reprinted by permission.

are significant disagreements both about the types of interpersonal bonds that give rise to special responsibilities and about how far such responsibilities extend. Notwithstanding these disagreements, however, the idea of special responsibilities counts for many people as one of their bedrock moral convictions, a rare fixed point in a world of rapid moral change. Not only do claims of special responsibility not strike most people as being, in general, objectionably self-serving, but on the contrary, such responsibilities may be viewed as a bulwark against the kind of sterile individualism that seems to characterize so much of modern life, particularly in affluent societies. Accordingly, the seriousness with which one takes one's special responsibilities may be seen as both a measure of one's moral virtue and a mark of one's success in avoiding the feelings of rootlessness and isolation that are so prevalent in highly individualistic societies. These considerations suggest that if the idea of global justice is to make headway among the affluent, the widespread resistance to that idea cannot be dismissed as just a manifestation of simple self-interest. Instead, if arguments for global justice are to be persuasive, they must engage with, and identify difficulties or limitations in, those notions of responsibility that appear to legitimate such resistance. The question is whether this can be done. In this essay, I will assess the force of one objection that might be offered, in the name of global justice, to claims of special responsibility. I have discussed this objection before, and I will begin by recapitulating my earlier presentation of it.[1]

The Distributive Objection

Suppose that none of three women, Alice, Beth, and Carla, has a special relationship with any of the others, and accordingly, none has special responsibilities to any of the others. The absence of such responsibilities, however, does not mean that none of the three women has any responsibilities whatsoever toward the others. On the contrary, each of them presumably has, for example, a responsibility not to harm or mistreat the others, and each may also have a responsibility to assist the others in certain types of situation. Let us call the responsibilities that the three women do have toward one another—despite the absence of any special relationships among them—their *general responsibilities*. For our purposes, the precise content of these general responsibilities is not very important. What is important is the fact that the distribution of these responsibilities is perfectly egalitarian in character; each woman has exactly the same responsibilities toward every other woman. Suppose, however, that, at some point, Alice and Beth become members of

---

[1] I first presented the objection in 'Families, Nations, and Strangers', Chapter Three in this volume. See also 'Liberalism, Nationalism, and Egalitarianism', Chapter Four in this volume.

a group of which Carla is not a member and which we may call the In Group. Let us also suppose that Alice and Beth attach considerable importance to their membership in this group and that they experience their participation in the group as extremely rewarding. We can imagine, if we like, that over time, each of them comes to see membership in the In Group as an important aspect of her identity.

If, as a result of their membership in the In Group, Alice and Beth come to have special responsibilities to each other, then by hypothesis, each of them will in certain contexts be required to give the other's interests priority over the interests of people like Carla. The relevant contexts may be of two importantly different kinds. First, in the absence of their special responsibilities to each other, Alice and Beth might on occasion have done certain things for Carla despite their not having a duty to do so. Now, however, discharging their responsibilities to each other must take priority over providing any sort of optional assistance to Carla. Second, there may now be situations in which Alice and Beth may have to give their responsibilities to each other priority, not over the provision of optional assistance to Carla, but over their general responsibilities to her. For example, Alice may sometimes have to help Beth rather than help Carla, if she cannot do both, even though she would have been obligated to help Carla had Beth too not needed help. Thus, in short, the special responsibilities that Alice and Beth have to each other will at times take priority over any *inclination* they may have to help Carla, and will at times take priority over any *responsibility* they may have to help her.

This means that if as a result of their membership in the In Group, Alice and Beth come to have special responsibilities to each other, the egalitarian distribution of responsibility that previously prevailed no longer obtains. Instead, Alice and Beth now have stronger claims on each other than Carla has on either of them. For each of them, correspondingly, Carla's claims have been demoted in relative importance. Thus Carla's claims on each of them are now weaker both than her claims on them were before they joined the In Group and than their claims on each other are now. Indeed, it would also appear that the claims that she now has on them are weaker than the claims that they now have on her. For we may suppose that Carla has no associates to whose interests she is required to give priority over the interests of Alice and Beth. Thus, their claims on her would appear not to have been weakened as a result of their joining the In Group, in the way that her claims on them have been. All things considered, then, it would seem that if Alice and Beth do indeed acquire special responsibilities to each other by virtue of their membership in the In Group, the overall distribution of responsibility that obtains once they have joined the group is both inegalitarian in character and notably unfavourable to Carla.

Now it may be objected that such a redistribution of responsibility would be unfair to Carla. For why should the fact that Alice and Beth have joined the In Group alter the distribution of responsibility in a manner that is so unfavourable to her? After all, it may be argued, since both Alice and Beth find their participation in the group to be very rewarding, they have already benefited from their membership independently of any redistribution of responsibility: they have already acquired an advantage that Carla lacks. Why, then, should they receive the additional advantage of having responsibility redistributed in a way that favours them?

It would be natural for anyone advancing this objection to qualify it in one way and to generalize it in another. The natural qualification is that the objection is waived if Carla herself had an opportunity to join the In Group and chose not to do so. The natural generalization is that the objection applies whenever Alice and Beth have significantly greater resources than Carla does, independent of any redistribution of responsibility, whether or not the greater resources that they have are actually a consequence of their membership. Thus, for example, if Alice and Beth happen to be wealthier than Carla, then the idea that morality requires them also to receive the advantage of having increased claims to each other's services may be seen as unjustifiably reinforcing the prior inequality in resources.

If we abstract from this example, we can see that the objection as generalized may be offered as a systematic objection to special responsibilities. It may be understood to hold that such responsibilities confer additional advantages on people who have already benefited from participating in rewarding groups and relationships and that this is unjustifiable whenever the provision of these additional advantages works to the detriment of those who are needier, whether they are needier because they are not themselves participants in rewarding groups and relationships or because they have significantly fewer resources of other kinds. This is what I call the *distributive objection*.

In so far as claims of special responsibility are invoked as a way of justifying resistance to the idea of global justice, the distributive objection may be presented by defenders of global justice as a challenge to that justification. The distributive objection challenges the idea that the members of affluent societies have special responsibilities to their associates that they do not have to other people. The objection need not deny that there are important differences of character and motivation between those who take such responsibilities seriously and those who act out of crudely self-interested motives. Nevertheless, it insists that special responsibilities serve to validate a natural tendency toward partiality or favouritism within groups, and that the effect of this form of validation is to confer unfair advantages on the members of wealthy groups while placing other people at an unfair disadvantage. In effect, such responsibilities provide the wealthy with the moral equivalent of a tax shelter. They provide those who are better off with a moral justification for channelling their time, energy, and other resources into rewarding relations and associations and away from people who are needier. For simply by entering into such relations and associations, one acquires special responsibilities to one's associates, and within limits, these responsibilities then take priority over, and thus serve to shield one from, the claims of others for assistance. Furthermore, fulfillment of these responsibilities normally contributes to the flourishing of the rewarding relations themselves. Thus, simply by entering into rewarding relations and associations, those who are better off can shelter their resources from potentially burdensome demands made in the name of global justice and invest those resources in enterprises that they find more satisfying.[2] Or so the distributive objection asserts.

Responses to the Distributive Objection

What is the force of the distributive objection? To what extent, if any, does it cast doubt on the legitimacy of claims of special responsibility? Is it successful in undermining the normative basis of resistance to the idea of global justice? Before trying to answer these questions, let us consider some possible responses to the objection.

First, it might be argued that the distributive objection rests on a misunderstanding, inasmuch as it assumes that one's special responsibilities to one's associates serve to weaken one's general responsibilities to other people. In reality, it might be said, the acquisition of special responsibilities to some people leaves unchanged both the content and the strength of one's general responsibilities to other people. Special responsibilities do not compete with general responsibilities; they simply are additional responsibilities. Thus their effect is not to weaken one's obligations to non-associates but, rather, to increase one's total share of responsibility.

If this argument were correct, the distributive objection as stated would indeed fail. Yet the argument would also undermine any attempt to use the idea of special responsibilities as a way of legitimating resistance to claims of global justice. The point of the argument is that the extent of our responsibilities to non-associates is fixed independently of our special responsibilities to our associates. Thus, if the argument were correct, we could not cite our special responsibilities to the latter by way of justifying our resistance to claims offered on behalf of the former. This means that if the argument were correct, it would indeed rebut the distributive objection but that in the process of doing so, it would concede the illegitimacy of the very conception of responsibility that the objection seeks to undermine. In rebutting the objection, in other words, it would nevertheless grant the conclusion that the objection seeks to establish.

In fact, however, although the argument is not altogether without merit, it is ultimately untenable. We may grant that special responsibilities serve

[2] For a related discussion, see Thomas Pogge, 'Loopholes in Moralities', *Journal of Philosophy* 89 (1992): 79–98.

in part to increase one's total share of responsibility. Yet at the same time, part of what it is to have such responsibilities to one's associates is to be required, within limits, to give their interests priority over the interests of non-associates, in cases in which the two conflict. This is the observation from which our discussion began, and it represents common ground between supporters and critics of special responsibilities. It is, of course, this feature of special responsibilities that leads them to be invoked in opposition to claims of global justice. And by the same token, it is this feature that exposes them to the distributive objection.[3]

Although the first response to the distributive objection is not persuasive, the recognition that special responsibilities serve in part to increase a person's total share of responsibility paves the way for a second response to the objection. This response complains that the distributive objection focuses exclusively on the benefits that special responsibilities confer on the participants in interpersonal relations while ignoring the burdens that such responsibilities also impose on them. For example, once Alice and Beth have joined the In Group, Alice may indeed benefit from Beth's newly acquired special responsibilities toward her. At the same time, however, Alice has also acquired special responsibilities toward Beth, which means that Alice's total share of responsibility has increased. And it may be argued that since Alice's overall moral burden has thus grown heavier, the claim that special responsibilities give her unfair advantages loses its force. More generally, the benefits that such responsibilities confer on the participants in interpersonal relationships are always offset by the burdens they impose. Special responsibilities confer no net advantage on participants and, *a fortiori*, no unfair net advantage.

There is an obvious complement to this argument. The complementary argument is that in addition to overlooking the disadvantages of special responsibilities for the participants in interpersonal relationships, the distributive objection overlooks the *advantages* of such responsibilities for *non-participants*. This argument begins by challenging something that our initial formulation of the distributive objection suggested, namely, that the acquisition by the participants in interpersonal relationships of special responsibilities to one another leaves undiminished their claims on non-participants. This argument maintains that on the contrary, when Alice and Beth join the In Group, the strengthening of their claims on each other is accompanied by a simultaneous weakening of their claims on Carla, even if Carla herself has no comparable special responsibilities to others. For the fact that Alice and Beth can

---

[3] However, Pogge appears to overlook the point when he writes, for example, 'I have no quarrel with the idea that persons, by becoming members of a social arrangement, may *increase* what they owe the other members and may thus come to owe them more than they owe all outsiders. What I find problematic is the idea that persons, by so increasing what they owe certain others, may *reduce* what they minimally owe everyone else' (ibid., 86–7, italics in original).

now call on each other for assistance is reason for Carla to give their interests less weight than she would previously have done.

Suppose, for instance, that Carla is in a position to help either Beth, who is a member of the In Group, or Denise, who is not. Suppose also that Beth and Denise are in equal need of assistance and that before Beth joined the In Group, their claims on Carla, which derive exclusively from Carla's responsibilities to other people in general, would have been equally strong. If, however, Beth now has special claims on Alice and the other members of the In Group, she has independent resources on which she can call and that Denise lacks. This, it may be argued, is reason for Carla to assign less weight to Beth's interests than she does to Denise's. This will obviously work to Denise's advantage, and presumably, Carla will receive a symmetrical advantage in the form of an increased priority assigned to her interests—relative to those of In Group members—by Denise and other non-members. Furthermore, the same consideration that gives Carla a reason to assign less weight to Beth's interests than she does to Denise's may in other circumstances make it appropriate for her to assign less weight to helping Beth than she does to pursuing her own projects and activities. Since Beth can turn to other In Group members for assistance, Carla may legitimately feel that there is less need for her to take time out from her own pursuits to help Beth. It is not unreasonable to expect Beth to look first to her fellow members for the assistance she needs. This means that the special responsibilities of In Group members work to Carla's advantage in two different ways. Not only do they strengthen her claims on Denise and other non-members, but they also reduce her total moral burden by allowing her to assign less weight to the interests of In Group members in deciding how to allocate her time and resources. Correlatively, it may be argued, those same special responsibilities can now be seen to work to the disadvantage of Alice and Beth in two different ways. In addition to increasing the total moral burden on each of them, they also weaken the claims of each on Carla, Denise, and other non-members. The upshot is that the advantages that special responsibilities confer on the participants in interpersonal relationships are fully offset by the disadvantages, and the disadvantages they confer on non-participants are fully offset by the advantages. Special responsibilities represent neither a net improvement for participants nor a net loss for non-participants, relative to a baseline situation in which everyone has only those responsibilities that arise independently of any special relationships. Thus there is no unfairness of the kind alleged by the distributive objection.

This argument makes it clear that the effects of special responsibilities on the overall distribution of responsibility are more complex than originally suggested. Yet the argument claims too much when it asserts that such responsibilities represent neither a net gain for the participants in interpersonal relationships nor a net loss for the non-participants. Consider first the case of the non-participants. The special responsibilities of In Group members are said to work to Carla's advantage by both strengthening her claims on

Denise and other non-members and allowing her to assign less weight to the interests of In Group members in deciding how much of her time and resources to devote to her own projects and pursuits. These points seem correct as far as they go, but they do not suffice to establish that the advantages mentioned fully offset the disadvantages for Carla of her reduced claims on In Group members. To see this, we only have to imagine that Carla is an inhabitant of a poor third-world country and that the In Group is the United States. Or, what amounts to the same thing, we have only to suppose—for the sake of argument at least—that Americans have a responsibility to give higher priority to one another's interests than they do to the interests of impoverished third-world residents. We may then ask ourselves whether the disadvantages of this fact for poor non-Americans are fully offset by their having stronger claims on one another or by its being permissible for them to pursue their own projects and plans without giving as much weight to the interests of the affluent. If, without underestimating the benefits of communal self-reliance, it seems clear that the answer to these questions is negative, that is presumably because the value of one's claims to other people's assistance depends in part on the extent of their resources and because the value of being permitted to pursue one's own projects and plans depends in part on the extent of one's own resources. Thus if the inhabitants of Chad or Bangladesh are told that the citizens of affluent Western societies have little responsibility to assist them, they are unlikely to take much comfort from the assurance that they may rely all the more heavily on one another or from the reflection that they may pursue their own projects unburdened by excessive concern for the welfare of affluent Westerners.

Consider next the case of the participants in interpersonal relationships. Obviously, the considerations just mentioned have some tendency to undermine the argument that the advantages of special responsibilities for them are fully offset by the disadvantages. For the participants, it seems, the advantages of having stronger claims on one another outweigh the disadvantages of having weaker claims on other people, at least in cases in which they already have greater resources than others do. Thus, for Americans, the advantages of having stronger claims on one another outweigh the disadvantages of having weaker claims on the citizens of Chad and Bangladesh. However, the original argument cited two putatively offsetting disadvantages for the participants, of which the weakening of their claims on non-participants was only the first. The other supposed disadvantage was that special responsibilities increase one's total moral burden and thereby place additional constraints on one's ability to advance legitimately one's projects and pursuits. If, as has now been suggested, the value of that ability is partly dependent on the extent of one's resources, it may seem to follow that the more affluent one is, the greater this disadvantage will be. But to one degree or another, it may appear to constitute a genuinely offsetting disadvantage for all participants.

However, this overlooks one of the legitimate insights of the distributive objection. The insight is that when one's participation in an interpersonal group or relationship is rewarding—quite apart from the responsibilities to which it gives rise—and when the fulfillment of those responsibilities in turn contributes to the flourishing of that very group or relationship, then although the responsibilities serve in part to increase one's total share of responsibility, it is misleading to conceive of that extra measure of responsibility solely as a burden for the person who bears it. Although special responsibilities are sometimes experienced as burdensome, and although fulfilling them can undoubtedly involve various kinds of costs, it is misleading to describe such responsibilities as placing constraints on one's ability to advance legitimately one's own projects and pursuits. The reason is that those responsibilities may enhance relationships and associations that must themselves be numbered among one's projects and pursuits broadly construed. Indeed, as we will soon see, it may even be argued that accepting special responsibilities not only enhances interpersonal relationships but is a necessary condition for their stable existence. The more valuable a relationship is and the more important the role is of one's special responsibilities in establishing and sustaining that relationship, the more misleading it will be to classify those responsibilities as burdens.

Where does this leave us? The argument we have been discussing purports to establish that special responsibilities represent neither a net improvement for the participants in interpersonal relationships nor a net loss for non-participants, relative to a baseline situation in which everyone has only those responsibilities that arise independently of any special relationships. However, we have found reason to doubt this claim. When non-participants have fewer resources than do participants, the disadvantages for them of such a redistribution of responsibility outweigh the advantages constituted by an increase in the strength of their claims on one another and a decrease in the strength of the participants' claims on them. In such circumstances, similarly, the advantages for the participants of having stronger claims on one another outweigh the disadvantages of having weaker claims on the non-participants. And in general, it is a mistake to suppose that the benefits for the participants in rewarding relationships of having stronger claims on one another are offset by the burdens of having greater responsibilities to one another. For the idea that such responsibilities constitute burdens for those who bear them is misleading. In short, then, the core of the distributive objection remains intact. It still maintains that special responsibilities confer additional advantages on people who have already benefited from participating in rewarding groups and relationships and that those additional advantages are unjustifiable whenever they work to the detriment of people who are needier.

Admittedly, it has not been shown that *only* those interpersonal relationships that are rewarding for the participants give rise to special responsibilities.

If this is not so, then the extent to which special responsibilities are advantageous for those who bear them may vary considerably from case to case, depending on the value of the relationships that generate them. Furthermore, it may be argued that it is wrong to assess the advantages and disadvantages of special responsibilities solely in terms of the strength or weakness of the claims they confer on people. A strong claim that is never exercised may benefit a person less than a weak claim that is exercised. And correspondingly, a more extensive responsibility to assist one's associate may prove less onerous than a more limited responsibility to assist a stranger, if it turns out that one's associate never needs the assistance to which he is entitled. Thus, it may be argued, a more accurate measure of the impact of special responsibilities on participants and non-participants alike would take into account not only the strength and weakness of the various claims conferred but also the extent to which those claims are actually exercised. And since this is a contingent matter that will vary from case to case, so too the advantages and disadvantages of special responsibilities—whether for participants or non-participants—will also be contingent and variable. Although those advantages and disadvantages may tend to conform to the patterns that have been identified, these will be only tendencies and not exceptionless regularities.

Yet these points require no significant modification of the distributive objection. Even if we suppose that some participants in unrewarding relationships also acquire special responsibilities, this does not undermine the claim that the participants in rewarding relationships receive additional advantages from the responsibilities to which their relationships give rise. And even if these additional advantages only *tend* to work to the detriment of those who are needier, that does not undermine the claim that they are unfair when they do.

Although the line of argument we have been pursuing does not, in the end, succeed in rebutting the distributive objection, it may provide a springboard for a third response to that objection. If the distributive objection claims only that special responsibilities arising out of certain kinds of relationships tend to work to the detriment of those who are needier and that they are unfair when they do, it may be said that the real target of the objection has been misidentified. The distributive objection is not an objection to special responsibilities *per se*. Rather, it is a response to the effects that such responsibilities tend to have in otherwise unjust situations. When there is already an unjust distribution of resources, special responsibilities may compound the injustice. But if the underlying injustice were eliminated, there would be no remaining objection to those responsibilities. Although they may reinforce existing injustices, they are not unjust in themselves, and they cannot by themselves transform just situations into unjust ones. Thus the real target of the distributive objection is the unjust distribution of resources and not special responsibilities. Admittedly, if such responsibilities do indeed reinforce or compound existing injustices, there is a way in which the relationships that give rise to those responsibilities are compromised. Those of us fortunate enough to participate in networks of rewarding interpersonal relationships in a world replete with injustice conduct our relationships under a kind of moral shadow. This is unfortunate, if not terribly surprising, but it does not constitute an objection to special responsibilities *per se*. Since they are not unjust in themselves, they remain genuine responsibilities and continue to possess normative authority even when they arise in the context of distributive injustice.

Although it aims to defend special responsibilities against the distributive objection, this argument implies that appeals to such responsibilities can at most justify only limited resistance to claims of global justice. For the argument provides no reason to doubt the legitimacy of those claims; it concedes that special responsibilities may serve to compound distributive injustice; and accordingly, it allows that interpersonal relations may be compromised by such injustice. It insists only that special responsibilities should be seen as genuine, or as possessing normative authority, even when they do compound injustice. If the argument were persuasive in other respects, this conclusion, limited though it is, would still require additional defence. It is not obvious why the normative authority of special responsibilities should not be called into question on those occasions when they do indeed compound injustice. But the argument is flawed in a more fundamental respect: the distributive objection does not limit itself to asserting that special responsibilities are unfair when they compound injustice. It asserts instead that such responsibilities are unfair whenever they work to the detriment of those who are already needier. This means that the alleged unfairness depends on the existence of prior inequalities, but as far as the distributive objection is concerned, those inequalities need not be unjust. In general, an unequal distribution that is not unjust may be transformed into an even more unequal distribution that is unjust, through the provision of additional benefits to those who were better off under the original distribution. And the distributive objection may be construed as holding that even if an initial inequality is not unjust, the effect of special responsibilities may be to introduce injustice where there was none before. It might be claimed, for example, that there is no injustice in the fact that Alice and Beth enjoy the personal rewards of membership in the In Group while Carla does not, but that it is unjust if, in consequence, Alice and Beth also acquire special responsibilities to each other and those responsibilities then work to Carla's disadvantage. Or it might be said that it need not be unjust if one society is richer in natural resources than another but that it is unjust if the members of the wealthier society are then required to give one another's interests priority over the interests of people in the poorer society. The central point is that, according to the distributive objection, it is unfair if special responsibilities work to the detriment of people who already have less, whether or not their already having less is also unfair.

This formulation highlights the way in which the distributive objection seems to treat the advantages conferred by special responsibilities as entirely separable from the other advantages that the participants in interpersonal relationships may enjoy, including the other rewards deriving from participation in those very relationships. In so doing, this formulation invites a fourth and final response to the distributive objection. This response challenges the idea that the other benefits of participation in an interpersonal relationship are secured independently of special responsibilities and that it is then an open question how, if at all, the relationship affects the distribution of responsibility. In fact, this response argues, the processes by which otherwise rewarding relationships are established and the processes by which special responsibilities are generated are inseparable. A commitment by the participants to give priority to one another's interests in suitable contexts is a precondition for the stable existence of a rewarding relationship, and it is these commitments that give rise to special responsibilities. Thus, one cannot secure the other benefits of participation in interpersonal relationships without acquiring special responsibilities in the process. Inasmuch as the distributive objection treats such responsibilities as conferring advantages that arise independently of the other benefits of rewarding relationships and that, accordingly, need not accompany them, the objection fails.

This response raises a variety of interesting questions that I cannot address here.[4] For our purposes, the fundamental point is this: by emphasizing the role of putatively responsibility-generating commitments in making rewarding relationships possible, the response just sketched implies that there is an important respect in which the acquisition of special responsibilities serves the interests of prospective participants in such relationships. But this is not something that the distributive objection denies. On the contrary, one of that objection's central aspirations is precisely to call attention to the ways in which special responsibilities work to the advantage of the participants in interpersonal groups and relationships. Its correlative observation, of course, is that such responsibilities may also work to the significant disadvantage of non-participants. And the response just sketched does not dispute this observation. So if, as that response maintains, people cannot obtain the benefits of participating in rewarding personal relations without acquiring special responsibilities in the process, the distributive objection will conclude that there must be constraints on the legitimacy of securing such benefits. More precisely, it will argue that the effects of special responsibilities on third parties serve to constrain the capacity of commitments to generate such responsibilities, the legitimacy of making those commitments that do generate responsibilities, and the content of the responsibilities that are in fact generated.

---

[4] I have discussed some of these questions in 'Families, Nations, and Strangers', Section IV.

Conclusion: The Force of the Distributive Objection

Once the conclusions of the distributive objection are framed in this way, it is clear that the objection does not delegitimate all claims of special responsibility or even show that such claims can never take precedence over considerations of global justice. The objection's ambition, it now seems, is merely to constrain those claims in various ways. On the other hand, it seems equally clear that none of the four responses we have considered provides a good reason for dismissing the objection or the concerns that underlie it. Instead, we are left with two ideas—the idea of special responsibilities and the idea of global justice—which are evidently in tension with each other, and each of which purports to limit the authority of the other. This kind of tension and mutual constraint is exactly what we should expect if, as I believe, each of these ideas is rooted in values that occupy a central place in the moral outlooks of many people. But this simple observation about the provenance of the two ideas, which should seem obvious, has lately been obscured by the widespread reliance in moral and political philosophy on a cluster of stylized and exaggerated contrasts: between universalism and particularism, between liberalism and communitarianism, between thin and thick ethical concepts, between Kantian ethics and an ethics of virtue, between Enlightenment morality and the morality of patriotism and loyalty. Each of these contrasts encourages the belief that the values of justice and equality, on the one hand, and the values of personal friendship and communal solidarity, on the other hand, derive from mutually exclusive and fundamentally opposed systems of ethical thought. I doubt whether this is correct as a matter of intellectual history. I am quite sure that it is false as a characterization of the experience of many people, including many who have come to rely more or less uncritically on dichotomies like those mentioned. I am quite sure that many people take seriously both sets of values, without any sense that they represent alien or mutually exclusive commitments. This does not mean, of course, that these values are never experienced as being in tension with each other. The point is, rather, that for many, to experience such a tension is not to register a clash between rival theories or philosophies but to feel torn by considerations internal to one's own moral outlook. I do not believe that tensions of this kind among our values can ever be eliminated, but such tensions may be more or less problematic. The tension between two values will be problematic to the extent that we are committed to both of them but have been unable to identify any way of accommodating one without slighting or doing violence to the other. We resolve such problems, to our own satisfaction at least, when we fix on a course of action, or design a policy or institution, or identify a set of principles, that will enable us to claim, in good faith, to have found a way of doing justice to both.

The real thrust of the distributive objection, and its contribution to arguments for global justice, is to suggest that the tension between our special responsibilities as we have interpreted them, on the one hand, and our commitment to the equal worth of persons, on the other hand, is more problematic than we normally suppose. It is to suggest, in other words, that in the name of those responsibilities, we have been prepared to acquiesce in policies and institutional arrangements that cannot be reconciled with any serious commitment to the proposition that all people are of equal worth. There is, in principle, nothing surprising about the idea that the tensions among certain of our values may be more problematic than we realize. In general, we have powerful incentives to overlook such problems. In the end, however, the force of the distributive objection in particular must rest on its success in evoking in us an uneasiness about the relations between the specific values with which it is concerned. To the extent that the objection does have force, its tendency, as I have said, is not to support the repudiation of special responsibilities. Indeed, the idea that the particular interpersonal relationships in which one participates help shape the normative landscape of one's life is so fundamental that I cannot imagine any argument powerful enough to overturn it. And although there are moral theories—such as utilitarianism—that do not treat it as fundamental, they invariably take care to accommodate it at some putatively derivative level, as indeed they must if they are to be taken seriously. Rather than supporting the repudiation of special responsibilities, the tendency of the distributive objection is to challenge us to find a better way of integrating our values if we can.

If the ubiquity of the stylized and exaggerated contrasts mentioned earlier is an obstacle at the level of theory to our meeting or even recognizing this challenge, the situation at the level of political practice is even more complex. The broad movement in recent years toward greater global integration has increased interest in the problem of global justice. Yet far from producing a solution to the problem, that movement seems instead to be transforming it. The 'traditional' problem of global justice, if it can be called that, is a problem concerning the relations between poor nations and wealthy nations. Inasmuch as appeals to special responsibility may be offered by the citizens of wealthy nations as a way of justifying their resistance to the idea of global justice, the bearing of special responsibilities on the traditional problem is relatively straightforward. But without solving this problem, the movement toward global integration has given rise to another problem as well. The new problem concerns the relations between an affluent, technologically sophisticated global élite and the large numbers of poor and undereducated people worldwide. The role of special responsibilities in relation to this new problem of global justice is less straightforward. Individual members of the cosmopolitan élite may, of course, seek to justify their resistance to proposed solutions of the problem by appealing, in the familiar way, to special responsibilities arising out of their own interpersonal relations. But unlike the citizenry of an affluent country, this élite is not itself united under any political authority, nor is it bound together by a sense of group loyalty or, indeed, by any shared ethos of responsibility. Certainly, individual members of the élite do not normally see themselves as having special responsibilities to their fellow members as such. Instead, appeals to special responsibility are more likely to be made, in this context, as part of the identity politics with which the movement toward global integration finds itself increasingly in conflict. And the function of such claims may be not to justify resistance to the idea of global justice but, rather, to call attention to the interests of those whom the movement toward global integration has left behind. To this extent at least, such claims may serve to express considerations of justice rather than to oppose them.

The traditional problem of global justice and the new problem coexist and cut across each other in ways that make the task of integrating justice and responsibility even more complex than it initially may have appeared. The challenge of reducing the tensions among our values and overcoming the oppositions within our thought is thus a formidable one, and there is no guarantee that it can be met, at the level of either theory or practice. But the stakes could hardly be higher, and we are almost certain to fail unless we try.

6

*Relationships and Responsibilities**

How do we come to have responsibilities to some people that we do not have to others? In our everyday lives, many different kinds of considerations are invoked to explain these 'special' responsibilities. Often we cite some kind of interaction that we have had with the person to whom we bear the responsibility. Perhaps we made this person a promise, or entered into an agreement with him. Or perhaps we feel indebted to him because of something he once did for us. Or, again, perhaps we once harmed him in some way, and as a result we feel a responsibility to make reparation to him. In all of these cases, there is either something we have done or something the 'beneficiary' of the responsibility has done that is cited as the source of that responsibility.

Not all of our explanations take this form, however. Sometimes we account for special responsibilities not by citing any specific interaction between us and the beneficiary, but rather by citing the nature of our relationship to that person. We have special duties to a person, we may say, because she is our sister, or our friend, or our neighbour. Many different types of relationship are invoked in this way. Perhaps the person is not a relative but a colleague, not a friend but a teammate, not a neighbour but a client. Sometimes the relationship may consist only in the fact that we are both members of a certain kind of group. We may belong to the same community, for example, or be citizens of the same country, or be part of the same nation or people. In some of these cases, we may never have met or had any interaction with the person who is seen as the beneficiary of the responsibility.

* Originally published in *Philosophy & Public Affairs* 26/3 (Summer 1997): 189–209. Copyright © 1997 by Princeton University Press. Reprinted by permission. This is a much-revised version of the paper that I delivered at the Eleventh Jerusalem Philosophical Encounter in December 1995. Versions of the paper were also presented to the NYU Colloquium in Law, Philosophy, and Political Theory; the Columbia Legal Theory Workshop; philosophy department colloquia at Arizona State, Stanford, the University of Miami, and the University of Michigan; and my fall 1995 graduate seminar at Berkeley. I am very grateful to all of these audiences for extremely helpful discussion. Special thanks also to Yael Tamir, who was my commentator in Jerusalem, and to Christopher Kutz, Jeff McMahan, Daniel Statman, Wai-hung Wong, and a reader for *Philosophy & Public Affairs* for providing me with valuable written comments.

We may nevertheless be convinced that our shared group membership suffices to generate such a responsibility. Of course, claims of special responsibility can be controversial, especially in cases of this kind. While some people feel strongly that they have special responsibilities to the other members of their national or cultural group, for example, other people feel just as strongly that they do not. Nevertheless, it is a familiar fact that such ties are often seen as a source of special responsibilities. Indeed, we would be hard pressed to find any type of human relationship to which people have attached value or significance but which has never been seen as generating such responsibilities. It seems that whenever people value an interpersonal relationship they are apt to see it as a source of special duties or obligations.

However, although it is clear that we do in fact cite our relationships to other people in explaining why we have special responsibilities to them, many philosophers have been reluctant to take these citations at face value. Instead, they have supposed that the responsibilities we perceive as arising out of special relationships actually arise out of discrete interactions that occur in the context of those relationships. Thus, for example, some special responsibilities, like the mutual responsibilities of spouses, may be said to arise out of promises or commitments that the participants have made to each other. Others, like the responsibilities of children to their parents, may be seen as arising from the provision of benefits to one party by the other. And in cases like those mentioned earlier, in which two people are both members of some group but have not themselves interacted in any way, it may be denied that the people do in fact have any special responsibilities to each other. As already noted, claims of special responsibility tend to be controversial in such cases anyway, and it may be thought an advantage of this position that it sees grounds for scepticism precisely in the cases that are most controversial.

Clearly, the view that duties arising out of special relationships can always be reduced to duties arising out of discrete interactions is compatible with the view that the relevant interactions, and hence the relevant duties, may be of fundamentally different kinds. Indeed, to some philosophers it seems clear that the relationships that have been seen as generating special responsibilities are so heterogeneous that the responsibilities in question cannot possibly have but a single ground. Nevertheless, one of the greatest pressures toward a reductionist position has come from those who believe that all genuine special responsibilities must be based on consent or on some other voluntary act. These voluntarists, as I will call them, are not hostile to the idea of special responsibilities as such. As I have argued elsewhere, however, they believe that such responsibilities can be costly and difficult to discharge, and thus quite burdensome for those who bear them.[1] It would be unfair, they believe, if people could be saddled with such burdens against their wills, and so it would be unfair if special responsibilities could be ascribed to people

---

[1] See 'Families, Nations, and Strangers' (Chapter Three in this volume) and 'Liberalism, Nationalism, and Egalitarianism' (Chapter Four in this volume).

who had done nothing voluntarily to incur them. In effect, then, voluntarists see a form of reductionism about special responsibilities as necessary if our assignments of such responsibilities are to be fair to those who bear them.

Voluntarism is an influential view, and many people find the voluntarist objection to unreduced special responsibilities quite congenial. At the same time, however, such responsibilities are also subject to a different kind of challenge in the name of fairness. In a series of essays, I have discussed what I call 'the distributive objection', which challenges the fairness of special responsibilities whether or not their source is thought of as lying in the voluntary acts of those who bear them.[2] The distributive objection asserts that the problem with such responsibilities is not that they may place unfair burdens on their bearers but rather that they may confer unfair benefits. The objection turns on the observation that special responsibilities give the participants in rewarding groups and relationships increased claims to one another's assistance, while weakening the claims that other people have on them. In this way, it asserts, such responsibilities provide the participants with significant advantages while working to the disadvantage of non-participants. The distributive objection insists that, unless these advantages and disadvantages are integrated into a fair distribution of resources of all kinds, special responsibilities will amount to little more than what one writer has called a 'pernicious'[3] form of 'prejudice in favor of people who stand in some special relation to us'.[4]

Thus, whereas the voluntarist objection asserts that fairness to the bearers of special responsibilities requires a version of reductionism with respect to those responsibilities, the distributive objection challenges the fairness of such responsibilities whether they are thought of as voluntarily incurred or not. If a non-reductionist account of special responsibilities is to be convincing, it will need to address both of these objections.

In this essay, I will sketch the rudiments of a non-reductionist account. My discussion will remain schematic, inasmuch as I will be concerned with the abstract structure of a non-reductionist position rather than with a detailed accounting of the specific responsibilities that such a position would assign people. Nevertheless, I hope that my sketch may suggest a new way of understanding non-reductionist claims of special responsibility and that, in so doing, it may make non-reductionism seem less implausible than it is often thought to be. In any event, I believe that the type of position I will describe merits careful consideration. As is no doubt evident, questions about the status of special responsibilities bear directly on a number of the liveliest controversies in contemporary moral and political philosophy. For

---

[2] In addition to the essays cited in footnote 1, see 'The Conflict Between Justice and Responsibility' (Chapter Five in this volume), which contains the most extensive discussion of the distributive objection.

[3] Robert Goodin, *Protecting the Vulnerable* (Chicago, IL: University of Chicago Press, 1985), 1.

[4] Ibid., 6.

example, such questions are central to the debate within moral philosophy between consequentialism and deontology. They are equally central to the debates within political philosophy between liberalism and communitarianism, and between nationalism and cosmopolitanism. Thus the way that we think about special responsibilities may have far-reaching implications, and it would be a mistake to dismiss non-reductionism without attempting to understand it sympathetically.

Non-reductionists are impressed by the fact that we often cite our relationships to people rather than particular interactions with them as the source of our special responsibilities. They believe that our perception of things is basically correct; the source of such responsibilities often does lie in the relationships themselves rather than in particular interactions between the participants. A non-reductionist might begin to elaborate this position as follows. Other people can make claims on me, and their needs can provide me with reasons for action, whether or not I have any special relationship to them. If a stranger is suffering and I am in a position to help, without undue cost to myself, then I may well have a reason to do so. This much is true simply in virtue of our common humanity. However, if I have a special, valued relationship with someone, and if the value I attach to the relationship is not purely instrumental in character—if, in other words, I do not value it solely as a means to some independently specified end—then I regard the person with whom I have the relationship as capable of making additional claims on me, beyond those that people in general can make. For to attach non-instrumental value to my relationship with a particular person just is, in part, to see that person as a source of special claims in virtue of the relationship between us. It is, in other words, to be disposed, in contexts which vary depending on the nature of the relationship, to see that person's needs, interests, and desires as, in themselves, providing me with presumptively decisive reasons for action, reasons that I would not have had in the absence of the relationship. By 'presumptively decisive reasons' I mean reasons which, although they are capable in principle of being outweighed or overridden, nevertheless present themselves as considerations upon which I must act. If there are no circumstances in which I would see a person's needs or interests as giving me such reasons, then, according to the non-reductionist, it makes no sense to assert that I attach (non-instrumental) value to my relationship with that person. But this is tantamount to saying that I cannot value my relationships (non-instrumentally) without seeing them as sources of special responsibilities.[5]

---

[5] The non-reductionist recognizes, of course, that it is possible for me to regard relationships in which I am not a participant as valuable. The non-reductionist's claim, however, is that valuing one's own relationship to another person is different, not because one is bound to see such a relationship as more valuable than other relationships of the same type, but rather because one is bound to see it as a source of reasons for action of a distinctive kind. For additional discussion of this point, see 'Conceptions of Cosmopolitanism', Chapter Seven in this volume.

If it is true that one cannot value one's relationship to another person (non-instrumentally) without seeing it, in effect, as a source of special responsibilities, then it hardly seems mysterious that such a wide and apparently heterogeneous assortment of relationships have been seen as giving rise to such responsibilities. Nor, given that different people value relationships of different kinds, does it seem mysterious that some claims of special responsibility remain highly controversial. On the non-reductionist view, differences in the kinds of relationships that people value lead naturally to disagreements about the assignment of special responsibility.

The non-reductionist position as thus far described takes us only so far. It asserts that relationships and not merely interactions are among the sources of special responsibilities, and it claims that people who value their relationships invariably see them as giving rise to such responsibilities. As so far described, however, the position says nothing about the conditions under which relationships actually do give rise to special responsibilities. Now there is, of course, no reason to expect that all non-reductionists will give the same answer to this question, any more than there is reason to expect that all reductionists will identify the same types of interactions as the sources of special responsibilities. In this essay, however, I wish to explore the specific suggestion that one's relationships to other people give rise to special responsibilities to those people when they are relationships that one has reason to value.[6] For ease of exposition, I will refer to this view simply as 'non-reductionism', but we should remember that this is just an expository device, and that other versions of non-reductionism are possible.

Several features of the formulation I have given require comment and clarification. First, the term 'value', as it occurs in that formulation and in subsequent discussion, should be taken to mean 'value non-instrumentally', and the term 'reason' should be taken to mean 'net reason'. In other words, if a person only has reason to value a relationship instrumentally, then the principle I have stated does not treat that relationship as a source of special responsibilities. And if a person has some reason to value a relationship but more reason not to, then again the principle does not treat it as generating such responsibilities. Furthermore, although the formulation I have given does not presuppose any particular conception of the kinds of reasons that people can have for valuing their relationships, reasons that are *reflexively instrumental*, in the sense that they derive from the instrumental advantages of valuing a relationship non-instrumentally, are to be understood as excluded. In other words, if attaching non-instrumental value to a certain relationship would itself be an effective means of achieving some independently desirable goal, the principle I have stated does not treat that as a reason of the responsibility-generating kind.

---

[6] On some views, membership in a group may give one special responsibilities *to the group* that transcend any responsibilities one has to the individual members. The view I am exploring is agnostic on this question.

Second, there is a perfectly good sense of 'relationship' in which every human being stands in some relationship to every other human being. However, as far as the view that I am presenting is concerned, only socially salient connections among people count as 'relations' or 'relationships'—two terms that I use interchangeably. Thus, for example, if you happen to have the same number of letters in your last name as John Travolta does, that does not mean that you have a relationship with him. Nor does the fact that you admire Travolta suffice to establish the existence of a relationship in the relevant sense, for the fact that one person has a belief about or attitude toward another does not constitute a social tie between them. On the other hand, two members of a socially recognized group do have a relationship in the relevant sense, even if they have never met, and if they value their membership in that group they may also value their relations to the other members. Thus, the fact that you are a member of the John Travolta Fan Club means that you have a relation to each of the other club members, and if you value your membership you may also value those relations.

Third, valuing my relationship with another person, in the sense that matters for non-reductionism, means valuing the relation of each of us to the other. So if, for example, I value my status as the Brutal Tyrant's leading opponent but not his status as my despised adversary, then I do not value our relationship in the sense that the non-reductionist principle treats as relevant. Similar remarks apply, *mutatis mutandis*, to having reason to value a relationship.

Fourth, non-reductionism as I have formulated it is not committed to a fixed view either of the strength or of the content of special responsibilities. It is compatible with the view that such responsibilities can be outweighed by other considerations. It is also compatible with the view that the strength of one's responsibilities depends on the nature of the relationships that give rise to them, and on the degree of value that one has reason to attach to those relationships. As far as the content of the responsibilities is concerned, we may assume that this too depends on the nature of the relationships in question, but that, at the most abstract level, it always involves a duty to give priority of various kinds, in suitable contexts, to certain of the interests of those to whom the responsibilities are owed.

Fifth, the non-reductionist principle states a sufficient condition for special responsibilities, not a necessary condition. Thus the principle does not purport to identify the source of all such responsibilities. In particular, it does not deny that promises and other kinds of discrete interactions can also give rise to special responsibilities. It merely claims to identify conditions under which interpersonal relations give rise to responsibilities that need not be fully accounted for in reductionist terms.

Sixth, non-reductionism makes it possible to claim both that people sometimes have special responsibilities that they think they lack, and that they sometimes lack special responsibilities that they think they have. For it is possible to think both that people can fail to value relationships that they have reason to value, and that they can succeed in valuing relationships that they have no reason to value. We may think, for example, that a neglectful father has reason to value his relations to the children he ignores, or that an abused wife lacks any reason to value her relation to the husband she cannot bring herself to leave. Similarly, we may feel that an ambitious young woman has good reasons to value her relationship with the devoted immigrant parents of whom she is ashamed, and little reason to value her relationship with the vain and self-absorbed classmate whose attention she prizes and whose approval she craves.[7]

Finally, however, our ability to sustain claims of this kind is clearly dependent on a conception of reasons, and, more specifically, on a conception of the conditions under which people may be said to have reasons to value their relations to others. The more closely a person's reasons are seen as linked to his existing desires and motivations, the less scope there will be for distinguishing between the relationships that he has reason to value and the relationships that he actually does value. On the other hand, the less closely reasons are thought of as tied to existing desires, the more room there will be to draw such distinctions. As I have indicated, non-reductionism does not itself put forward a conception of reasons. Its claim, rather, is that many judgments of special responsibility are dependent on the ascription to people of reasons for valuing their relations to others, so that any substantive conception of such responsibilities is hostage to some conception of reaons.[8]

Non-reductionism of the kind I have described makes possible the following simple defence of unreduced special responsibilities. We human beings are social creatures, and creatures with values. Among the things that we value are our relations with each other. But to value one's relationship with another person is to see it as a source of reasons for action of a distinctive kind. It is, in effect, to see oneself as having special responsibilities to the person with whom one has the relationship. Thus, in so far as we have good reasons to value our interpersonal relations, we have good reasons to see ourselves as having special responsibilities. And, accordingly, scepticism about

[7] Of course, since the non-reductionist principle does articulate only a sufficient and not a necessary condition for special responsibilities, the fact that one has no reason to value one's relationship to a particular person does not by itself show that one has no special responsibilities whatsoever to that person—only that one has no responsibilities arising under the non-reductionist principle.

[8] This means that it would be possible for a reductionist to argue that people's reasons for valuing their relations to others derive exclusively from discrete interactions that occur in the context of those relations. Even if this argument were accepted, however, it would remain the case that, according to the principle under consideration, the source of the relevant responsibilities lies in the relationships rather than the interactions. Furthermore, it may not be possible without loss of plausibility to translate reductionism about special responsibilities into reductionism about people's reasons for valuing their relationships. For some of the types of interaction that have been seen as generating such responsibilities do not seem plausibly construed as generating reasons for valuing relationships.

such responsibilities will be justified only if we are prepared to deny that we have good reasons to value our relationships.

It may seem that this argument is fallacious. For consider: even if I have reason to promise that I will meet you for lunch on Tuesday, and even though I would be obligated to meet you if I were so to promise, it does not follow that, here and now, I actually have such an obligation. On the contrary, I acquire the obligation only if I make the promise. Similarly, it may seem, even if I have reason to value my relationship with you, and even if I would acquire special responsibilities to you if I did value our relationship, it does not follow that, here and now, I actually have such responsibilities. On the contrary, I acquire the responsibilities only if I value the relationship. However, the non-reductionist will resist this analogy. In the promising case, I have reason to perform an act which, if performed, will generate an obligation. But the non-reductionist's claim about special responsibilities is different. The claim is not that, in having reason to value our relationship, I have reason to perform an act which, if performed, will generate responsibilities. The claim is rather that, to value our relationship *is*, in part, to see myself as having such responsibilities, so that if, here and now, I have reason to value our relationship, then what I have reason to do, here and now, is to see myself as having such responsibilities. In the promising case, the promise generates the obligation, and no obligation arises in the absence of the promise. But the existence of a relationship that one has reason to value is itself the source of special responsibilities, and those responsibilities arise whether or not the participants actually value the relationship. Or so the non-reductionist claims.

Even if the disanalogy with the promising case is conceded, it may nevertheless be said that the non-reductionist argument stops short of establishing that we really do have special responsibilities. As we have seen, the non-reductionist claims that, in so far as we have reason to value our interpersonal relationships, we also have reason to see ourselves as having such responsibilities. But, it may be said, even if we have reason to see ourselves as having such responsibilities, that is compatible with our not actually having them. This seems to me misleading, however. If the non-reductionist argument establishes that we have good reason to see ourselves as having special responsibilities, then that is how we should see ourselves. There is no substantive difference, in this context, between the conclusion that we do have special responsibilities and the conclusion that, all things considered, we have good reasons for thinking that we do.

Some may worry that the non-reductionist principle as I have formulated it focuses too much attention on the bearers of special responsibilities and too little on the beneficiaries. Sometimes, it may be said, the source of a special responsibility does not lie in the fact that the relationship is one that the bearer has reason to value, but rather in the vulnerability created by the beneficiary's trust in or dependence on the bearer. However, this suggestion is not incompatible with the principle I have articulated. For that principle purports to identify only a sufficient condition, and not a necessary condition, for a relationship to give rise to special responsibilities. Thus it no more precludes the possibility that relations of trust and vulnerability may also give rise to such responsibilities than the principle that one ought to keep one's promises precludes the possibility that there are other kinds of obligations as well.

How, then, might a non-reductionist respond to the voluntarist and distributive objections? The voluntarist objection, we may recall, points out that special responsibilities may constitute significant burdens for those who bear them, and asserts that it would be unfair if such responsibilities could be ascribed to individuals who had done nothing voluntarily to incur them. The first thing that non-reductionists may say in response to this objection is that, in addition to our special responsibilities, there are other moral norms that govern our treatment of people in general. These moral norms, they may point out, apply to us whether or not we have agreed to them. For example, one cannot justify one's infliction of harm on a person by saying that one never agreed not to harm people. There are, in other words, general moral responsibilities that can be ascribed to us without our having voluntarily incurred them. And although these general responsibilities, like special responsibilities, may be costly or burdensome, we do not ordinarily regard their imposition as unfair. So why, non-reductionists may ask, should special responsibilities be any different? If voluntarists do not require that general responsibilities be voluntarily incurred, how can they insist that special responsibilities must be? The voluntarist may reply that special responsibilities, unless voluntarily incurred, give other people undue control over one's life. If certain people can make claims on you without your having done anything to legitimate those claims, then, the voluntarist may argue, those people enjoy an unreasonable degree of authority over the way you live. However, since general moral norms also enable people to make claims on individuals who have done nothing to legitimate those claims, non-reductionists will again want to know why special responsibilities that have not been voluntarily incurred should be objectionable in a way that general responsibilities are not.

One reason for the voluntarist's concern about special responsibilities may be as follows. Our most significant social roles and relations determine, to a considerable extent, the ways that we are seen by others and the ways that we see ourselves. They help to determine what might be called our social identities. To the extent that we choose our roles and relations, and decide how much significance they shall have in our lives, we shape our own identities. But to the extent that these things are fixed independently of our choices, our identities are beyond our control. What disturbs the voluntarist about special responsibilities may be this: if our relations to other people can generate responsibilities to those people independently of our choices, then, to that extent, the significance of our social relations is not up to us to determine.

And if the significance of such relations is not up to us to determine, then we may be locked into a social identity we did not choose. This suggests that special responsibilities may be troubling to the voluntarist, in a way that general responsibilities are not, because special responsibilities may seem to threaten our capacity for self-determination—our capacity to determine who, in social terms, we are. On this interpretation, it is not wrong to suggest that the voluntarist views special responsibilities, unless voluntarily incurred, as giving other people undue control over our lives. However, the problem is not simply that others may be able to make unwelcome claims on our time and resources. That much would be true even if we had only general responsibilities. The more fundamental problem is that other people may be able to shape our identities in ways that run counter to our wishes.

Seen in this light, the voluntarist's position has obvious appeal. The ability to have our social identities influenced by our choices is something about which most of us care deeply, and which seems to us an important prerequisite for the forms of human flourishing to which we aspire. We regard societies in which one's social identity is rigidly fixed, as a matter of law or social practice, by features of one's birth or breeding over which one has no control, as societies that are inhospitable to human freedom. This does not mean that we are committed to repudiating whatever communal or traditional affiliations may have been conferred upon us at birth. It only means that we want the salience in our lives of such affiliations to be influenced by our own wishes and decisions, rather than being determined by the dictates of the society at large. This is, of course, one reason why liberals insist that the legal status of citizens should be insensitive to facts about their race or religion or social class.

And yet, despite the value that we attach to having our social identities influenced by our choices, and despite the particular importance of protecting this value against political interference, it is clear that the capacity to determine one's identity has its limits. Each of us is born into a web of social relations, and our social world lays claim to us long before we can attain reflective distance from it or begin making choices about our place in it. We acquire personal relations and social affiliations of a formative kind before we are able to conceive of them as such or to contemplate altering them. Thus there is obviously no question, nor can the voluntarist seriously think that there is, of our being able actually to choose all of the relations in which we stand to other people. What the voluntarist can hope to claim is only that the significance of those relations is entirely up to us. However, this claim too is unsustainable. For better or worse, the influence on our personal histories of unchosen social relations—to parents and siblings, families and communities, nations and peoples—is not something that we determine by ourselves. Whether we like it or not, such relations help to define the contours of our lives, and influence the ways that we are seen both by ourselves and by others. Even those who sever or repudiate such ties—in so far as it is possible to do so—can never escape their influence or deprive them of all significance, for to have repudiated a personal tie is not the same as never having had it, and one does not nullify social bonds by rejecting them. One is, in other words, forever the person who has rejected or repudiated those bonds; one cannot make oneself into a person who lacked them from the outset. Thus, while some people travel enormous social distances in their lives, and while the possibility of so doing is something that we have every reason to cherish, the idea that the significance of our personal ties and social affiliations is wholly dependent on our wills—that we are the supreme gate-keepers of our own identities—can only be regarded as a fantasy. So if, as the non-reductionist believes, our relations to other people can generate responsibilities to them independently of our choices, then it is true that, in an important respect, the significance of our social relations is not fully under our control; but since the significance of those relations is in any case not fully under our control, this by itself does not rob us of any form of self-determination to which we may reasonably aspire.

In the end, then, the non-reductionist's response to the voluntarist objection is to insist that, although the significance of choice and consent in moral contexts is undeniable, nevertheless, the moral import of our relationships to other people does not derive solely from our own decisions. Nor, the non-reductionist may add, need we fear that this is tantamount to conceding the legitimacy of systems of caste or hierarchy, or that it leaves the individual at the mercy of oppressive social arrangements. For the relationships that generate responsibilities for an individual are those relationships that the individual has reason to value. No claims at all arise from relations that are degrading or demeaning, or which serve to undermine rather than to enhance human flourishing. In other words, the alternative to an exaggerated voluntarism is not an exaggerated communitarianism or historicism. In recognizing that the significance of our social relationships does not stem exclusively from our choices, we do not consign ourselves to a form of social bondage. In surrendering the fantasy that our own wills are the source of all our special responsibilities, we do not leave ourselves defenceless against the contingencies of the social world.

Yet even if these remarks constitute an effective response to the voluntarist objection, they may seem only to highlight the non-reductionist's vulnerability to the distributive objection. For, if relationships that are destructive of an individual's well-being do not, in general, give that individual special responsibilities, then presumably the relationships that do give him special responsibilities either enhance or at least do not erode his well-being. But, according to the distributive objection, special responsibilities may themselves work to the advantage of the participants in special relationships, and to the disadvantage of non-participants. And, it may be asked, why should a relationship that enhances the well-being of the participants give rise to a distribution of moral responsibility that further advances their interests, while working against the interests of non-participants? How can the non-reductionist respond to the charge that, unless the benefits and burdens of special responsibilities are integrated into an overall distribution that is fair, such responsibilities will themselves provide unfair advantages to the participants in interpersonal relations, while unfairly penalizing non-participants?

The non-reductionist may begin by reiterating that, as long as people attach value to their interpersonal relations, they will inevitably see themselves as having special responsibilities. And as long as they have good reasons for attaching value to those relations, we must allow that they also have good reasons to see themselves as having such responsibilities. There may, of course, be room for general scepticism about people's reasons for valuing their interpersonal relations. But it seems unlikely that proponents of the distributive objection can afford to be sceptics of this sort. For the distributive objection is animated by a concern for fairness in the allocation of benefits and burdens, and if, as the sceptic asserts, people never have reason to value their social relations, then it is unclear why considerations of fairness should weigh with them at all. Rather than providing grounds for the rejection of special responsibilities in particular, general scepticism about our reasons for valuing personal relations seems potentially subversive of morality as a whole.

Provided that the distributive objection is not taken to support a wholesale repudiation of special responsibilities, however, non-reductionists may concede that it makes a legitimate point. There are important respects in which special responsibilities may work to the advantage of the participants in personal relationships, and to the disadvantage of other people. These facts seem undeniable once they are called to our attention. That we sometimes lose sight of them is due in large measure to the influence of voluntarism, which focuses exclusively on the respects in which special responsibilities can be burdensome for the people who bear them, and sees the task of legitimating such responsibilities solely as a matter of justifying those burdens. Once we face the facts to which the distributive objection calls attention, however, we must agree that there is another side to special responsibilities: that they may also provide significant advantages for the participants in interpersonal relations and significant disadvantages for non-participants. In so far as the distributive objection insists only on the desirability of integrating these advantages and disadvantages into an overall distribution of benefits and burdens that is fair, non-reductionists have no reason to disagree.

Indeed, once the distributive objection is understood in this way, it may be seen as illustrating a more general point, with which non-reductionists also have no reason to disagree. The general point is that special responsibilities need to be set within the context of our overall moral outlook and constrained in suitable ways by other pertinent values. On a non-reductionist view, such constraints may, in principle, operate in at least three different ways. Some may affect the content of special responsibilities, by setting limits to the circumstances in which, and the extent to which, people are required to give priority to the interests of those to whom they have such responsibilities. Other constraints may affect the strength of special responsibilities, by supplying countervailing considerations that are capable of outweighing or over-riding those responsibilities in various contexts. Still other constraints may affect people's reasons for valuing their relationships. Perhaps, for example, people have no (net) reason to value relationships which themselves offend against important moral values or principles, so that such relationships do not generate special responsibilities even if people do in fact value them.[9]

The upshot is that, although non-reductionism insists that unreduced special responsibilities must be part of any adequate moral scheme, it is not hostile to the idea that there are a variety of other moral values—including the values underlying the distributive objection—by which such responsibilities must be constrained and with which they must be integrated if they are to be fully satisfactory. For example, there is nothing to prevent the non-reductionist from agreeing that considerations of distributive fairness serve to limit both the strength and the content of people's special responsibilities. Of course, the mere fact that non-reductionism is open to such possibilities does not suffice to show that a single moral outlook will be capable of accommodating special responsibilities while fully satisfying the values underlying the distributive objection. In fact, I believe that there is a deep and persistent tension between these two features of our moral thought, and nothing in the non-reductionist position guarantees that we will be able simultaneously to accommodate both features to our own satisfaction.[10]

Although this is a serious problem, however, it is no more of a problem for non-reductionist accounts of special responsibilities than it is for reductionist accounts. In fact, it is a problem for any view that takes special responsibilities seriously, while remaining sensitive to the values underlying the distributive objection. Any such view, and indeed any view that recognizes a diversity of moral values and principles, needs to ask how far that diversity can be accommodated within a unified moral outlook. Too often it is simply taken for granted either that a unified outlook must in principle be available, or that any tension at all among our values means that there is no possibility of jointly accommodating them. Neither assumption seems to me to be warranted. Instead, it seems to me a substantive question, the answer

---

[9] Might it be said, by someone sympathetic to the distributive objection, that relationships that run afoul of that objection violate this last type of constraint, and thus do not give rise to special responsibilities after all? This is unpersuasive because the distributive objection is not an objection to a class of relationships. In other words, it does not allege that certain relationships offend against important moral values. Instead, it claims only that considerations of distributive fairness prevent some relationships, which may be entirely unobjectionable in themselves, from giving rise to special responsibilities. But the constraint in question applies only to relationships that themselves offend against important moral values.

[10] See, generally, Thomas Nagel, *Equality and Partiality* (New York, NY: Oxford University Press, 1991).

to which remains open, to what extent the diverse moral values that we recognize can be jointly accommodated within a unified scheme of thought and practice.

Pending an answer to that question, non-reductionism appears to have the following advantages as an account of special responsibilities. To begin with, it has the virtue of cohering, better than do reductionist accounts, with our actual practice, which is to cite relationships as well as interactions as sources of special responsibilities. It also has the advantage of being able to explain, in simple and straightforward terms, why it is that people have seen such a diverse and apparently heterogeneous assortment of relationships as giving rise to such responsibilities. Furthermore, non-reductionism makes it possible to agree that our ordinary practices of ascribing special responsibilities to the participants in significant relationships are broadly correct. Like those ordinary practices themselves, however, it also leaves room for the criticism of particular ascriptions of responsibility. Admittedly, the content of the non-reductionist principle depends on some conception of the kinds of reasons people have for valuing their relations to others. Thus, given this principle, disagreements about reasons will inevitably lead to disagreements about the circumstances under which special responsibilities should be ascribed to people. Even this may seem like an advantage, however. For there are many disagreements about the ascription of such responsibilities that do seem plausibly understood as reflecting a more fundamental disagreement about the reasons people have for valuing their relationships. To the extent that this is so, non-reductionism locates controversies about the ascription of special responsibilities in the right place, and provides an illuminating explanation of them. Finally, non-reductionism is sensitive to the concerns underlying the voluntarist and distributive objections, yet it provides reasons for insisting that neither objection supports the complete repudiation of unreduced special responsibilities.

Let me close by returning to a point that I made earlier. The non-reductionist position I have outlined, if it can be persuasively developed, may have implications for a number of important controversies in moral and political philosophy. Inasmuch as it offers a defence of special responsibilities that is non-consequentialist in character, for example, it points to a possible defence of at least some sorts of 'agent-centred restrictions'.[11] Similarly, I believe, it suggests some constraints that any adequate formulation of cosmopolitanism may need to respect. Detailed discussion of these implications, however, must await another occasion.[12]

---

[11] See *The Rejection of Consequentialism* (Oxford: Clarendon Press, 1994 [rev. ed.]), esp. Chap. Four.

[12] See 'Conceptions of Cosmopolitanism' for discussion of some constraints on an adequate cosmopolitan view.

7

Conceptions of Cosmopolitanism*

In recent years, political philosophy has seen a resurgence of interest in the idea of cosmopolitanism.[1] In common parlance, the term 'cosmopolitanism' suggests a posture of worldly sophistication which is naturally contrasted with more provincial or parochial outlooks. Philosophical usage, although not un-related, tends to be more specialized. Interestingly enough, however, there is no consensus among contemporary philosophers and theorists about how the precise content of a cosmopolitan position is to be understood, and this despite the fact that cosmopolitanism as a political doctrine has a rich history dating back to ancient times. Accordingly, one of my central aims in this essay is to call attention to two different strands in recent thinking about cosmopolitanism. One strand presents it primarily as a doctrine about justice. The other presents it primarily as a doctrine about culture and the self. Cosmopolitanism about justice and cosmopolitanism about culture are not

* Originally published in *Utilitas* 11/3 (November 1999): 255–76. © Edinburgh University Press 1999. Reprinted by permission. Earlier versions of this paper were presented to the Columbia Colloquium in Political Theory, the Harvard Program in Ethics and the Professions, a Stanford Conference on Cosmopolitanism and Nationalism, the Department of Philosophy at Uppsala University, and the School of Law (Boalt Hall) at Berkeley. I am grateful to all of these audiences for valuable discussion. I also owe special thanks to David Hollinger for helpful comments on an early draft.
   [1] See, for example, Bruce Ackerman, 'Rooted Cosmopolitanism', *Ethics*, 104 (1994); Kwame Anthony Appiah, 'Cosmopolitan Patriots', *Critical Inquiry*, 23 (1997); Charles Beitz, 'Cosmopolitan Ideals and National Sentiment', *Journal of Philosophy*, 80 (1983); *Perpetual Peace: Essays on Kant's Cosmopolitan Ideal*, ed. J. Bohman and M. Lutz-Bachmann, Cambridge, MA, 1997; *Cosmopolitics: Thinking and Feeling beyond the Nation*, ed. P. Cheah and B. Robbins, Minneapolis, MN, 1998; David Hollinger, 'Nationalism, Cosmopolitanism, and the United States', *Immigration and Citizenship in the Twenty-First Century*, ed. N. Pickus, Lanham, MD, 1998; David Hollinger, *Postethnic America*, New York, NY, 1995; Will Kymlicka, 'From Enlightenment Cosmopolitanism to Liberal Nationalism', *The Enlightenment: Then and Now*, ed. S. Lukes and M. Hollis, forthcoming; Judith Lichtenberg, 'National Boundaries and Moral Boundaries: A Cosmopolitan View', *Boundaries: National Autonomy and its Limits*, ed. P. Brown and H. Shue, Totowa, NJ, 1981; Martha Nussbaum *et al.*, *For Love of Country: Debating the Limits of Patriotism*, Boston, MA, 1996; Thomas Pogge, 'Cosmopolitanism and Sovereignty', *Ethics*, 103 (1992); Jeremy Waldron, 'Minority Cultures and the Cosmopolitan Alternative', *University of Michigan Journal of Law Reform*, 25 (1992).

the only possible forms of the view, and they are not mutually exclusive. Yet some defenders of cosmopolitanism seem clearly to have one form rather than the other in mind.

One way of coming to appreciate the difference between cosmopolitanism about justice and cosmopolitanism about culture is by taking note of the different positions to which they are opposed. Cosmopolitanism about justice is opposed to any view that posits principled restrictions on the scope of an adequate conception of justice. In other words, it opposes any view which holds, as a matter of principle, that the norms of justice apply primarily within bounded groups comprising some subset of the global population. For example, this type of cosmopolitanism rejects communitarian and nationalist arguments to the effect that the principles of distributive justice can properly be applied only within reasonably cohesive social groups: groups that share a common history, culture, language, or ethnicity, or which, for other reasons, are sufficiently cohesive that the identities of their members are partly constituted and defined by their membership.[2] At the same time, however, cosmopolitanism about justice is equally opposed to liberal theories which set out principles of justice that are to be applied in the first instance to a single society, conceived of as a co-operative scheme or an arrangement for reciprocal advantage, and considered more or less in isolation from all others. Indeed, some of the most vigorous proponents of a cosmopolitan approach to distributive justice have explicitly formulated their views in opposition not to communitarianism but rather to Rawls's doctrine that the principles of justice are to be applied to the basic structure of an individual society.[3] While remaining otherwise sympathetic to Rawls's ideas, these cosmopolitan critics have sought to defend the application of his principles of justice to the global population as a whole.[4] In short, although its proponents typically situate themselves within the liberal tradition broadly construed, cosmopolitanism about justice is no less opposed to liberal restrictions on the scope of justice than to communitarian or nationalist restrictions.

Cosmopolitanism about culture and the self, meanwhile, is opposed to any suggestion that individuals' well-being or their identity or their capacity for effective human agency normally depends on their membership in a determinate cultural group whose boundaries are reasonably clear and whose stability and cohesion are reasonably secure. Cosmopolitans see these ideas as involving a distorted understanding of culture and unduly restrictive conceptions of individual identity, agency, and well-being. Cultures, they maintain, are always in flux; change is the normal condition for a living culture. For the population that sustains a culture is itself constantly changing. Old generations with their memories and ties to the past gradually fade away. New

---

[2] See, for example, Michael Sandel, *Liberalism and the Limits of Justice*, Cambridge, 1982.

[3] See John Rawls, *A Theory of Justice*, Cambridge, MA, 1971.

[4] See, for example, Charles Beitz, *Political Theory and International Relations*, Princeton, NJ, 1979; Thomas Pogge, *Realizing Rawls*, Ithaca, NY, 1989.

generations with new problems and experiences gradually attain maturity. And any cultural group may at any time be called upon to respond to new challenges—to wars, diseases, or natural disasters, for example, or to new discoveries, creations, or inventions. A group's responses to such challenges are then absorbed into, and thus serve to modify, the culture's history and self-understanding. Furthermore, the population that sustains any one culture will almost always have multiple forms of contact with other populations and their ideas, languages, artefacts, traditions, and practices. Through these multiple communicative routes, cultures routinely appropriate—sometimes in altered or distorted from and often with only partial comprehension—more or less coherent fragments of materials from other cultures. And when they do not appropriate the products of other cultures, often they react against those products—trying to ward them off and to resist their influence. But, of course, this too is a form of influence. In short, the cosmopolitan argues, cultures are constantly in flux, constantly changing, constantly being modified, updated, altered, supplemented, recast, and reconceived. Nor is this a sign of weakness or ill health. On the contrary, it is those extremely rare cultures whose populations are isolated from all others and which therefore exist like museum pieces, protected against the normal rough-and-tumble jostling of intercultural exchange, which are the likeliest to be brittle, fragile, and unable to perpetuate themselves when change comes, as, inevitably, it must do.

In addition to insisting on the ubiquity of cultural change, cosmopolitanism about culture emphasizes the fluidity of individual identity, people's remarkable capacity to forge new identities using materials from diverse cultural sources, and to flourish while so doing. Far from requiring immersion in a single, pristine culture if they are to achieve a coherent sense of self or to have available to them the kinds of choices that make a good life possible, some human beings flourish by exercising their inventiveness and creativity to construct new ways of life using the most heterogeneous cultural materials. In so doing, they demonstrate the very capacities that make it possible for human beings to create culture in the first place, and they enrich humanity as a whole by renewing the stock of cultural resources on which others may draw. In a marvellous article defending cultural cosmopolitanism, Jeremy Waldron quotes a passage from an essay by Salman Rushdie that makes the point quite eloquently. '*The Satanic Verses*', Rushdie says of the novel that changed his life forever,

celebrates hybridity, impurity, intermingling, the transformation that comes of new and unexpected combinations of human beings, cultures, ideas, politics, movies, songs. It rejoices in mongrelization and fears the absolutism of the Pure. *Melange*, hotchpotch, a bit of this and a bit of that is *how newness enters the world*. (Quoted in Jeremy Waldron, 'Minority Cultures and the Cosmopolitan Alternative', 751).

The claims to which cosmopolitanism about culture is opposed, play an important role in much communitarian and nationalist thought, as well as in many formulations of multiculturalism, and in that capacity they are routinely deployed as premises in anti-liberal arguments. Yet some liberals, too, have accepted such claims, and have sought to show that they can be effectively accommodated within a modified liberal framework.[5] Cosmopolitanism about culture opposes these claims whether they are offered by communitarians, nationalists, multiculturalists, or liberals. Thus, like cosmopolitanism about justice, cosmopolitanism about culture, although appealing primarily to thinkers who situate themselves within a broadly liberal tradition, nevertheless finds itself in opposition to some formulations of liberalism as well as to many forms of nationalism and communitarianism.

Although the two kinds of cosmopolitanism differ in content, it is certainly no accident that the term 'cosmopolitanism' is applied to both positions. For the root idea of cosmopolitanism is the idea that each individual is a citizen of the world, and owes allegiance, as Martha Nussbaum has put it, 'to the worldwide community of human beings'.[6] Cosmopolitanism about justice and cosmopolitanism about culture can both be seen as variants of this idea. For the cosmopolitan about justice, the idea of world citizenship means that the norms of justice must ultimately be seen as governing the relations of all human beings to each other, and not merely as applying within individual societies or bounded groups of other kinds. For the cosmopolitan about culture, meanwhile, the idea of world citizenship means that individuals have the capacity to flourish by forging idiosyncratic identities from heterogeneous cultural sources, and are not to be thought of as constituted or defined by ascriptive ties to a particular culture, community, or tradition.

There is, however, an ambiguity in the idea of world citizenship, and that ambiguity gets transmitted to these two variants. What is ambiguous is the way in which one is to understand the normative status of one's particular interpersonal relationships and group affiliations, once one is thought of as a citizen of the world. More specifically, the question is what kinds of reasons one can have, compatibly with one's status as a world citizen, for devoting differential attention to those individuals with whom one has special relationships of one kind or another—either relationships that are personal in character or ones that consist instead in co-membership in some larger group.

On one interpretation, world citizenship is fundamental, in the sense that the devotion of special attention to some people rather than others is legitimate only if it can be justified by reference to the ideal of world citizenship itself. This is the interpretation apparently favoured by Nussbaum. She says that '[n]one of the major thinkers in the cosmopolitan tradition denied that we can and should give special attention to our own families and to our own ties of religious and national belonging'.[7] Cosmopolitans believe, according

[5] See, for example, Will Kymlicka, *Liberalism, Community, and Culture*, Oxford, 1989. See also David Miller, *On Nationality*, Oxford, 1995; Yael Tamir, *Liberal Nationalism*, Princeton, NJ, 1993.

[6] Nussbaum, 4.   [7] Ibid., 135.

to her, 'that it is right to give the local an additional measure of concern'.[8] However, she adds, 'the primary reason a cosmopolitan should have for this is not that the local is better *per se*, but rather that this is the only sensible way to do good'.[9] Rather than attempting to divide one's attention equally among all the children of the world, for example, one should devote special attention to one's own children, but only because that is the most effective way of allocating one's benevolence. One must not suppose that one's own children are worth more than other children. This seems to imply that, in trying to justify our particular attachments and loyalties, we are faced with a dilemma. Either we must argue, as Nussbaum does, that devoting special attention to the people we are attached to is an effective way of doing good for humanity at large, or else we must suppose that the people we are attached to are simply worth more than others. I shall return to this dilemma later. For now, it suffices to note that, on the interpretation of world citizenship that Nussbaum appears to favour, special attention to particular people is legitimate only if it can be justified by reference to the interests of all human beings considered as equals. Cosmopolitanism, in this view, implies that particular human relationships and group affiliations never provide independent reasons for action or suffice by themselves to generate special responsibilities to one's intimates and associates.[10]

There is a more moderate way of understanding the idea of world citizenship. On this alternative interpretation, to say that one is a citizen of the world is to say that, in addition to one's relationships and affiliations with particular individuals and groups, one also stands in an ethically significant relation to other human beings in general. There is no suggestion, on this interpretation, that one's special relationships and affiliations need to be justified by reference to the ideal of world citizenship itself, or that any legitimate reasons we have for promoting the interests of the people we care specially about must be derivative from the interests of humanity as a whole. Instead, world citizenship is one important form of membership among others, one important source of reasons and responsibilities among others. Cosmopolitanism, on this more moderate interpretation, insists only that one's local attachments and affiliations must always be balanced and constrained by consideration of the interests of other people.

As I have said, the idea of world citizenship is ambiguous as between the two interpretations I have mentioned, the one more extreme and the other more moderate, and this ambiguity gets transmitted to the two variants of cosmopolitanism I have been discussing: cosmopolitanism about justice and cosmopolitanism about culture. Within cosmopolitanism about justice, the ambiguity manifests itself as an ambiguity about whether individual societies and other bounded groups are thought ultimately to be insignificant from the

---

[8] Ibid.   [9] Ibid., 135 f.
[10] I have discussed Nussbaum's position at greater length in my review of *For Love of Country*, which appeared in the *Times Literary Supplement*, December 27, 1996.

standpoint of justice or whether the claim is merely that traditional theories of justice greatly exaggerate their significance. In other words, the question is whether there is anything that the members of an individual society owe each other, as a matter of justice, that they do not owe to non-members. Or, to put the point in still another way, are there *any* norms of *social* as opposed to *global* justice: any norms that apply only within an individual society and not to the global population as a whole? The extreme view denies that there are, at least at the level of fundamental principle, although its proponents may concede that some distinction between social and global norms is justified on practical or instrumental grounds. The moderate view, by contrast, treats such a distinction as fundamental; it denies that global justice takes the place of social justice, even at the level of basic principle, and it accepts that the members of an individual society owe each other some things, as a matter of justice, that they do not owe to non-members. The cosmopolitan character of the moderate view lies in its insistence that there are, in fact, substantive norms of global justice in addition to the norms that apply within a single society, and in its denial that the content of social justice can be arrived at by considering the individual society as a closed system in isolation from all others. The principles of social justice, according to the moderate cosmopolitan, are not replaced, but they are constrained, by the principles of global justice.

Within cosmopolitanism about culture, the ambiguity in the idea of world citizenship manifests itself as an ambiguity about whether what is claimed is merely that individuals need not be situated within a single cultural tradition in order to flourish, or whether it is asserted, more ambitiously, that people cannot flourish in that way. In other words, the question is whether those who do not forge idiosyncratic identities from heterogeneous cultural materials, but whose aims and aspirations are structured instead by the values and traditions of a particular cultural community, are deemed just as capable of flourishing as people who are culturally more adventurous, and, relatedly, whether participation in the life of such a community is recognized as a potential source of special responsibilities to one's fellow members. The extreme view denies that adherence to the values and traditions of a particular community represents a viable way of life in the modern world, and, accordingly, is not inclined to treat an individual's relationship to a particular cultural community as a potential source of special responsibilities. The moderate view, by contrast, maintains only that people do not need to situate themselves squarely within a particular cultural tradition in order to thrive. It is quite happy to accept that some people will continue to do so, and that those who do may acquire special responsibilities to the other members of their communities.

The tension between these two versions of cosmopolitanism about culture is clearly exhibited in the article by Waldron mentioned earlier. At a minimum, Waldron argues, the fact 'that a freewheeling cosmopolitan life, lived in a kaleidoscope of cultures, is both possible and fulfilling' undercuts any suggestion that 'all people *need* their rootedness in the particular culture in which they and their ancestors were reared'. While 'immersion in the culture of a particular community . . . may be something that particular people like and enjoy . . . they no longer can claim that it is something that they need'.[11] But Waldron is also tempted by a stronger claim, namely, 'that the hybrid lifestyle of the true cosmopolitan is in fact the only appropriate response to the modern world in which we live'.[12] Since Waldron never makes it clear whether, in the end, he is prepared to endorse this claim, the net result is that his paper exhibits an unresolved ambivalence with respect to the choice between moderate and extreme cosmopolitanism about culture.

The appeal of moderate cosmopolitanism, both about culture and about justice, is not difficult to appreciate. The fact that some people can and do flourish while drawing in idiosyncratic ways on culturally eclectic materials seems perfectly evident. Thus, the possibility that 'a freewheeling cosmopolitan life' can be fulfilling is undeniable. And moderate cosmopolitanism about justice seems equally plausible. Those people who do not happen to belong to our society, nation, or community are no less valuable than those who do, and their antecedent claims to a share of the earth's resources are no weaker. Furthermore, we interact with them at least indirectly, through our common participation in a network of interlocking economic, political, and technological structures and arrangements.[13] Given all of this, it seems implausible to deny that there are substantive principles of global justice that govern our relations to them, or to insist that the principles of justice for a single society can be fully determined without reference to its relations to other societies.

Indeed, the moderate versions of cosmopolitanism that I have articulated may strike some people as being so plausible as to amount to little more than a set of platitudes. Yet Waldron is right to insist that some influential claims about the necessity of immersion in a single, cohesive culture appear to be undermined by the very possibility that moderate cosmopolitanism about culture affirms—the possibility of a fulfilling cosmopolitan way of life. Nor should we forget how threatening that possibility has sometimes seemed to people who wished to maintain the purity of their own culture, or the pathological forms that hostility to cosmopolitan eclecticism has all too often taken. And moderate cosmopolitanism about justice is no more vacuous or platitudinous than moderate cosmopolitanism about culture. Although it may not sound

[11] Waldron, 762. One might wonder whether Waldron is not here conflating the denial that *all* people need immersion in their culture with the denial that *anyone* does. For related criticism of this passage, see Will Kymlicka, *Multicultural Citizenship*, Oxford, 1995, 85 f. See also J. Waldron, 'Multiculturalism and Melange', *Public Education in a Multicultural Society*, ed. R. Fullinwider, Cambridge, 1996.

[12] Waldron, 'Minority Cultures and the Cosmopolitan Alternative', 763.

[13] I have discussed this point at greater length in 'Individual Responsibility in a Global Age', Chapter Two in this volume.

particularly radical to assert that there are substantive principles of global justice which supplement and constrain the principles of justice for an individual society, the complete internalization of this claim would require far-reaching changes in many traditional theories of justice, not to mention the actual political practice of existing states and societies.

Whereas the moderate versions of cosmopolitanism may strike some people as being so obvious as to be vacuous or platitudinous, the extreme versions may seem so implausible as to be difficult to take seriously. For each denies the ultimate moral and justificatory significance of social affiliations whose importance in most people's lives, and whose *de facto* political importance, could hardly be greater. It may look as if the extreme versions of cosmopolitanism about culture and justice simply inherit the implausibility of the extreme interpretation of world citizenship, which implies that particular human relationships and group affiliations cannot by themselves give rise to special responsibilities or independent reasons for action. Since the conviction that we have special responsibilities to our families, friends, and communities is so deeply embedded within common-sense moral thought that even to call attention to it is to risk belabouring the obvious, it can seem puzzling that extreme versions of cosmopolitanism have managed to tempt as many philosophers and theorists as they have.

Part of the explanation may lie in what I will call 'Nussbaum's dilemma'. As we saw earlier, Nussbaum appears to think that, in trying to justify our particular attachments and loyalties, we are faced with a choice. Either we must argue that devoting special attention to the people we are attached to is an effective way of doing good for humanity at large, or else we must suppose that those people are simply worth more than others. What we cannot do is to affirm that all people are of equal worth, while simultaneously insisting that our special relationships to particular people obligate us to devote special attention to those people, whether or not doing so will promote the good of humanity at large. In other words, Nussbaum's dilemma implies that there is a price to be paid for treating particular relationships and affiliations as independent sources of reasons and responsibilities, and the price is that we must deny the equal worth of persons. This makes the appeal of extreme forms of cosmopolitanism look less puzzling. Given Nussbaum's dilemma, extreme cosmopolitanism is simply the inevitable consequence of a serious commitment to equality.

Yet this only pushes the puzzle back one level. The question at the next level is why 'Nussbaum's dilemma' should be regarded as a genuine dilemma. Surely many people who wish to affirm the equality of persons also take themselves to have underived special responsibilities to their families, friends and communities—responsibilities, in other words, that do not have their source in considerations about the good of humanity as a whole. It is, therefore, not at all apparent why a commitment to equality should be thought incompatible with a recognition of underived special responsibilities.

Interestingly, some of the strongest proponents of the idea that there is such an incompatibility have not been extreme cosmopolitans at all, but have rather been communitarian critics of liberalism, who have argued that the values of justice and equality, which they see as characteristic of liberalism and the Enlightenment, cannot be reconciled with the values of loyalty, tradition, and communal solidarity. A case in point is Alasdair MacIntyre's argument that there is a fundamental incompatibility between 'a morality of liberal impersonality' and what he calls 'the morality of patriotism'.[14] In decisions about the allocation of scarce but essential resources, MacIntyre says, the standpoint of impersonal morality requires that the interests of all people be given equal weight, whereas the patriotic standpoint demands that one put the interests of one's own community ahead of the interests of other communities.[15] No attempt to combine these two perspectives, he suggests, can ever 'be carried through without incoherence'.[16] Thus, it seems that, for MacIntyre, 'Nussbaum's dilemma' is a genuine dilemma. A commitment to the equal worth of persons is incompatible with a recognition of underived special responsibilities to the members of one's own community. This implies that moderate cosmopolitanism, which purports to recognize both values, is untenable. Beyond this, MacIntyre also believes that, given the need to choose between equality and special responsibilities, consistent liberals must choose equality, which implies that they must end up as extreme cosmopolitans. Of course, MacIntyre would presumably see this as a reason for being suspicious of liberalism rather than as a reason for embracing extreme cosmopolitanism. But many extreme cosmopolitans would agree with him not only about the untenability of moderate cosmopolitanism, but also about the reality of 'Nussbaum's dilemma' and about the need for consistent liberals to accept the extreme cosmopolitan position.

Despite this, the reality of the dilemma cannot be taken for granted, for it flies in the face of the experience and conviction of many people. And if there is, in fact, no incompatibility between a commitment to equality and a recognition of underived special responsibilities, then the argument in favour of extreme cosmopolitanism that we are considering simply collapses. Equally, however, the argument against moderate cosmopolitanism collapses. Thus, a great deal turns on the question of whether 'Nussbaum's dilemma' is indeed a genuine dilemma. The fact that so many people actually do affirm the equal worth of persons, while acknowledging underived special responsibilities, establishes at least a weak presumption against the reality of the dilemma. At a minimum, we need persuasive reasons for thinking that people who suppose they can embrace both values simultaneously are mistaken.

---

[14] Alasdair MacIntyre, 'Is Patriotism a Virtue?', The Lindley Lecture, Lawrence, Kansas, 1984, 18. For additional discussion of MacIntyre's position, see my 'Liberalism, Nationalism, and Egalitarianism', Chapter Four in this volume.
[15] MacIntyre, 6.   [16] Ibid., 19.

There are at least two different arguments that may appear to support the claim of incompatibility. The first begins from the premise that the equal worth of persons, if it is not to be just an empty slogan, must have implications for the way people are treated. It does not, of course, imply that each person must treat every other person equally in all respects. That would be an insane—as well as an unsatisfiable—requirement. However, it may be argued, the proposition that all people are of equal worth does imply that people should be treated equally unless there are good reasons for treating them unequally. And, it may be said, the fact that I have a special relation to a particular person is not a good reason. There is, as Godwin famously insisted, no magic in the pronoun 'my':[17] no way the mere fact that a person is *my* friend or daughter or compatriot can provide a legitimate reason for assigning more weight to that person's interests than to the interests of other equally worthy people. So if one is genuinely committed to the equal worth of persons, one must, unless one believes in magic, reject the idea that one has special responsibilities to particular people simply because of the nature of one's relationship to those people.

The second argument that may appear to vindicate Nussbaum's dilemma is this. Special responsibilities, it may be said, do not merely constitute a departure from equal treatment; taken seriously, their effect is to legitimate and, indeed, greatly to exacerbate global inequalities of wealth and power. For when the members of rich and powerful societies give each other's interests priority over the interests of people in poor societies, the inevitable result is that material inequality is increased: the rich get richer and the poor get poorer. Thus, the reason why the recognition of special responsibilities cannot be reconciled with a commitment to equality is that the actual effects of taking such responsibilities seriously are predictably and massively inegalitarian. Given the way special responsibilities actually function, people who are committed to discharging them cannot possibly do more than pay lip service to the idea of equality.

We have, then, two arguments for the incompatibility of equality and special responsibilities. The first, which I will call the conceptual argument, is that a commitment to the equality of persons sets up a presumption in favour of equal treatment from which special responsibilities represent a conceptually unjustified departure. The second argument, which I will call the substantive argument, is that equality and special responsibilities require policies and practices that are diametrically opposed to each other. If we take equality seriously, we must act in ways that are incompatible with discharging our special responsibilities. And if we take our special responsibilities seriously, we must act in ways that contribute to the perpetuation of material inequality.

---

[17] William Godwin, *An Enquiry Concerning Political Justice*, London, 1793, bk. 2, ch. 2.

I believe that the first of these arguments—the conceptual argument—is not only mistaken but quite deeply mistaken. The fact that a particular relationship is mine is not only a legitimate reason for departing from equal treatment, it is the basic reason. What I mean by this is that if we attend closely to what interpersonal relationships involve, we will see that the participants in such relationships cannot attach value to them, in the ways that they manifestly do, without seeing them as providing reasons for unequal treatment. This means that interpersonal relationships cannot play the fundamental role that they do in human life unless people treat their own relationships as independent sources of reasons for action. Indeed, in certain cases, something even stronger is true. Since certain kinds of relationships—to put the point paradoxically—cannot exist at all unless the participants value them, and since the participants cannot value them without seeing them as providing reasons for unequal treatment, certain kinds of relationships cannot exist at all unless they are seen as providing reasons for unequal treatment. Thus, the claim that the 'mere' fact that a relationship is one's own cannot provide one with legitimate reasons for action involves a deep error. Interpersonal relationships could not play the role they do in our lives, and in some cases could not even exist, unless they were treated by the participants as providing such reasons.

The crucial point, which I have developed at greater length elsewhere,[18] is this. It is possible to attach purely instrumental value to a personal relationship. For example, one may value one's relationship to a certain person solely because one sees it as a way to advance one's career, or to realize one's social aspirations. However, it is pathological to attach nothing but instrumental value to any of one's personal relationships. And to value one's relationship to another person non-instrumentally is, in part, to be disposed, in contexts that may vary depending on the nature of the relationship, to see that person's needs, interests, and desires as, in themselves, giving one presumptively decisive reasons for action, reasons that one would not have had in the absence of the relationship. To say that these reasons are seen as presumptively decisive is not to say that they can never, in the end, be outweighed by other considerations. It is merely to say that, in the first instance, they present themselves as considerations upon which one must act. Thus, if one values one's relationship to a particular person non-instrumentally, one will inevitably see it as a source of reasons for action: as a source, more specifically, of presumptively decisive reasons for treating that person differently from others. And this in turn is tantamount to saying that one will see the relationship as a source of special responsibilities. Furthermore, there are, as I have said, certain kinds of relationships that cannot be said to obtain at all if the participants do not value their relations to each other. For example, a relationship does not qualify as a friendship unless the participants attach non-instrumental

---

[18] 'Relationships and Responsibilities', Chapter Six in this volume.

value to it. Two people may interact on cordial and familiar terms, and their dealings with each other may, in that sense, be 'friendly'; nevertheless, their relationship does not count as a friendship if they do not value it. It follows that there can be no genuine friendships that are not seen by the participants as reasons for differential treatment.

One implication of these considerations is that there is a fundamental difference between regarding a relationship in which one is not a participant as valuable and valuing a relationship of one's own. Both affect one's reasons for action, but they do so in different ways. If I believe that some relationship in which I am not a participant is a valuable relationship, then I will, for example, believe that I should not gratuitously act so as to undermine it. But I need not see that relationship as providing me with reasons for action that differ in strength or character from the reasons that other comparably valuable relationships provide. By contrast, to value my own relationship to another person is precisely to see that person's needs and interests as reason-giving in a way that other people's needs and interests are not, even if those other people are themselves participants in equally valuable relationships of the very same kind. This is not because there is some magic in the pronoun 'my'. To suppose that it is a matter of magic is to misunderstand the structure of the human relationships in which people find fulfilment. More specifically, it is to overlook the fact that valued human relationships are partly constituted by patterns of perceived reasons.

It is worth emphasizing that these considerations apply to those who lead 'freewheeling cosmopolitan' lives no less than to people whose lives are situated within more traditional cultural frameworks. So long as 'freewheeling cosmopolitans' participate in and attach value to particular interpersonal relationships, they must inevitably see those relationships as sources of reasons for action. The fact that the cosmopolitan's relationships may cross national, cultural, or communal lines is beside the point, as is the fact that those relationships may defy custom or convention or may break new social ground. In so far as a cosmopolitan way of life is indeed a *way of life*—a way of orienting oneself toward and participating in the social world—it can be expected to generate an array of human relationships and associations no less rich and varied, and no less valued by the participants, than those associated with more traditional ways of life. And so long as the participants do indeed value those relationships, they will inevitably see them as generating reasons for differential treatment. This means that there is an ineliminably particularistic dimension to any way of life worthy of the name.

If this is correct, then the conceptual argument fails. It is simply not true that the idea of special responsibilities represents a conceptually unjustified departure from the kind of equal treatment that a commitment to the equal worth of persons requires. Or, to put the same point another way, there is no conceptual incoherence in affirming both that all people are of equal worth and that one has special responsibilities to those particular people with whom one stands in relationships of certain significant kinds.

That leaves the substantive argument. According to this argument, the practical implications of special responsibilities are sufficiently inegalitarian that a general practice of honouring such responsibilities precludes the implementation of substantively egalitarian policies or institutions. It may perhaps be compatible with a sincere affirmation of the abstract proposition that all people are of equal value, but it leaves no room for policies designed to reduce material inequality. It is, therefore, compatible only with a kind of formal commitment to abstract equality, a commitment that is devoid of significant practical implications.

But this argument is overstated. It is true, as I have said, that people cannot value their relationships at all without seeing them as providing reasons for differential treatment. However, the kinds of differential treatment for which those relationships are seen as providing reasons are highly variable. They depend not only on the nature of the relationships involved but also on the content of the background norms and institutions that fix the social context within which the relationships arise. In other words, people's judgements about the circumstances in which, and the extent to which, they have reason to give special weight to the interests of their intimates and associates are highly sensitive to the norms they have internalized and to the character of the prevailing social practices and institutions. Behaviour that is seen in one social setting as an admirable expression of parental concern, for example, may be seen in another setting as an intolerable form of favouritism or nepotism.

This means that social institutions can vary considerably in their character while still leaving ample room for people to behave in ways that give expression to the value they attach to their interpersonal relationships. Within a fairly broad range, people can modify the behaviour that serves this function to fit the institutional and normative context in which they find themselves. In particular, they can adapt their behaviour to more or less egalitarian institutions and policies. People who live in societies with relatively more extensive social welfare programmes, or more extensive policies of redistributive taxation, are not thereby prohibited from giving meaningful expression to the value they place on their most treasured relationships. To be sure, this kind of flexibility is not unlimited, and it is an interesting question where the limits lie. However, it is not necessary to fix those limits with any precision to see that a general practice of honouring special responsibilities need not preclude the implementation of significantly egalitarian policies, or deprive a professed commitment to equality of all practical implications.

This is not to deny that there is a tension between equality and special responsibilities. It is clear that the deployment of resources—whether material, motivational, or institutional—in the service of one value can often lead to a reduction in the resources devoted to the other. Thus, psychologically and politically, a focus on special responsibilities can and often does lead to a neglect of egalitarian concerns—and *vice versa*—even if it does not have to. This is the truth that the substantive argument exaggerates. Stripped of the exaggeration, what it tells us is that, despite the ways in which the two values are compatible, we should not expect that principles capable of accommodating them both will be easy to identify. And even if such principles were in hand, we should not suppose that it would then be easy, at the level of practice, to develop institutions, policies, and habits of conduct that would make possible their stable implementation. On the contrary, it is likely to require considerable social imagination and ingenuity, psychological sophistication and sensitivity, and political determination and skill. Nevertheless, none of this goes to show that a practice of taking special responsibilities seriously precludes a substantive commitment to equality.

If, as I have been maintaining, neither the conceptual argument nor the substantive argument is successful, then there is little reason to regard 'Nussbaum's dilemma' as a genuine dilemma. There is little reason, in other words, to suppose that a commitment to the equality of persons is incompatible with a recognition of underived special responsibilities. And if that is so, then we have been given no reason to accept the claims of extreme cosmopolitanism either with respect to justice or with respect to culture. Moreover, if equality and special responsibilities are neither substantively nor conceptually incompatible, and if many people do in fact take both values seriously, then moderate forms of cosmopolitanism have much to recommend them.[19]

Lest this make the case for moderate cosmopolitanism sound too pat, however, let me complicate matters by mentioning one limitation of my argument, along with two difficulties confronting even moderate forms of cosmopolitanism about culture.

The limitation is this. I have argued against extreme cosmopolitanism about justice and culture only in so far as those doctrines rely on the general scepticism about the legitimacy of underived special responsibilities that is characteristic of the extreme version of the cosmopolitan ideal of world citizenship. However, both doctrines might in principle be defended on narrower grounds. Thus, for example, there is room for a thoroughly globalist conception of justice which allows that individuals have special responsibilities to the members of their families and to other intimate acquaintances, but denies that they have such responsibilities to their fellow citizens or conationals. The claim, in other words, would be that, even though people do have some underived special responsibilities, the members of any given society owe nothing more to each other, as a matter of fundamental principle, than they owe to non-members. There is also room for a form of extreme cultural cosmopolitanism which agrees that individuals normally acquire special responsibilities through participation in personal relationships, but

[19] For a defence of 'moderate nationalism' which argues that it converges with a moderate form of 'global humanism', see Stephen Nathanson, 'Nationalism and the Limits of Global Humanism', in R. McKim and J. McMahan (eds.) *The Morality of Nationalism*, New York, NY, 1997.

denies that membership in a cultural community can give rise to responsibilities of this sort. Whatever the merits of these positions, nothing I have said rules them out. I have argued against extreme cosmopolitanism about justice and culture only in so far as those views depend on general scepticism about underived special responsibilities.

Let me now turn to the first of the two difficulties facing even moderate forms of cosmopolitanism about culture. Particular communities, societies, and cultural groups, when they are in reasonably good order, typically incorporate relatively specific norms and standards that set out the responsibilities of individual members. Thus, individuals whose aims and aspirations are structured by their membership in such groups, and who see themselves as having special responsibilities to the other members of their groups, are typically confronted with a reasonably well-articulated set of expectations concerning the content of those responsibilities. They know, at least roughly, what their community or tradition expects of them. Furthermore, the community normally provides an institutional framework within which those responsibilities may be discharged, as well as a set of mechanisms, often of considerable psychological sophistication, which serve to nurture and support the motivations that individuals must have if they are reliably to fulfil their responsibilities. In short, the community normally supplies individuals with a reasonably clear statement of their responsibilities and encourages the development of the motivations that will lead them to discharge those responsibilities. It provides for them what might be called the 'infrastructure of responsibility'.

By contrast, those who lead freewheeling, cosmopolitan lives, having cut themselves free of the bonds tying them to particular communities and traditions, are deprived of the infrastructure that such a community provides. Indeed, individuals are often attracted to a cosmopolitan way of life precisely because they find a particular community's infrastructure too confining or oppressive, and seek to distance themselves from it. But then the difficulty is that the cosmopolitan life may not have a ready-made alternative infrastructure to offer. Despite my argument that even cosmopolitans will have particular relationships that they see as independent sources of reasons for action, there may be no developed institutions that serve to identify the responsibilities arising out of those relationships, or to encourage and channel the motivations that would lead individuals reliably to discharge them. Precisely because the relationships in question tend to be culturally eclectic and to cut across communal lines, they are unlikely to fall within a socially well-developed framework of institutional norms and expectations capable of supplying an infrastructure of responsibility. The danger for cosmopolitans, then, is the danger of moral isolation—of being cut off from the forms of social support that structure and sustain individual responsibility. As citizens of the world, ironically, cosmopolitans may find themselves without any social world in which they function as citizens.

The second difficulty that even moderate forms of cosmopolitanism about culture must overcome is this. Recall the terms of Salman Rushdie's cosmopolitan celebration of hybridity, impurity, and mongrelization. '*Melange*, hotchpotch, a bit of this and a bit of that', Rushdie wrote, 'is *how newness enters the world.*' But of course, what non-cosmopolitan traditionalists fear, to put the matter symmetrically if inelegantly, is that it is also how oldness leaves the world. And although, as I have argued, there is clearly something both correct and important about what Rushdie says, the fears of the traditionalist also have something to be said for them. When rich and vibrant traditions, practices, and ways of life are modified or supplanted through the emergence of new cultural combinations and social possibilities, one of the results may be real loss: not simply the disappearance of primitive or benighted forms of thought and practice, but the loss of entire social worlds with their particular rhythms, forms of beauty and achievement, and patterns of personal interaction, and with their different ways of ordering human experience so as to create distinctive modes of fulfilment, of solidarity, and of consolation.

It goes without saying that elegiac reverence about older cultural forms can be as dangerous—and as silly—as triumphal optimism about newer ones, partly because each attitude needs to repress some banal but important truths: about the inevitability of change in the one case, and about the inescapability of the past in the other. It also goes without saying that the stances people take on matters of tradition and cultural innovation are legitimately dependent on variations in individual temperament and outlook. For all I know, they may be dependent on variations in birth order, genetic make-up, or social class. Yet these considerations themselves suggest, what should in any case be evident, namely, that it is as undesirable to have a political philosophy that rests on contempt or indifference toward the past as it is to have one that rests on anxiety or insecurity about the future. And if the challenge for communitarians and traditionalists is to counteract the impression that they sometimes violate the second of these provisos, the challenge for cosmopolitans is to counteract the impression that they sometimes violate the first.

Of course, the whole point of moderate cosmopolitanism is to combine a respect for traditional loyalties with an openness to cultural innovation. Yet there remains a suspicion that those of a liberal, cosmopolitan temperament cannot really make sense of the putative moral claims of the past as they are understood by those who take them seriously. There are a number of closely related reasons for this. The first has to do with the foundational role of choice within liberal theory. Although, in my judgement, communitarian critics of liberalism sometimes exaggerate that role, there can be no denying the fundamental justificatory significance of choice within at least the contractarian branch of liberal thought. Because the central function of choice within contractarian liberalism is precisely to deny the validity of structures of authority and obligation that cannot command the voluntary consent of those who are subject to them, the idea that unchosen ties to a community or tradition can carry moral weight may seem, at the very least, completely alien in spirit.

Furthermore, freedom is a defining political value for any form of liberalism, whether contractarian or not. And it may seem that the content of the relevant forms of freedom cannot even be described without using the language of choice. The freedom of religion, for example, must mean that people can choose their religious affiliations without fear of penalty or loss of political status. The freedom of association, similarly, must mean that people may choose their own associates. But then it seems to follow that liberalism is committed to viewing traditional and communal affiliations as objects of choice, and to construing any moral claims those affiliations may generate as entirely dependent on the wills of the affiliates. Since this is not, of course, how individual affiliates may themselves interpret the force of their traditional or communal ties, liberalism seems committed to repudiating their moral self-understanding and to substituting a more thoroughly voluntaristic interpretation of the moral significance of such ties.

Finally, notwithstanding moderate cosmopolitanism's professed respect for traditional loyalties, its openness to the hybridizing and mongrelization of cultures may appear to render it incapable of attributing any moral significance to unchosen communal or traditional bonds. For the cosmopolitan endorsement of the intermingling of cultures may seem to carry with it a view of cultural affiliations as being, morally speaking, entirely optional. And this in turn may seem incompatible with accepting the capacity of inherited affiliations to make valid claims on individuals independently of their own choices or acts of will. Yet it is precisely to claims of this sort that those with traditional loyalties often see themselves as responding. Thus, cosmopolitanism's receptiveness to cultural innovation may seem to require a repudiation of the moral authority of established cultures and traditions, at least as it is understood by their adherents.

In view of these familiar considerations, many have concluded that a liberal cosmopolitan outlook must inevitably be tone-deaf with respect to the claims of tradition and the past. However, although no form of liberal cosmopolitanism can simply endorse the self-understandings of traditional communities, moderate versions of the view may argue that one can treat cultural affiliations as a matter of choice for political purposes without accepting a voluntaristic understanding of their moral significance. More specifically, moderate cosmopolitans may argue that, although the state should, within broad limits, give citizens the freedom to do as they choose, it need not claim, in so doing, that it is only the choices citizens make— rather than the reasons for those choices—that have normative significance. On the contrary, it may be argued, the state is perfectly capable of recognizing that people choose on the basis of what they see as compelling reasons and that those reasons sometimes include perceived obligations deriving from inherited affiliations. Nor need the state deny the validity of such reasons. As a legal matter, it grants each individual the final word concerning his or her cultural affiliations; nobody is legally entitled to interfere coercively with the individual's determinations, and changes of affiliation are not subject to legal penalty or loss of political status. However, this does not mean that the state views the moral significance of such affiliations as deriving exclusively from acts of individual will, nor, for that matter, does the state endorse any particular analysis of their moral significance. In short, the state merely disallows the coercive enforcement of cultural affiliations; it does not offer a voluntaristic theory of their ultimate moral import.

This argument draws on two familiar liberal distinctions: between the public and the private, and between political values and moral values. More specifically, it may be viewed as an extension of a claim by Rawls, who says that an insistence on the right of citizens to alter their ends and attachments without jeopardizing their legal standing or 'institutional identity' is compatible with a recognition that many citizens will view their existing ends and attachments as essential to their 'moral' or 'noninstitutional' identity.[20] The argument is open to the objection that, if one allows that unchosen affiliations may indeed be a source of genuine obligations, then it is no longer clear why the state should disallow their coercive enforcement. But this, it may be replied, is just an instance of the familiar question of how liberal tolerance can be justified without relying on scepticism about value, rather than a special question about the capacity of liberal cosmopolitanism to accommodate the putative moral force of communal and traditional affiliations.

If this line of argument can be successfully developed, then moderate cosmopolitans may continue to maintain that the claims of the past and the lure of the future can both be accommodated through a kind of cultural division of labour. Those who see themselves as having compelling reasons to live within a traditional framework are free to do so; moderate cosmopolitanism neither denies the force of those reasons nor insists on a Procrustean redescription of them in voluntaristic terms. At the same time, those who see things otherwise and who seek to forge new cultural ties are equally free to do that; moderate cosmopolitanism certainly does not pass judgement on their failure to treat the claims of tradition or community as decisive.

Yet this irenic solution may not go deep enough. Cosmopolitans point to the ubiquity of cultural change in support of their openness to cultural innovation and their hostility to ideals of cultural purity. As we have seen, this often creates the impression that cosmopolitanism is insensitive to the claims of tradition. Yet to insist that cultures are always in flux is not to deny the very existence of distinct cultural traditions, and to oppose the idea of cultural purity is not to deny that allegiance to a particular cultural tradition can ever make sense. In fact, a proper appreciation of the ubiquity of

[20] John Rawls, *Political Liberalism*, New York, NY, 1993, 30–2.

cultural change should make it easier to see that genuine allegiance to a tradition can never be just a matter of blind adherence to past practices, but must always involve decisions about how earlier values and practices can best be applied in novel circumstances and about the form in which those values and practices can be extended and projected into an uncertain future. By highlighting these facts, cosmopolitan insights about the ubiquity of cultural change should promote sympathy for a certain kind of traditionalist project. The sort of project I have in mind would be concerned not with the purity of a cultural tradition but with its integrity. More specifically, it would be concerned with the question of how the integrity of a tradition can be maintained, and what would count as maintaining it, given the inevitability of cultural change, and given the mutual influence that diverse cultures are bound to exert on each other in an ever more densely interconnected world.

Those whose traditionalism takes this form will think it important to identify and perpetuate the values and practices on whose continuity the integrity of their tradition rests. At the same time, however, they will be prepared to reconceive those elements of the tradition that are no longer credible as they stand but which admit of illuminating reinterpretation; to abandon elements of the tradition that have come to seem unacceptable and which resist reinterpretation; and to promote the intelligent selection and incorporation into the tradition of new ideas and practices whose inspiration may be drawn from external sources, but which can be embraced without doing violence to the integrity of the tradition, and can instead serve to enrich it. This is, if you like, traditionalism with a cosmopolitan inflection. It affords a model of traditional engagement that incorporates the central insight of cosmopolitanism about culture, and, to the extent that it is viable, it suggests that the repertoire of cosmopolitan responses to the claims of tradition can extend beyond mere toleration.

Conclusion

I take the two difficulties just mentioned to reinforce one general moral of this essay, namely, that the task of defending moderate cosmopolitanism should not be thought of as a narrowly philosophical undertaking. In other words, it is not just a matter of producing cogent arguments in support of some abstract formulation of the view. Instead, moderate cosmopolitanism about justice will be a compelling position only if it proves possible to devise human institutions, practices, and ways of life that take seriously the equal worth of persons without undermining people's capacity to sustain their special loyalties and attachments. And moderate cosmopolitanism about culture will be compelling only if two things turn out to be true. The first is that some people succeed in developing recognizably cosmopolitan ways of living that incorporate the sort of stable infrastructure of responsibility that more traditional ways of life have always made available to their adherents. The second is that other people succeed in preserving the integrity of their traditions without succumbing to the temptation to engage in the doomed and deadly pursuit of cultural purity. Thus, some of the most important arguments in favour of moderate cosmopolitanism about culture will have to come not from philosophers or other academic theorists but from people engaged in a wide variety of what Mill called 'experiments in living'. And the vindication of either form of moderate cosmopolitanism will require not just argument but the exercise of creativity and imagination in the development of new practices, institutions, and modes of social organization. I have maintained that certain arguments purporting to undermine moderate cosmopolitanism from the outset are unsuccessful. Ultimately, however, the viability of moderate cosmopolitanism must depend on the success of human beings in negotiating a series of ineliminable distinctions—between justice and loyalty, tradition and choice, past and future, ourselves and others—without allowing those distinctions to calcify into rigid and destructive dichotomies.

8

The Appeal of Political Liberalism *

The appeal of liberalism derives to a considerable extent from its commitment to tolerating diverse ways of life and schemes of value. Yet this same commitment is also responsible for much of what is puzzling about liberalism. For what is the basis of liberal toleration? One answer rests the case for toleration on a pluralistic understanding of the nature of human value, on a conviction that the realm of value is irreducibly heterogeneous. Diverse ways of life should be tolerated, on this view, because they are routes to the realization of diverse human goods. A very different answer rests the case for tolerance on a general scepticism about value, on a conviction that there is no good sense to be made of the idea of objective value or the notion of a good life. On this view, diverse ways of life should be tolerated because there is nothing to the thought that some ways of life are better than others, and so there is no legitimate basis for *in*tolerance.

If the case for liberal toleration rests on some pluralistic thesis about the nature of human values, then both the depth of such toleration and the extent of its appeal seem called into question. For, inevitably, the pluralistic thesis will itself be controversial. Thus, on this interpretation, liberalism's professed toleration of differing conceptions of value turns out to depend on a more fundamental commitment to a particular conception of value, a conception which will be uncongenial or even abhorrent to some of the very evaluative outlooks that liberalism purports to tolerate, and which will not, therefore, serve to recommend liberal institutions to people who share those outlooks. Much the same will be true, it seems, if toleration is seen as the outgrowth of scepticism rather than pluralism about value. For scepticism no less than pluralism represents a controversial understanding of the nature of values.

* Originally published in *Ethics* 105 (1994): 4–22. © 1994 by The University of Chicago. All rights reserved. Reprinted by permission of The University of Chicago Press. This essay is a slightly revised version of a paper presented at the Third Annual Philosophy Conference at the University of California, Riverside, on May 1, 1993. I am indebted to those present on that occasion for helpful discussion, and especially to David Gill, who raised the question that prompted most of the revisions in the present version. I am also indebted to John Rawls for illuminating discussion of his work over a period of many years.

The most obvious way of defending liberal toleration, apart from the two just mentioned, is as a *modus vivendi*, a strategic compromise among contending social groups, none of whom is in a position to impose its preferred way of life on the others without intolerable cost, and each of whom therefore accepts a policy of mutual tolerance as the best that it can hope to achieve under the circumstances. That it will sometimes be possible to make a strong case for liberal toleration on pragmatic grounds of this sort seems hard to deny. Historically, the role played by such considerations has often been crucial. Yet a defence of toleration that rests entirely on pragmatic grounds seems unable to account for the moral appeal of the idea of tolerance, and, in any case, it retains its force only so long as the necessary balance of power in society is preserved. If one group gains enough strength that a policy of intolerance comes to seem tempting, the pragmatic argument provides no reason to resist the temptation.

The need to understand the basis of liberal toleration has taken on a renewed urgency at this historical moment. The liberal societies of the West are beset by a host of social problems whose source, according to many critics, lies ultimately in a culture of individualism and a breakdown of communal values for which liberal thought itself is responsible. While the tendency of this criticism is to suggest a need for greater social unity and cohesion, the very idea of a liberal society as a single national community with a common culture is also under attack, as such societies, with their increasingly diversified populations, struggle to come to terms with their own histories of exclusion and to accommodate the claims of 'multiculturalism'. In this context, it is more important than ever to arrive at a clear understanding of the basis of liberal toleration. More generally, liberalism needs to understand how it is to conceive of its relations to the diverse ways of life and forms of culture that characterize modern societies. The importance of this project of liberal self-understanding, as I shall refer to it, is only intensified by the need for liberal societies to orient themselves both in relation to those other societies, in Eastern Europe and elsewhere, that are struggling to establish liberal institutions for the first time, and in relation to societies like Iran, whose fundamentalist character presents a radical challenge to liberal thought.

John Rawls's book *Political Liberalism* constitutes a major contribution to this project of liberal self-understanding.[1] Rawls offers us a new way of thinking about the basis of liberal toleration. His 'political liberalism' addresses itself to the following question: 'How is it possible for there to exist over time a just and stable society of free and equal citizens who still remain profoundly divided by reasonable religious, philosophical, and moral doctrines?' (47). The core of political liberalism's answer to this question is that for such a society to be possible, its basic structure must be 'effectively regulated by a political

---

[1] John Rawls, *Political Liberalism* (New York, NY: Columbia University Press, 1993). Page references to this book will be given parenthetically in the text.

conception of justice that is the focus of an overlapping consensus of at least the reasonable comprehensive doctrines affirmed by its citizens' (48). To understand this answer, obviously, we need to understand what is meant by notions like a 'political conception of justice' and an 'overlapping consensus'.

To begin, we know from *A Theory of Justice* that a conception of justice is a 'set of principles for assigning basic rights and duties and for determining . . . the proper distribution of the benefits and burdens of social cooperation'.[2] A political conception of justice, Rawls now tells us, is one that has 'three characteristic features' (11). First, it is a moral conception, but 'a moral conception worked out for a specific kind of subject' (11), namely, for the 'basic structure' of society, by which Rawls means a society's main social, political, and economic institutions. Second, a political conception of justice 'is presented as a freestanding view' (12). This means that 'it is neither presented as, nor as derived from, [a comprehensive moral] doctrine applied to the basic structure of society, as if this structure were simply another subject to which that doctrine applied' (12). Rather, a political conception 'is a module, an essential constituent part, that fits into and can be supported by various reasonable comprehensive doctrines that endure in the society regulated by it' (12). Third, the content of a political conception of justice 'is expressed in terms of certain fundamental ideas seen as implicit in the public political culture of a democratic society' (13). The suggestion here is that despite the diversity of people's comprehensive moral doctrines, there may be certain fundamental ideas implicit in a society's culture and institutions that command widespread agreement. A political conception of justice is one that is developed on the basis of this common ground.

If a political conception of justice can indeed be derived solely from ideas that are latent in the public political culture, then it may become the object of an 'overlapping consensus'. That is, it may be accepted by people who affirm very different comprehensive moral doctrines, because all of these people accept, albeit for different reasons, the fundamental ideas that function, in effect, as premises in the argument for the conception of justice. In an overlapping consensus, Rawls writes, 'the reasonable [comprehensive] doctrines endorse the political conception, each from its own point of view. Social unity is based on a consensus on the political conception; and stability is possible when the doctrines making up the consensus are affirmed by society's politically active citizens and the requirements of justice are not too much in conflict with citizens' essential interests as formed and encouraged by their social arrangements' (134).

Not only will people's reasons for accepting the political conception vary, depending on which comprehensive moral doctrine they affirm, but in addition, different comprehensive moral doctrines may stand in different relations to the political conception. For example, some comprehensive doctrines

[2] John Rawls, *A Theory of Justice* (Cambridge, MA: Harvard University Press, 1971), 5.

may provide the political conception with a deductive basis, while others may provide reasons of other kinds for accepting it. Rawls says that 'the point to stress here is that . . . citizens individually decide for themselves in what way the public political conception all affirm is related to their own more comprehensive views' (38). What matters, he writes, is that 'citizens themselves, within the exercise of their liberty of thought and conscience, and looking to their comprehensive doctrines, view the political conception as derived from, or congruent with, or at least not in conflict with, their other values' (11).

These ideas enable Rawls to offer a model of liberal pluralism and toleration that represents an alternative to the three I canvassed at the outset. Like the model of liberalism as a *modus vivendi*, Rawls's model treats with utmost seriousness the deep differences in people's values and ways of life, and the potential for deadly conflict arising out of those differences. Yet, as he insists, the overlapping consensus that he envisions is not itself a mere *modus vivendi*. For, first, the object of the consensus is not just a set of institutional arrangements but is, rather, a moral conception, a conception of justice. And, second, all those who participate in the consensus accept that conception for moral reasons of one sort or another. As Rawls says, 'All those who affirm the political conception start from within their own comprehensive view and draw on the religious, philosophical, and moral grounds it provides. The fact that people affirm the same political conception on those grounds does not make their affirming it any less religious, philosophical, or moral, as the case may be, since the grounds sincerely held determine the nature of their affirmation' (147–8). Because of these two differences between an overlapping consensus and a *modus vivendi*, there will also, Rawls says, be a third difference. An overlapping consensus will enjoy greater stability than a *modus vivendi*, because the commitment to the political conception of those who participate in the consensus is based on moral considerations rather than calculations of self or group interest, and hence is not liable to be undermined by changes in the balance of power within the society. One's moral reasons for accepting the political conception are not weakened by an increase in one's power that would make it easier to press for a more advantageous set of institutional arrangements.

In a sense, then, Rawls's explanation of the basis of liberal toleration, if successful, may manage to combine the advantages of an appeal to a *modus vivendi* with those of an appeal to a pluralistic conception of value, while avoiding the pitfalls of either. Like the explanation in terms of a *modus vivendi* and unlike the one in terms of a pluralistic conception of value, Rawls combines respect for the facts of disagreement and diversity with a reluctance to rely on any controversial moral premises. However, like the explanation in terms of a pluralistic conception of value and unlike the one in terms of a *modus vivendi*, Rawls represents citizens as having moral reasons for their allegiance to the structures of toleration and the institutions of the liberal society. His aim, in other words, is to provide liberal institutions with a basis in moral reasons, without himself presupposing any controversial and contentious moral outlook. This aspiration is descended from Rawls's earlier aspiration, in *A Theory of Justice*, to derive a substantive conception of justice from the set of putatively 'weak and widely shared' conditions and constraints that make up the original position. If Rawls can succeed in achieving his newer aim, then the earlier one is also vindicated, at least in part. For the notion of an overlapping consensus on fundamental ideas implicit in the public political culture supplies new content for the claim that the original position—construed now as a device for representing certain of those fundamental ideas—is made up of weak and widely shared assumptions.

Thus, from the standpoint of the project of liberal self-understanding, the potential advantages of 'political liberalism' seem clear. Ultimately, however, the appeal of the view must depend, at least in part, on whether an overlapping consensus on something like Rawls's political conception of justice is a realistic possibility. In chapter 4 of *Political Liberalism*, Rawls offers what he calls 'a model case' of such a consensus:

It contains three views: one affirms the political conception because its religious doctrine and account of free faith lead to a principle of toleration and underwrite the fundamental liberties of a constitutional regime; while the second view affirms the political conception on the basis of a comprehensive liberal moral doctrine such as those of Kant or Mill. The third . . . is not systematically unified: besides the political values formulated by a freestanding political conception of justice, it includes a large family of nonpolitical values. It is a pluralist view, let us say, since each subpart of this family has its own account based on ideas drawn from within it, leaving all values to be balanced against one another, either in groups or singly, in particular kinds of cases. (Rawls, *Political Liberalism*, 145).

By itself, this model case does little to encourage the thought that an overlapping consensus on Rawlsian principles could actually be achieved in a modern liberal society. For the three views it contains are not fully representative of the diverse schemes of value one finds in such societies; instead, all three appear to be drawn from the same relatively narrow portion of the broad spectrum of evaluative conviction. Although it seems plausible enough that these three views might converge on a liberal conception of justice, that tells us little about the prospects for a more inclusive consensus.

Later in chapter 4, Rawls presents a modified version of this model case which also includes classical utilitarianism. 'This utilitarianism,' he writes, 'supports the political conception for such reasons as our limited knowledge of social institutions generally and on our knowledge about ongoing circumstances. It stresses further the bounds on complexity of legal and institutional rules as well as the simplicity necessary in guidelines for public reason. These and other reasons may lead the utilitarian to think a political conception of justice liberal in content a satisfactory, perhaps even the best, workable approximation to what the principle of utility, all things tallied up, would require' (170).

Although the inclusion of classical utilitarianism serves to broaden the range of outlooks contained in the model consensus, and although its explicit purpose is just to illustrate the point that the different comprehensive doctrines represented in an overlapping consensus may stand in different relations to the political conception on which they converge, it is in some ways a puzzling addition. Rawls emphasizes that an overlapping consensus is a consensus not just on principles of justice but also on the fundamental ideas implicit in the public political culture from which those principles are derivable (149). Indeed, what makes an overlapping consensus on a political conception of justice possible is precisely the fact that the political conception is developed from shared ideas. Accordingly, the original position is now to be construed as modelling certain of those shared ideas, and Rawls's arguments to the effect that his principles would be chosen in the original position are to be interpreted as beginning from those ideas. Yet many of these arguments are explicitly directed against utilitarianism. If utilitarianism is said to be included in the overlapping consensus on Rawls's two principles, then are we to imagine that utilitarians endorse Rawls's arguments for the rejection of utilitarianism even as they continue to affirm that view? This seems incoherent.

Moreover, even the fundamental ideas from which the arguments for the two principles proceed, and which the original position helps to model, are ideas which, according to Rawls himself, utilitarianism does not accept. For example, the 'fundamental organizing idea' to which Rawls appeals is 'that of society as a fair system of social cooperation between free and equal persons viewed as fully cooperating members of society over a complete life' (9). Crucial to this idea of fair co-operation is said to be a notion of reciprocity, according to which 'all who are engaged in cooperation and who do their part as the rules and procedures require, are to benefit in an appropriate way as assessed by a suitable benchmark of comparison' (16). Yet in *A Theory of Justice* Rawls tells us that 'the principle of utility is incompatible with the conception of social cooperation among equals for mutual advantage. It appears to be inconsistent with the idea of reciprocity implicit in the notion of a well-ordered society.'[3] Elaborating on this point, he writes: 'Implicit in the contrasts between classical utilitarianism and justice as fairness is a difference in the underlying conceptions of society. In the one we think of a well-ordered society as a scheme of cooperation for reciprocal advantage regulated by principles which persons would choose in an initial situation that is fair, in the other as the efficient administration of social resources to maximize the satisfaction of the system of desire constructed by the impartial spectator from the many individual systems of desires accepted as given.'[4] If this is right, then it really is quite unclear how utilitarianism can be included in an overlapping consensus on Rawls's principles of justice, since it rejects the fundamental ideas that serve as premises in the arguments for those principles, as well as the arguments themselves.

---

[3] Rawls, *A Theory of Justice*, 14.   [4] Ibid., 33.

Of course, as Rawls says, a utilitarian might conclude that, 'given normal social conditions' (171), Rawls's two principles represent 'a satisfactory, perhaps even the best, workable approximation to what the principle of utility, all things tallied up, would require' (170). The question is whether such a conclusion would be sufficient for utilitarianism to be included in an overlapping consensus, if it is also committed to rejecting the fundamental ideas from which Rawls's principles are derived as well as the arguments used to derive them. Moreover, the precise content and spirit of the imagined utilitarian conclusion are less clear than they may initially appear. We may recall that in *A Theory of Justice* Rawls considers two possible attitudes a utilitarian might take toward apparently non-utilitarian principles of justice. On the one hand, some utilitarians may say that such principles 'have but a subordinate validity as secondary rules; they arise from the fact that under the conditions of civilized society there is great social utility in following them for the most part and in permitting violations of them only under exceptional circumstances'.[5] Rawls's project in *A Theory of Justice* is to a large extent motivated by the conviction that this attitude does not accord sufficient primacy to the principles of justice. On the other hand, a utilitarian might, Rawls suggests, argue that utility will actually be maximized if Rawls's two principles are 'publicly affirmed and realized as the basis of the social structure'.[6] However, Rawls maintains, such an argument would be tantamount to conceding the inadequacy of utilitarianism. For the publicity condition means that utilitarianism must be 'defined' as 'the view that the principle of utility is the correct principle for society's public conception of justice'.[7] In other words, Rawls says, 'what we want to know is which conception of justice characterizes our considered judgments in reflective equilibrium and best serves as the public moral basis of society. Unless one maintains that this conception is given by the principle of utility, one is not a utilitarian.'[8] The upshot is that of the two possible attitudes that a utilitarian might take toward non-utilitarian principles of justice, the first represents too weak a form of endorsement, while the second is tantamount to the abandonment of utilitarianism. Thus neither attitude provides a model of how a committed utilitarian might genuinely affirm Rawls's principles as part of an overlapping consensus, and this only reinforces the doubts already mentioned about whether utilitarianism could indeed be included in such a consensus.

Even if it could, the question of how widespread a consensus on Rawls's principles of justice might realistically be achieved would remain. For a stable overlapping consensus in a modern liberal society would require the inclusion not only of fully articulated philosophical theories like utilitarianism but also of the many moral, religious, and broadly philosophical outlooks actually endorsed by citizens in such societies. A stable overlapping consensus, one might say, must be a consensus of citizens, not of theories. Rawls recognizes this, and in chapter 4 of *Political Liberalism*, he tries to turn the

---

[5] Ibid., 28.   [6] Ibid., 181.   [7] Ibid., 182.   [8] Ibid.

point to his advantage. He argues, in effect, that in judging the prospects of an overlapping consensus on his conception of justice, it is a mistake to focus exclusively on committed partisans of fully articulated philosophical theories with clearly recognized implications for the justice of the basic structure of society. For most citizens in a liberal society do not hold any fully articulated and fully comprehensive moral doctrine. What they may well have instead is a loose network of values and convictions of varying degrees of generality, whose implications concerning Rawls's principles may or may not be clear to them. However, many of these people, having been raised in a liberal society, will have internalized the fundamental idea of society as a fair system of co-operation on which Rawls's political conception rests and will have developed a strong allegiance to broadly liberal values and institutions. Indeed, rather than accepting liberal ideas as the consequence of their comprehensive moral doctrine, they may instead allow their commitment to a liberal order to shape the rest of their values. For example, they may find themselves shaping their understanding of their faith to render it consistent with such an order—perhaps emphasizing those strands in their tradition that lend support to tolerance and downplaying those that conflict with it. If this is correct, and if Rawls can in fact elaborate his conception of justice solely on the basis of ideas implicit in the public political culture of a liberal society, then such people may have strong reasons to affirm that conception. As Rawls puts it, 'the comprehensive doctrines of most people are not fully comprehensive, and this allows scope for the development of an independent allegiance to the political conception that helps to bring about a consensus' (168).

Although this argument has some force, there is an important ambiguity in Rawls's account of the sort of overlapping consensus he envisions, and this ambiguity affects the plausibility of his position. Recall that in an overlapping consensus, what people are said to affirm is a political conception of justice. And 'a distinguishing feature of a political conception is that it is presented as freestanding' (12), that is, as independent of any comprehensive moral doctrine. Now this suggests two puzzles. First, by whom must a conception be presented as freestanding in order to count as political? One possibility is that Rawls's presentation of his own conception is authoritative, so that that conception is political because *he* presents it as freestanding. But then, in order to know whether a given conception of justice is political we must be able to identify its authoritative presentation. What, for example, is the authoritative presentation of utilitarianism? Another possibility is that conceptions of justice are to be individuated partly by features of their presentation. Thus if you argue for Rawls's conception of justice by appealing to your comprehensive moral doctrine and I argue for it as a freestanding view, we are actually arguing for two different conceptions of justice, one political and the other not. But this seems needlessly confusing and potentially misleading, and in any case, it is a peculiar position to take if one is attempting to emphasize the possibility of consensus—to explain how people with divergent moral outlooks may nevertheless converge on a particular conception of justice. Still another interpretation is suggested when Rawls remarks at one point that what is characteristic of a political conception is only 'that it *can* be presented without saying, or knowing, or hazarding a conjecture about, what . . . [comprehensive] doctrines it may belong to, or be supported by' (12–13; emphasis added). This leaves open the possibility that all conceptions of justice may be political, if all of them *can* be 'presented as' freestanding. (How plausible would the presentations have to be?)

None of these three options seems to me especially attractive. It might be less confusing and more illuminating to use the adjective 'political' to describe arguments for conceptions of justice rather than the conceptions themselves. A political argument for a conception of justice would be one that appealed to ideas implicit in the public political culture, whereas a non-political argument, say, would be one that appealed to a comprehensive moral doctrine. Thus one and the same conception of justice might in principle be supported by arguments of either type. Rawls might then be interpreted as asserting not that his conception of justice is a political conception but, rather, that his arguments for that conception are political arguments. And political liberalism might be construed as comprising two theses: first, that given the pluralistic character of modern societies, a just and stable order is possible only if the basic structure of society is effectively regulated by a conception of justice that is the focus of an overlapping consensus and, second, that the possibility of an overlapping consensus on a particular conception of justice is signaled by the availability of persuasive political arguments for that conception.

There is, however, a second and deeper puzzle underlying the one just mentioned, and it concerns the attitude that participants in an overlapping consensus are expected to have toward the 'political conception of justice' on which they converge. In particular, the question is whether participation in such a consensus requires that one *regard* the conception of justice as a 'political conception': that is, as a 'freestanding' conception whose content 'is expressed in terms of certain fundamental ideas seen as implicit in the public political culture of a democratic society'. We know, in other words, that the participants in an overlapping consensus accept certain principles of justice as well as certain fundamental ideas implicit in the public political culture from which those principles are derivable. The question is whether they themselves also think of the principles as being expressed in terms of what they take to be ideas implicit in the public political culture, and as capable of being derived independently of any particular comprehensive moral doctrine. On the face of it, it would appear unwise to make this a requirement for participation in an overlapping consensus. For the more things that people must believe in order to be included in such a consensus, the more difficult it will be for a consensus actually to be achieved. In other words, if participation in the consensus requires affirmation not only of a particular set of principles of justice but also of certain metatheses about the status of those principles, then, other things equal, one would expect the consensus to include fewer people. Furthermore, Rawls's whole reason for drawing our attention to the possibility of an overlapping consensus is to suggest that people may affirm the same principles of justice even though they view these principles in very different ways, depending on which comprehensive moral doctrine they accept. Thus any requirement that the participants in an overlapping consensus must view the conception of justice as political would appear to be incongruous with the motivation for introducing the idea of such a consensus in the first place.

Suppose, for example, that someone—call her Jane—accepts Rawls's two principles of justice because she believes them to be implied by her comprehensive moral doctrine, which we may suppose to be some version of what Rawls calls 'comprehensive liberalism'. Jane does not, let us assume, think of the two principles as constituting a freestanding conception of justice, nor does she characterize them as such when she is explaining or defending them to others. Rather, she presents them to others as she herself conceives of them, namely, as derived from a certain comprehensive moral outlook. And although she recognizes that the two principles may be seen as giving expression to the idea of society as a fair system of co-operation, it does not occur to her to think of that idea as implicit in the public political culture; still less does she see the fact that it is implicit in the culture as crucial to its justificatory role. The importance to her of the idea of society as a fair system of co-operation derives instead from its relation to the ideal of 'ethical autonomy' (77–8) that is at the core of her comprehensive doctrine. Yet Jane is, we may suppose, a sincere and indeed committed advocate of the two principles of justice and, as such, she is of course a staunch defender of the right of other people to affirm and defend comprehensive moral doctrines other than her own. If, by virtue of her failure to conceive of the two principles as amounting to a political conception of justice, a person like Jane does not qualify for inclusion in an overlapping consensus, then surely the prospects of achieving a widespread consensus are open to serious doubt. Moreover, to exclude Jane would seem inconsistent with the motivation for introducing the idea of an overlapping consensus to begin with.

Nevertheless, Rawls does at times appear to require that the participants in an overlapping consensus regard the conception of justice as political. He writes, for example, that 'citizens are to conduct their fundamental discussions within the framework of what each regards as a political conception of justice based on values that the others can reasonably be expected to endorse and each is, in good faith, prepared to defend that conception so understood' (226). Rawls makes this claim in the context of his discussion of 'the idea of public reason'. This idea arises because, Rawls believes, 'it is essential that a liberal political conception include, besides its principles of justice, guidelines of inquiry that specify ways of reasoning and criteria for the kinds of information relevant for political questions' (223). He therefore maintains that 'the parties in the original position, in adopting principles of justice for the basic structure, must also adopt guidelines and criteria of public reason for applying those norms' (225). These guidelines and criteria are to specify the modes of reasoning that may be used and the types of considerations that may be appealed to in discussing and resolving political questions in a society regulated by the principles of justice. They impose constraints on acceptable forms of political argument, constraints that Rawls refers to as 'the limits of public reason'. These limits hold not only for public officials but also for 'citizens when they engage in political advocacy in the public forum, and thus for members of political parties and for candidates in their campaigns and for other groups who support them' (215). Indeed, the limits govern 'how citizens are to vote' (215), at least when 'the most fundamental political questions' are at stake (216). Among the most important of the constraints imposed by the limits of public reason is that 'in discussing constitutional essentials and matters of basic justice we are not to appeal to comprehensive religious and philosophical doctrines—to what we as individuals or members of associations see as the whole truth' (224–5). In other words, the limits of public reason tell us that we are 'to conduct our fundamental discussions in terms of what we regard as a political conception. We should sincerely think that out view of the matter is based on political values everyone can reasonably be expected to endorse' (241).

Rawls's discussion of public reason raises a variety of questions. For one thing, it seems puzzling to suggest that the parties in the original position adopt guidelines that specify, among other things, that we are 'to conduct our fundamental discussions in terms of what we regard as a political conception' of justice. For the idea of a political conception of justice is not one that is obviously available to the parties in the original position. What makes Rawls's conception political is the fact that it is elaborated on the basis of fundamental ideas that are implicit in the public political culture. The function of the parties in the original position is to help model certain of those fundamental ideas, not to endorse them or to argue from them to something the parties regard as a political conception. In other words, the parties' sole concern is to choose a conception of justice that will maximize their share of primary social goods. They do not themselves decide that they want a political conception of justice based on ideas implicit in the public political culture; rather, the fact that they model such ideas means that *we* have reason to regard the principles they select as having the status of a political conception.

More generally, the idea that the parties in the original position adopt 'guidelines of inquiry' which include 'principles of reasoning and rules of evidence' (224) requires further explanation. Rawls says that the 'argument for those guidelines . . . is much the same as, and as strong as, the argument for the principles of justice themselves' (225). Perhaps so; but in the case of the guidelines, the array of options from which the parties choose and the basis of their choice require further elaboration. Moreover, there is the following difference between the choice of such guidelines and the choice of principles of justice. In order to make their choice among rival conceptions of justice, the parties do not themselves need to employ any particular conception of justice. If they did, the justificatory force of their choice would be open to serious doubt. In choosing among candidate principles of reasoning and methods of inquiry, however, the parties must already be employing certain methods of reasoning and modes of inquiry, which are given by stipulation as part of the original position construction. Thus, in the absence of some further explanation of the relation between the methods of inquiry the parties employ and the methods of inquiry they adopt, there is a danger that any choice they make will appear question-begging.

For present purposes, however, what is most striking about Rawls's discussion of public reason is how emphatically it serves to reinforce the concern that by requiring the participants in an overlapping consensus to conceive of the conception of justice they endorse as political, Rawls risks undermining the plausibility of the idea that an overlapping consensus might actually be achieved. The principle that ordinary citizens, when engaged in political advocacy and even when voting, must appeal only to what they regard as a political conception of justice and never to their own comprehensive moral doctrines is an extraordinarily strong one. Accordingly, it seems much harder to envision a wide variety of comprehensive doctrines converging on this principle of public reason in addition to the two principles of justice than it does to envision them converging on the principles of justice alone. Indeed, the plausibility of this putative principle of public reason is open to serious challenge. For it does not seem difficult to think of cases in which people in the United States, for example, have appealed to comprehensive moral doctrines in ways that many would regard as appropriate, or at least not inappropriate. Toward the end of his discussion of public reason, Rawls himself considers the examples of the abolitionists and of Martin Luther King, Jr., and in the face of these examples he modifies his principle to allow that citizens may in certain circumstances appeal to their comprehensive doctrines if this is necessary to strengthen the ideal of public reason itself. But there are many other examples that could be cited in addition to the two that Rawls mentions: such as the religiously inspired opposition of Quakers and others to the war in Vietnam; the religiously motivated opposition of many people to capital punishment; the central role traditionally played by black churches in the political life of the African-American community; the opposition by certain religious denominations to United States policies in Central America during the 1980s and the associated movement to provide sanctuary in churches for Central American refugees; and the religiously-based advocacy of policies to eliminate homelessness and poverty. Note, moreover, that all of the examples I have cited are instances in which comprehensive religious doctrines have been drawn on in the context of public political advocacy, in ways generally congenial to the political left. If we broaden our horizons to include non-religious appeals to moral principles, to include citizens' reasons for voting as well as the content of their public advocacy, and to include positions taken across a wider range of the political spectrum, then the number of examples will only multiply. The idea, that in all such examples the reliance on a comprehensive moral or religious doctrine must either be necessary to strengthen the ideal of public reason or else unjustified, seems highly questionable. And in any event, the availability of so many examples does nothing to enhance the plausibility of the idea that an overlapping consensus might actually converge not only on Rawls's two principles of justice but also on the guidelines of public reason as he describes them.

Given the contentiousness of some of Rawls's claims about the limits of public reason, and given that their effect is also to make the achievement of an overlapping consensus seem less likely, it is natural to wonder how important it is for Rawls's purposes to insist on those claims. In an attempt to ascertain this, let us imagine a society in which an overlapping consensus on Rawls's two principles of justice has actually been achieved and in which a constitution consistent with those two principles has been adopted. Let us further suppose, however, that citizens in this society view the status of the two principles in different ways, depending on their comprehensive moral doctrines. Thus there is no consensus on the proposition that the two principles of justice constitute a political conception, still less on the proposition that citizens are to conduct their discussion of constitutional essentials and basic justice in terms of what they regard as a political conception. Despite the absence of consensus on these two points, the constitution of the society guarantees the basic rights and liberties of all citizens, in accordance with the principles of justice, and this excludes any attempt to use the coercive power of the state to enforce a particular comprehensive doctrine. Similarly, any attempt to deny basic justice to some people in the name of a particular comprehensive doctrine is ruled out. Moreover, since all citizens, by hypothesis, affirm that the two principles are to regulate the basic structure of their society, they all regard those principles as the 'final court of appeal for ordering the conflicting claims of moral persons'.[9] Thus it is to the two principles, rather than their own comprehensive moral doctrines, that citizens naturally appeal when discussing constitutional essentials and matters of basic justice. In addition, citizens are aware of the existence both of widespread agreement on the principles of justice and of widespread disagreement in people's comprehensive moral doctrines. This awareness, when coupled with the commitment to mutual respect that is implied by citizens' common affirmation of the two principles, gives rise to an ethos of restraint, a reluctance on the part of many citizens to appeal in the public arena to

---

[9] Ibid., 135.

their own comprehensive moral doctrines. After all, the fact that they are in agreement about the principles to regulate the basic structure of their society is what matters for fundamental political purposes, and, we may suppose, they have no need and little desire to alienate those they respect by insisting on divisive moral or religious claims.

The upshot of this discussion is that some limits of public reason may be a consequence of, and still others may be encouraged by, the existence of an overlapping consensus on the two principles alone, without any need for citizens to conceive of those principles as a political conception of justice or to agree that they must conduct their discussion of fundamental political questions in terms of what they regard as a political conception. If this is correct, and if the requirement that citizens view the conception of justice as political has the disadvantages I have said it does, then Rawls may have little reason to insist on that requirement.

The point I have been trying to make may be put another way. One of Rawls's aims in *Political Liberalism*, if I understand him correctly, is to respond to those critics of his earlier work who charged that while purporting to offer a neutral and universal justification for his principles of justice, it rested tacitly but unmistakably on a liberal conception of value. In response, Rawls denies that his theory aspires to universal validity but also that it rests on any comprehensive conception of value. Instead, he argues, his theory is addressed to societies of a certain type at a particular historical moment. These societies have a tradition of democratic thought and constitutional interpretation, but there exist within them deep disagreements about fundamental political questions and also a wide diversity of comprehensive moral and religious doctrines. Given these historical facts, there is a real question about how a shared and workable conception of justice for these societies can be arrived at. It is to this question that Rawls's theory is addressed, and his answer involves not the endorsement of a particular comprehensive doctrine but, rather, an attempt to bypass the disagreements among such doctrines. What he tries to do, as we know, is to identify certain bases of agreement that are implicit in the public political culture and which therefore represent common ground among the citizens of democratic societies. He then attempts to use these 'fixed points' as premises in an argument for a conception of justice to which all or nearly all may be able to agree. This is what Rawls is trying to do: to argue from views that are widely shared in our culture to a definite conclusion about justice, thereby offering a conception of justice that may command widespread agreement despite the pluralism and disagreement that characterize our society. If his argument is successful, then the conception he identifies may serve as the object of an overlapping consensus among people who have different comprehensive moral doctrines and whose affirmation of the theory is therefore based ultimately on different reasons. In order to be successful, it is important that Rawls's argument be a 'political' one: that is, that it rely as much as possible on shared ideas and avoid reliance on any comprehensive moral doctrine. However, if what I have been urging is correct, it is not important that the citizens who are included in the overlapping consensus should themselves think of Rawls's conception as political. Any requirement that they do so would make an over-lapping consensus more difficult to achieve, would add little that is plaus-ible to an adequate account of public reason, and would mandate a degree of metaethical uniformity that is incongruous with the motivation for intro-ducing the idea of an overlapping consensus in the first place. For all of these reasons, such a requirement would weaken rather than strengthen Rawls's reply to his critics. Or so it seems to me.

This conclusion is not altered, incidentally, if we take into account the added complication that Rawls characterizes his conception of justice not only as political but also as constructivist. It is constructivist because its principles 'may be represented as the outcome of a certain procedure of construction' (89–90). That is, the principles are constructed from ideas of society and the person via the device of the original position. A constructivist conception, Rawls says, neither asserts nor denies that its principles are true; it 'does with-out the concept of truth' altogether (94). Political constructivism, which is 'part of' political liberalism, asserts instead that the constructivist conception is 'reasonable for a constitutional regime' (126). Although many citizens 'may want to give the political conception a metaphysical foundation as part of their own comprehensive doctrine' (126), political constructivism refrains from doing this and restricts itself to the claim that the conception is reasonable. 'The advantage of staying within the reasonable,' Rawls writes, 'is that there can be but one true comprehensive doctrine, though . . . many reasonable ones. Once we accept the fact that reasonable pluralism is a permanent condition of public culture under free institutions, the idea of the reasonable is more suitable as part of the basis of public justification for a constitutional regime than the idea of moral truth. Holding a political conception as true, and for that reason alone the one suitable basis of public reason, is exclusive, even sectarian, and so likely to foster political division' (129). The question, how-ever, is who exactly is supposed to believe that 'the idea of the reasonable is more suitable as part of the basis of public justification for a constitutional regime than the idea of moral truth'. It is easy to see that there may be an advantage to Rawls in offering a purely constructivist argument for his prin-ciples—in asserting, that is, not that the principles are true but merely that their source in ideas implicit in the public political culture enables them to provide a reasonable basis of public justification. For if he can give people a reason to affirm his principles whether or not they accept the idea of moral truth, he maximizes the appeal of those principles and enhances the prospects of an overlapping consensus. He makes it possible, in other words, for people to agree on the principles even if they disagree about the meta-physical status of those principles. But if citizens are also required to agree that 'the idea of the reasonable is more suitable as part of the basis of public justification . . . than the idea of moral truth', then Rawls risks squandering these very gains, for he is then insisting on a partial but nevertheless significant degree of uniformity in the way people regard his principles.

Up to this point, I have been exploring the appeal of political liberalism by examining the prospects for an overlapping consensus on a political conception of justice in a modern democratic society. Before concluding, I want to take up one other issue that bears on the appeal of political liberalism, and this concerns the relevance of this form of liberalism for those societies whose traditions are not liberal or democratic. Thus I want to turn from political liberalism's domestic policy, as it were, to its foreign policy. As we have seen, Rawls's work as he now presents it is addressed to modern democratic societies at a certain historical moment. His political liberalism seeks to establish a liberal conception of justice on the basis of ideas that are implicit in the public political culture of such societies. If, however, political liberalism appeals in this way to the public political culture of democratic societies, then the justification of liberal principles and institutions that it offers appears to presuppose a society in which liberal values are already well entrenched. It is not clear that political liberalism provides any reason for establishing liberal institutions in societies that do not already have liberal traditions. Thus, to put it another way, it is not clear that political liberalism could ever provide the original justification for a society's liberal institutions. Liberal traditions and institutions must, it seems, precede political liberalism: that is, they must already exist in order to create the conditions that make possible the sort of justification offered by political liberalism. This is not merely a historical problem; it raises doubts about whether political liberalism has anything to offer to those aspiring democracies in Eastern Europe and elsewhere that have no liberal traditions and whose public political cultures therefore lack the implicit ideas to which Rawls appeals. If in fact political liberalism has nothing to offer such societies, then its defence of liberal principles and institutions may seem intolerably weak. In renouncing any universalistic ambitions, Rawls may now seem to have gone too far in the other direction and to have produced a version of liberalism that is so historically specific and so dependent on a prior history of liberal institutions as to be of little relevance in those situations where the justification of liberalism matters most: that is, where liberalism is confronted by, and must engage with, societies whose traditions and practices are not liberal.

In his essay on 'The Law of Peoples', Rawls makes clear that his defence of liberalism does not in fact aspire to the kind of universality that some liberals would prefer.[10] In that essay, he attempts to develop what he calls a 'liberal law of peoples', which applies even to societies that are not themselves liberal. Yet he also makes it clear that this law does not require non-liberal societies to become liberal. On the contrary, Rawls argues that 'not all

---

[10] John Rawls, 'The Law of Peoples', *Critical Inquiry* 20 (1993): 36–68.

regimes can be reasonably required to be liberal', and that a society that is not liberal may nevertheless be 'well ordered and just'.[11] Rawls's development of the law of peoples raises many questions that I cannot pursue here. For present purposes, however, what is noteworthy is that it appears to confirm the suspicion that Rawls's justification of liberal institutions is limited in certain striking ways. Political liberalism makes no general claim about the superiority of liberal over non-liberal societies, nor does it provide arguments as to why heretofore non-liberal societies should become liberal. Rawls seems to regard this reticence as a virtue, in part because he is sensitive to the charge that more ambitious claims on behalf of liberalism represent a form of Western ethnocentrism, and because he believes that it is not necessary to make such claims in order to develop a law of peoples that applies to all nations and which specifies certain minimum standards of acceptable conduct.

Yet, it may be objected, political liberalism does not merely refrain from asserting that all societies should become liberal; what is more disturbing is that it cannot give any non-liberal society a reason why it should become liberal. It simply has nothing to offer to those societies that may be attempting, in the face of considerable opposition and without the benefit of any significant democratic tradition, to develop liberal institutions for the first time and which look naturally to the liberal philosophers of the democratic West for what is literally 'moral support'.

This seems to me a legitimate concern, although Rawls might respond that there is in fact a difference between the reasons why liberal institutions take root in a society for the first time and the justifications for such institutions that become available at later stages. Thus it might be said that liberal institutions take hold, when they do, for a variety of reasons—which may include the need for a *modus vivendi*, the collapse of alternative institutional schemes, or the desire to emulate the perceived economic success of existing liberal democracies—but which almost certainly do not include a society's happening to converge from the outset on a particular liberal comprehensive moral doctrine. Moreover, and this may be one of the sobering messages of *Political Liberalism*, liberal institutions founded on the sorts of reasons just mentioned are bound to be precarious until a society has lived under them long enough to develop a tradition of tolerance, a commitment to the virtues of liberal citizenship, and an ethos of reasonableness and fair reciprocity. These things are resources that can help to stabilize liberal institutions by making an overlapping consensus on liberal values and principles possible. But their development takes time and reasonably favourable conditions. It cannot happen overnight at the drop of an argument, even a good one. Once it does happen, however, and this may be the more encouraging message of *Political Liberalism*, then a liberal society may be able to flourish despite the deep disagreements that are bound to persist.

[11] Ibid., 37, 44.

If this response seems insufficiently robust, there is one further thing that might be said consistently with the spirit of Rawls's book, namely, that if an overlapping consensus on liberal principles can indeed be achieved in modern democracies, then accepting any one of the doctrines included in such a consensus may give one reason to support a liberal scheme. In other words, the distinctive contribution of political liberalism may be to suggest that there are many ways to arrive at liberal principles and that that very fact is a source of liberalism's strength. For if the reasonable comprehensive doctrines that thrive under conditions of freedom all converge on liberal principles, then what may be said to those in societies seeking to establish liberal institutions is that such institutions represent common ground among the various outlooks likely to endure under conditions that encourage the free exercise of human reason. Of course, however, this can be said only if an overlapping consensus is a realistic possibility in modern, pluralistic democracies. This brings us back to the questions raised earlier. Until those sorts of questions are convincingly answered, the suspicion is likely to persist, especially among those who would defend liberalism on the basis of a comprehensive moral doctrine, that Rawls's position depletes the moral resources of liberalism without managing in exchange to broaden its justificatory appeal.

9

*Rawls and Utilitarianism**

In the Preface to *A Theory of Justice*,[1] Rawls observes that '[d]uring much of modern moral philosophy the predominant systematic theory has been some form of utilitarianism' (TJ vii). Critics of utilitarianism, he says, have pointed out that many of its implications run counter to our moral convictions and sentiments, but they have failed 'to construct a workable and systematic moral conception to oppose it' (TJ viii). As a result, Rawls writes, 'we often seem forced to choose between utilitarianism and intuitionism'. In the end, he speculates, we are likely to 'settle upon a variant of the utility principle circumscribed and restricted in certain ad hoc ways by intuitionistic constraints'. 'Such a view,' he adds, 'is not irrational; and there is no assurance that we can do better. But this is no reason not to try' (TJ viii). Accordingly, what he proposes to do 'is to generalize and carry to a higher order of abstraction the traditional theory of the social contract as represented by Locke, Rousseau, and Kant'. Rawls believes that, of all traditional theories of justice, the contract theory is the one 'which best approximates our considered judgments of justice'. His aim is to develop this theory in such a way as to 'offer an alternative systematic account of justice that is superior . . . to the dominant utilitarianism of the tradition' (TJ viii).

Rawls sounds a similar note toward the end of Chapter One, where he observes that 'the several variants of the utilitarian view have long dominated our philosophical tradition and continue to do so', and this 'despite the persistent misgivings that utilitarianism so easily arouses' (TJ 52). This is, he says, a 'peculiar state of affairs', which is to be explained by 'the fact that no constructive alternative theory has been advanced which has the comparable virtues of clarity and system and which at the same time allays these doubts' (TJ

* From *The Cambridge Companion to Rawls*, ed. Samuel Freeman (Cambridge University Press, forthcoming). Reprinted by permission. Earlier versions of this paper were presented to a philosophy department colloquium at UCLA, a symposium in Stockholm sponsored by the Royal Swedish Academy of Sciences and the Rolf Schock Foundation, and the 2000 Conference of the International Society for Utilitarian Studies, held at Wake Forest University. I am grateful to all of these audiences for helpful discussion. I am also indebted to Samuel Freeman for his comments on a previous draft and to Nicholas Kolodny for valuable research assistance.
[1] Harvard University Press, 1971. Cited hereafter as TJ, with page references given parenthetically in the text.

52). Rawls's 'conjecture is that the contract doctrine properly worked out can fill this gap' (TJ 52).

Rawls's claim to have outlined a theory—'justice as fairness'—that is superior to utilitarianism has generated extensive debate. Despite his opposition to utilitarianism, however, it seems evident from the passages I have quoted that he also regards it as possessing theoretical virtues that he wishes to emulate. In particular, he admires utilitarianism's 'systematic' and 'constructive' character, and thinks it unfortunate that the views advanced by critics of utilitarianism have not been comparably systematic or constructive. This aspect of Rawls's attitude toward utilitarianism has attracted less attention. Yet it marks an important difference between his view and the views of other prominent critics of utilitarianism writing at around the same time, even when those critics express their objections in language that is reminiscent of his. For example, where Rawls says that '[u]tilitarianism does not take seriously the distinction between persons' (TJ 27), Robert Nozick, explicitly citing Rawls, says that to sacrifice one individual for the greater social good 'does not sufficiently respect and take account of the fact that he is a separate person, that his is the only life he has'.[2] And Bernard Williams, developing a different but not entirely unrelated criticism, argues that utilitarianism makes personal 'integrity as a value more or less unintelligible'.[3] But neither Nozick nor Williams stresses the importance of providing a *systematic* alternative to utilitarianism.

I have said that Rawls's appreciation for utilitarianism's systematic and constructive character has attracted less comment than his claim to have identified a theory of justice that is preferable to utilitarianism. However, a number of critics have argued that Rawls's position has important features in common with utilitarianism, features in virtue of which his view is open to some of the very same objections that he levels against the utilitarian. Whether or not these arguments are successful, they may be seen in part as responses to the emphasis on system that is a feature both of Rawls's theory and of utilitarianism. To the extent that this is so, they can help to illuminate Rawls's complex attitude toward utilitarianism: an attitude that is marked by respect and areas of affinity as well as by sharp disagreements. They can also help us to see that some people may be troubled by Rawls's arguments against utilitarianism, not because they sympathize with those aspects of the view that he criticizes, but rather because they are critical of those aspects of the view with which he sympathizes.

In this essay, I will begin by reviewing Rawls's main arguments against utilitarianism. I will then examine an argument by Nozick and by Michael Sandel to the effect that there is a tension between certain aspects of Rawls's theory and his criticisms of utilitarianism. I will explain why I do not regard

---

[2] *Anarchy, State, and Utopia* (New York, NY: Basic Books, 1974), 33.
[3] 'A Critique of Utilitarianism', in *Utilitarianism For and Against*, ed. J. J. C. Smart and Bernard Williams (Cambridge University Press, 1973), 77–150, at 99.

this argument as persuasive, but will also indicate how it points to some genuine affinities between justice-as-fairness and utilitarian ideas, affinities that I will then explore in greater depth. My hope is to arrive at a balanced assessment of Rawls's attitude toward utilitarianism. I will conclude by discussing some apparent differences between Rawls's position in *A Theory of Justice* and his position in *Political Liberalism*.[4]

Rawls's criticisms of utilitarianism comprise a variety of formulations which depend to varying degrees and in various ways on the apparatus of the original position. Formally, his aim is to show is that the parties in the original position would prefer his own conception of justice—justice as fairness—to a utilitarian conception. Thus his 'official' arguments against utilitarianism take the form of arguments purporting to show that it would be rejected by the parties. Yet the most important of those arguments can also be formulated independently of the original position construction and, in addition, there are some arguments that are not offered from the vantage point of the original position at all.

Rawls gives distinct arguments against two forms of utilitarianism: the classical version and the principle of average utility. Classical utilitarianism, as he understands it, holds 'that society is rightly ordered, and therefore just, when its major institutions are arranged so as to achieve the greatest net balance of satisfaction summed over all the individuals belonging to it' (TJ 22). It is, according to Rawls, a teleological theory, by which he means that it defines the good independently from the right and defines the right as maximizing the good. The principle of average utility, as its name suggests, 'directs society to maximize not the total but the average utility' (TJ 162). Although classical and average utilitarianism 'may often have similar practical consequences' (TJ 189), and although those consequences will coincide completely so long as population size is constant, Rawls argues that the two views are 'markedly distinct conceptions' whose 'underlying analytic assumptions are far apart' (TJ 161).

Rawls observes that the distribution of satisfaction within the society has no intrinsic significance for classical utilitarianism. If a radically inegalitarian distribution—either of satisfaction itself or of the means of satisfaction—will result in the greatest total satisfaction overall, the inequality of the distribution is no reason to avoid it. Of course, as Rawls recognizes, utilitarians frequently argue that, given plausible empirical assumptions, the maximization of satisfaction is unlikely to be achieved in this way. The fact remains, however, that classical utilitarianism attaches no intrinsic importance to questions of distribution, and that it imposes no principled limit on the extent to which aggregative reasoning may legitimately be employed in making social decisions. The losses of some people may, in principle, always be outweighed by the greater gains of other people.

[4] Columbia University Press, 1993 (paperback edition, 1996). Cited hereafter as PL, with page references to the paperback edition given parenthetically in the text.

Rawls argues that this commitment to unrestricted aggregation can be seen as the result of extending to 'society as a whole the principle of rational choice for one man' (TJ 26–7). In other words, we normally think that it is reasonable for a single individual to seek to maximize satisfaction over the course of a lifetime. It is reasonable, for example, to 'impose a sacrifice on ourselves now for the sake of a greater advantage later' (TJ 23). The classical utilitarian, Rawls argues, reasons in much the same way about society as a whole, regarding it as legitimate to impose sacrifices on some people in order to achieve greater advantages for others. This extension to society as a whole of the principle of choice for a single individual is facilitated, Rawls believes, by treating the approval of a perfectly sympathetic and ideally rational and impartial spectator as the standard of what is just. Since the impartial spectator 'identifies with and experiences the desires of others as if these desires were his own', his function is to organize 'the desires of all persons into one coherent system of desire' (TJ 27). In this way, 'many persons are fused into one' (TJ 27). In summary, Rawls argues, the classical utilitarian 'view of social cooperation is the consequence of extending to society the principle of choice for one man, and then, to make this extension work, conflating all persons into one through the imaginative acts of the impartial sympathetic spectator' (TJ 27). This is what leads Rawls to make the claim that this form of utilitarianism 'does not take seriously the distinction between persons'. This is a decisive objection provided 'we assume that the correct regulative principle for anything depends on the nature of that thing, and that the plurality of distinct persons with separate systems of ends is an essential feature of human societies' (TJ 29).

It is noteworthy that this argument against classical utilitarianism is developed without reference to the apparatus of the original position and is not dependent on that apparatus. Rawls does, of course, offer an additional argument to the effect that the parties in the original position would reject the classical view. The argument is that the parties, knowing that they exist and wishing only to advance their own interests, would have no desire to maximize the net aggregate satisfaction, especially since doing so might require growth in the size of the population even at the expense of a significant reduction in the average utility per person. This argument is straightforward and appears decisive. At any rate, it has attracted far less controversy than Rawls's claim that the parties would reject the principle of average utility. Yet is probably fair to say that it has been less influential, as an argument against classical utilitarianism, than the argument offered independently of the original position construction.

Rawls goes on to suggest that if the terms of the original position were altered in such a way that the parties were 'conceived of as perfect altruists, that is, as persons whose desires conform to the approvals' (TJ 188–9) of an impartial, sympathetic spectator, then classical utilitarianism would indeed be adopted. This leads him to the 'unexpected conclusion' that the classical view

is 'the ethic of perfect altruists', by contrast with the principle of average utility which, from the perspective afforded by the original position, emerges as
'the ethic of a single rational individual (with no aversion to risk)' (TJ 189).
Thus, in looking at the two versions of utilitarianism from the standpoint
of the original position, a 'surprising contrast' (TJ 189) between them is
revealed. This suggests to Rawls that 'even if the concept of the original position served no other purpose, it would be a useful analytic device' (TJ 189),
enabling us to see the 'different complex[es] of ideas' (TJ 189) underlying the
two versions of utilitarianism. However, the characterization of classical utilitarianism as the ethic of perfect altruists seems puzzling, given the fact that
the classical view is said to conflate all persons into one. It seems peculiar to
suppose that perfect altruists would neglect the distinctness of persons and
support the unrestricted interpersonal aggregation to which such neglect is
said to give rise. After characterizing classical utilitarianism as the ethic of
perfect altruists, moreover, Rawls goes on in the next several pages to ask
what theory of justice would be preferred by an impartial, sympathetic spectator who did not conflate all systems of desires into one. In response, he
argues that a 'benevolent' person fitting this description would actually prefer justice-as-fairness to classical utilitarianism. But this makes it even less clear
why classical utilitarianism should be associated with perfect altruism. If that
association is unwarranted, then the contrast between the classical and average views may be less dramatic than Rawls suggests, and the claims of the
original position as an illuminating analytic device may to that extent be
reduced.

Of course, this is not to deny that the principle of average utility would
have more appeal than classical utilitarianism for the parties in the original
position. Indeed, whereas Rawls's assertion that the parties would reject classical utilitarianism has attracted little opposition, his claim that his conception of justice would be preferred to the principle of average utility has been
quite controversial.[5] Most of the controversy has focused on Rawls's argument that it would be rational for the parties to use the maximin rule for
choice under uncertainty when deciding which conception of justice to select.

[5] See, for example, Kenneth Arrow, 'Some Ordinalist-Utilitarian Notes on Rawls's Theory
of Justice', *Journal of Philosophy* 70 (1973): 245–63; Brian Barry, *The Liberal Theory of
Justice* (Oxford: Clarendon Press, 1973), Ch. 9; Holly Smith Goldman, 'Rawls and
Utilitarianism', in *John Rawls' Theory of Social Justice: An Introduction*, ed. H. Gene Blocker
and Elizabeth H. Smith (University of Ohio Press, 1980), 346–94; R. M. Hare, 'Rawls'
Theory of Justice', in *Reading Rawls*, ed. Norman Daniels (Stanford University Press,
1989), 81–107; John Harsanyi, 'Can the Maximin Principle Serve as a Basis for
Morality? A Critique of John Rawls's Theory', in *Essays on Ethics, Social Behavior, and
Scientific Explanation* (Dordrecht, Holland: D. Reidel, 1976), 37–63; David Lyons,
'Nature and Soundness of the Contract and Coherence Arguments', in *Reading Rawls*,
141–67; Jan Narveson, 'Rawls and Utilitarianism', in *The Limits of Utilitarianism*, ed.
Harlan B. Miller and William H. Williams (University of Minnesota Press, 1982),
128–43; Robert Paul Wolff, *Understanding Rawls* (Princeton University Press, 1977), Ch.
15.

If they do use this rule, then they will reject average utility in favour of his two principles, since the maximin rule directs choosers to select the alternative whose worst outcome is superior to the worst outcome of any other alternative, and the two principles are those a person would choose if he knew that his enemy were going to assign him his place in society. However, as Rawls acknowledges, the maximin rule is very conservative, and its employment will seem rational only under certain conditions. Unless the decision facing the parties in the original position satisfies those conditions, the principle of average utility may be a better choice for the parties even if it is riskier, since it may also hold out the prospect of greater gain (TJ 165–6). Yet Rawls argues that the original position does have features that make reliance on the maximin rule appropriate and that the parties would reject average utility as unduly risky.

In general, the use of maximin is said to be rational when there is no reliable basis for assessing the probabilities of different outcomes, when the chooser cares very little for gains above the minimum that could be secured through reliance on maximin, and when the other options have possible consequences that the chooser would find intolerable. Rawls's strategy is to try to establish that the choice between average utility and his two principles satisfies these conditions because (1) the parties have no basis for confidence in the type of probabilistic reasoning that would support a choice of average utility, (2) his two principles would assure the parties of a satisfactory minimum, and (3) the principle of average utility might have consequences that the parties could not accept. Although Rawls first outlines this strategy in section 26, it is important to emphasize that what he provides in that section is only a sketch of 'the qualitative structure of the argument that needs to be made if the case for these principles is to be conclusive' (TJ 150).

With respect to the first condition, Rawls observes in section 28 that, from the standpoint of the original position, the *prima facie* appeal of average utility depends on the assumption that one has an equal chance of turning out to be anybody once the veil of ignorance is lifted. Yet Rawls says that this assumption 'is not founded upon known features of one's society' (TJ 168). Instead, it is based on the principle of insufficient reason, which, in the absence of any specific grounds for the assignment of probabilities to different outcomes, treats all the possible outcomes as being equally probable. Rawls says that, given the importance of the choice facing the parties, it would be rash for them to rely on probabilities arrived at in this way. This is presumably because the maximization of average utility could, in societies with certain features, require that the interests of some people be seriously compromised. Thus, the excessive riskiness of relying on the principle of insufficient reason depends on the claim about the third condition, that is, on the possibility that average utility might lead to intolerable outcomes. This possibility arises, Rawls suggests, because utilitarianism relies entirely on certain 'standard assumptions' (TJ 159) to demonstrate that its calculations will not

normally support severe restrictions on individual liberties. Given the importance that the parties attach to the basic liberties, Rawls maintains that 'they
would prefer to secure their liberties straightaway rather than have them depend
upon what may be uncertain and speculative actuarial calculations' (TJ
160–1). They would be unwilling to take the chance that, in a society governed by utilitarian principles, a utilitarian calculation might someday provide the basis for a serious infringement of their liberties, especially since they
have the more conservative option of the two principles available to them.

If the conclusion that the parties would regard the principle of average utility as excessively risky depends on the claim that, under certain conditions,
it would justify the sacrifice of some people's liberties in order to maintain
the average level of well-being within the society at as high a level as possible, then Rawls's arguments against average utility are not as different from
his arguments against classical utilitarianism as his talk of a 'surprising contrast' might suggest. In both cases, the parties are said to fear that their own
interests might be sacrificed for the sake of the larger utilitarian goal. And in
both cases, this argument from the perspective of the parties corresponds to
an independent criticism of utilitarianism as being excessively willing to sacrifice
some people for the sake of others.

Defenders of the principle of average utility have challenged Rawls's
arguments in a variety of ways. First, they have argued that the 'standard
assumptions' are sufficiently robust that it would not be excessively risky for
the parties to choose average utility even if this meant relying on the principle of insufficient reason. Second, however, they have wondered why, if
Rawls believes that it would be unduly risky for the parties to rely on probabilities that are not grounded in information about their society, he fails to
provide them with that information. So long as the veil of ignorance prevents the parties from knowing their own identities, providing them with
the relevant information about their society need not compromise their impartiality. Third, they have questioned whether Rawls's principles can truly be
said to guarantee the parties a satisfactory minimum and whether the parties, who are ignorant of their conceptions of the good, can truly be said to
care little for gains above such a minimum. Fourth, they have argued that
Rawls's own principles of justice are not altogether risk-free, since the 'general conception' of justice-as-fairness would permit the infringement of basic
liberties under extraordinary conditions. Thus, they have maintained, there
is less of a difference than Rawls indicates between average utility and his
own view in respect of their riskiness. Under normal conditions neither would
permit serious infringements of liberty while under extraordinary conditions
either might. Finally, critics have argued that there is a fundamental obscur-
ity in Rawls's account of the way that the parties assess risk. He says that
the choice of principles should not depend on the parties' 'special attitudes'
toward risk, and that the veil of ignorance therefore prevents them from knowing 'whether or not they have a characteristic aversion to taking chances' (TJ

172). Instead, the aim is to show that 'choosing as if one had such as aversion is rational given the unique features of ... [the original position] irrespective of any special attitudes toward risk' (TJ 172). However, defenders of average utility have questioned whether it makes sense to suppose that there is an attitude toward risk that it is rational to have if one is ignorant of one's 'special attitudes' toward risk.

These issues have been extensively discussed, and I will here simply assert that, despite some infelicities in Rawls's presentation, I believe he is correct to maintain that the parties would prefer his two principles to the principle of average utility. In arriving at this conclusion, it is important to guard against an excessively narrow, formalistic interpretation of the 'maximin argument'.[6] As already noted, Rawls's initial account in section 26 of the reasons for relying on the maximin rule is merely an outline of what he will attempt to establish subsequently. It should not be interpreted, as it sometimes has been, as the self-contained presentation of a formal decision-theoretic argument which is independent, for example, of the appeals to stability, self-respect, and the strains of commitment in section 29. The inevitable effect of such an interpretation is to make Rawls's argument seem both more formal and less plausible than it really is.

In fact, Rawls states explicitly that the arguments of section 29 'fit under the heuristic schema suggested by the reasons for following the maximin rule. That is, they help to show that the two principles are an adequate minimum conception of justice in a situation of great uncertainty. Any further advantages that might be won by the principle of utility ... are highly problematical, whereas the hardship if things turn out badly are [sic] intolerable' (TJ 175). In other words, the arguments of section 29 are intended to help show that the choice confronting the parties has features that make reliance on the maximin rule rational. They are not unrelated arguments.

Indeed, the point goes further. The arguments set out in section 29 explicitly invoke considerations of moral psychology that are not fully developed until Part III. In other words, section 29's appeals to psychological stability, self-respect, and the strains of commitment are all intended as contributions to the overarching enterprise of demonstrating that Rawls's principles would provide a satisfactory minimum whereas the principle of average utility might have consequences with which the parties would find it difficult to live. In slightly different ways, however, all of these appeals are underwritten by the contrast that Rawls develops at length in Part III between the moral psychologies of the two theories. Rawls argues there that because his principles embody an idea of reciprocity or mutual benefit, and because reciprocity is the fundamental psychological mechanism implicated in the development of moral motivation, the motives that would lead people to internalize and uphold his principles are psychologically continuous with developmentally

---

[6] My discussion follows those of Steven Strasnick, in his review of Robert Paul Wolff's *Understanding Rawls*, *Journal of Philosophy* 76 (1979): 496–510, and Joshua Cohen, 'Democratic Equality', *Ethics* 99(1989): 727–51.

more primitive mechanisms of moral motivation. This means that, in a society whose basic structure was regulated by the two principles, allegiance to those principles would, under favorable conditions, develop naturally out of pre-existing psychological materials. By contrast, utilitarianism does not embody an idea of reciprocity. If people are to be stably motivated to uphold utilitarian principles and institutions, even when those principles and institutions have not worked to their advantage, the capacity for sympathetic identification will have to be the operative psychological mechanism. Yet that capacity is, as a rule, not strong enough nor securely enough situated within the human motivational repertoire to be a reliable source of support for utilitarian principles and institutions.

As I have indicated, substantial portions of Part III are devoted to the detailed elaboration of this contrast along with its implications for the relative stability of the two rival conceptions of justice and their relative success in encouraging the self-respect of citizens.[7] Furthermore, Rawls says explicitly that much of the argument of Part II, which applies his principles to institutions, is intended to help establish that they constitute a workable conception of justice and provide a satisfactory minimum (TJ 156). The upshot is that the reasons for relying on the maximin rule, far from being fully elaborated in section 26, are actually the subject of much of the rest of the book.[8,9] In effect, the

[7] In *Political Liberalism* (xvii–xx and xlii–xliv) Rawls says that the account of stability given in Part III of the *Theory* is defective, because it tests the rival conceptions of justice by asking whether the well-ordered society associated with each such conception would continue to generate its own support over time and, in so doing, this account implicitly assumes that in a well-ordered society everyone endorses the conception on the basis of a shared 'comprehensive moral doctrine'. In view of the inevitable diversity of reasonable comprehensive doctrines in a modern democratic society, Rawls argues, this is not a realistic assumption and hence the test of stability is inadequate. Perhaps so, but Rawls shouldn't concede too much here. He may be correct in thinking he needs to show how a society regulated by his conception of justice could be stable despite the prevalence of diverse comprehensive doctrines. Surely, however, if it is true that the well-ordered utilitarian society would not continue to generate its own support even if everyone initially endorsed utilitarian principles of justice on the basis of a shared commitment to utilitarianism as a comprehensive philosophical doctrine, then that remains a significant objection to the utilitarian view.

[8] Thus, I believe it is misleading when Rawls says, at the end of his discussion of relative stability in section 76: 'These remarks are not intended as justifying reasons for the contract view. The main grounds for the principles of justice have already been presented. At this point we are simply checking whether the conception already adopted is a feasible one and not so unstable that some other choice might be better. We are in the second part of the argument in which we ask if the acknowledgment previously made should be reconsidered' (TJ 504). After all, he had said in section 29 a) that the stability argument is one of the 'main arguments for the two principles' (TJ 175), b) that it fits 'under the heuristic schema suggested by the reasons for following the maximin rule' (TJ 175), and c) that it depends 'on the laws of moral psychology and the availability of human motives', which are only discussed 'later on (sections 75–76)' (TJ 177). These points imply that the discussion in section 76 is an indispensable part of the presentation of 'the main grounds for the principles of justice'.

[9] In 'Justice and the Problem of Stability', (*Philosophy & Public Affairs* 18 (1989): 3–30), Edward McClennen acknowledges that a 'careful reading of *A Theory of Justice* makes it clear that it would be a mistake to treat the rational choice argument of the analytic construction [i.e., the original position] and the psychological theory pertaining

'maximin argument' functions as a master argument within which many of the book's more specific arguments are subsumed. Viewed in this light, the argument's significance as a contribution to the criticism of utilitarianism is easier to appreciate. By itself, the claim that even the average version of utilitarianism is unduly willing to sacrifice some people for the sake of others is not a novel one. However, by anchoring the parties' unwillingness to accept the sacrifices associated with average utility in a carefully elaborated moral psychology and a developed account of how a workable and efficient set of social institutions could avoid such sacrifices, Rawls considerably strengthens and enriches that familiar criticism. At the very least, his argument challenges utilitarians to supply a comparably plausible and detailed account of utilitarian social and economic institutions and of the processes by which, in a society regulated by utilitarian principles, motives would develop that were capable of generating ongoing support for those institutions and principles. The force of this challenge, moreover, is largely independent of Rawls's claims about the justificatory significance of the original position construction. Even if utilitarians reject the original position as a device for adjudicating among rival conceptions of justice, in other words, this challenge is not one they can easily ignore.

Whereas the maximin argument is presented as a reason why the parties would not choose utilitarianism, Rawls develops another important line of criticism whose ostensible relation to the original position construction is less straightforward.[10] This line of criticism turns on a contrast between those views that take there to be but a single rational good for all human beings and those that conceive of the human good as heterogeneous. We may speak here of a contrast between *monistic* and *pluralistic* accounts of the good. Rawls believes that teleological theories, which define the good independently of the right and define the right as maximizing the good, tend also to interpret the good in monistic terms. He thinks this is true of those teleological theories he describes as perfectionist, of certain religious views, and also of classical utilitarianism in so far as its account of the good is understood hedonistically. Non-teleological forms of utilitarianism, such as the principle of average utility,[11] are also monistic if they rely on a hedonistic interpretation

to the sense of justice as completely disjoint' (6–7). McClennen himself, however, believes that Rawls's conception of justice can best be defended independently of the original position construction by a rational choice argument that makes a more direct appeal to considerations of psychological stability.

[10] For helpful discussions of this line of criticism, see Samuel Freeman, 'Utilitarianism, Deontology, and the Priority of Right', *Philosophy & Public Affairs* 23 (1994): 313–49; T. M. Scanlon, 'Rawls' Theory of Justice', *University of Pennsylvania Law Review* 121 (1973): 1020–69.

[11] See TJ 166, where Rawls says that the principle of average utility 'is not a teleological doctrine, strictly speaking, as the classical view is', since it aims to maximize an average and not a sum. Note, however, that under the index entry for average utilitarianism (606), there is a subheading that reads: 'as teleological theory, hedonism the tendency of'.

of the good. Admittedly, hedonistic forms of utilitarianism recognize that different individuals will take pleasure in very different sorts of pursuits, and so they are superficially hospitable to pluralism in a way that other monistic views are not. For this very reason, Rawls suggests, utilitarianism offers 'a way of adapting the notion of the one rational good to the institutional requirements of a modern state and pluralistic democratic society'.[12] So long as the good is identified with agreeable feeling, however, the account remains monistic.[13]

Rawls suggests that teleological views may be drawn to monistic accounts out of a desire to avoid indeterminacy in the way the good is characterized, since for teleological views 'any vagueness or ambiguity in the conception of the good is transferred to that of the right' (TJ 559). He also suggests that part of the attraction of monistic accounts, and of teleological theories that incorporate such accounts, may derive from a conviction that they enable us to resolve a fundamental problem about the nature of rational deliberation. The problem is to explain how rational choices among apparently heterogeneous options can ever be made. Unless there is some one ultimate end at which all human action aims, this problem may seem insoluble. If, however, there is some 'dominant end' to which all of our other ends are subordinated, then 'a rational decision is always in principle possible, since only difficulties of computation and lack of information remain' (TJ 552). Moreover, if there is indeed a dominant end at which all rational human action aims, then it is but a short step to construing that end as the 'sole intrinsic good' (TJ 556) for human beings. In this way, we may be led to a monistic account of the good 'by an argument from the conditions of rational deliberation' (TJ 556). And once we have accepted a monistic account of the good, a teleological view directing us to maximize that good may seem plausible. As Rawls says: 'Teleological views have a deep intuitive appeal since they seem to embody the idea of rationality. It is natural to think that rationality is maximizing something and that in morals it must be maximizing the good' (TJ 24–5). Furthermore, hedonism is 'the symptomatic drift of teleological theories' (TJ 560) both because agreeable feeling may appear to be an 'interpersonal currency' (TJ 559) that makes social choice possible and because hedonism's superficial hospitality to varied ways of life enables it 'to avoid the appearance of fanaticism and inhumanity' (TJ 556). Thus, Rawls believes, there is a chain of argument that begins with a worry about the possibility of rational decision and concludes with an endorsement of hedonistic utilitarianism.

Against this line of thought, Rawls argues, first, that there simply is no dominant end: no one overarching aim for the sake of which all our other ends

---

[12] 'Social Unity and Primary Goods', in *Utilitarianism and Beyond*, ed. Amartya Sen and Bernard Williams (Cambridge University Press, 1982), 159–85, at 182.

[13] In light of this assessment of the utilitarian conception of the good and his own defence of a pluralistic conception, Rawls's comment in section 15, that utilitarianism and his theory agree that 'the good is the satisfaction of rational desire' (TJ 92–3) seems misleading at best.

are pursued. Pleasant or agreeable feeling, in particular, cannot plausibly be thought to constitute such an aim. Nor, he maintains, does the irreducible diversity of our ends mean that rational choice is impossible. All it means is that formal principles play a limited role in determining such choices. Rational choice must often rest instead on self-knowledge: on a careful attempt to ascertain which one of a diverse set of ends matters most to us. In making such determinations, we may do well to employ 'deliberative rationality'—to reflect carefully, under favourable conditions, in light of all the relevant facts available to us—but there is no formal procedure that will routinely select the rational course of action. And since there is no dominant end of all rational human action, Rawls continues, it is implausible to suppose that the good is monistic. Instead, he says, the '[h]uman good is heterogeneous because the aims of the self are heterogeneous' (TJ 554). This drains away much of the motivation for a teleological view. Whereas the idea of arranging social institutions so as to maximize the good might seem attractive if there were a unique good at which all rational action aims, it makes more sense, in light of the heterogeneity of the good, to establish a fair framework of social co-operation within which individuals may pursue their diverse ends and aspirations.

The significance of this criticism is subject to doubts of two different kinds. First, it may seem that the criticism simply does not apply to contemporary versions of utilitarianism which do not, in general, purport to construe the good hedonistically. When such views advocate the maximization of total or average satisfaction, their concern is with the satisfaction of people's preferences and not with some presumed state of consciousness. Yet in 'Social Unity and Primary Goods', where he builds on an argument first broached in the final four paragraphs of Section 28 of TJ, Rawls contends that even contemporary versions of utilitarianism are often covertly or implicitly hedonistic. For they rely on something like a 'shared highest order preference function' as the basis for interpersonal comparisons of well-being, and such a function treats citizens as subscribing to a common ranking of the relative desirability of different packages of material resources and personal qualities—including traits of character, skills and abilities, attachments and loyalties, ends and aspirations. Rational citizens are then assumed to desire an overall package with as high a ranking as possible. This assumption, Rawls argues, implies 'the dissolution of the person as leading a life expressive of character and of devotion to specific final ends', and it is only 'psychologically intelligible'[14] if one thinks of pleasure as a dominant end for the sake of which a rational person is willing to revise or abandon any of his other ends or commitments. If this analysis is correct, then Rawls's argument may apply to a broader range of utilitarian theories than was initially evident.

However, the argument's oblique relation to the original position construction may give rise to doubts of another kind. The argument is not presented

---

[14] 'Social Unity and Primary Goods', 181.

to the parties in the original position as a reason for rejecting utilitarianism or teleological views in general. Rather, it appears to play a role in motivating the design of the original position itself. It helps to explain why the parties are denied knowledge of any specific conception of the good, and why they are instead stipulated to accept the thin theory of the good, with all that that involves. Given these starting points, it seems antecedently unlikely that the parties will accept any theory of justice that relies on a hedonistic or other monistic conception of the good. As Rawls says: 'The parties . . . do not know what final aims persons have, and all dominant-end conceptions are rejected. Thus it would not occur to them to acknowledge the principle of utility in its hedonistic form. There is no more reason for the parties to agree to this criterion than to maximize any other particular objective' (TJ 563). But this suggests that the parties reject theories of justice that incorporate monistic conceptions of the good because Rawls's argument for pluralism has led him to design the original position in such a way as to guarantee that they will do so. This in turn may cast doubt on the justificatory significance of the parties' choice. And since their choice represents the core of Rawls's 'official' case against utilitarianism, one effect of the way he deploys the argument against monism may be to jeopardize that case. In his later writings, Rawls himself expresses misgivings about the role played in TJ by his defense of a pluralistic theory of the good. In 'Justice as Fairness: Political not Metaphysical' he describes it as one of the 'faults' of TJ that the account of goodness developed in Part III 'often reads as an account of the complete good for a comprehensive moral conception'.[15] And in *Political Liberalism*, he recasts the argument against monistic conceptions of the good; the point is no longer that they are mistaken but rather that no such conception can serve as the basis for an adequate conception of justice in a pluralistic society.[16]

These considerations implicate some significant general issues—about the justificatory function of the original position and about the changes in Rawls's views over time—which lie beyond the scope of this essay. However, even if the role of the argument against monism in *Theory* raises questions about the justificatory significance of the original position construction, and even if the philosophical character of the argument is in tension with the 'political' turn taken in Rawls's later writings, I believe that the argument can stand on its own as an important challenge to utilitarian thought. The same, as I have already suggested, is true of Rawls's claim that utilitarianism tolerates unacceptable interpersonal trade-offs. Indeed, I believe that those two arguments represent his most important and enduring criticisms of the utilitarian tradition.

Despite the vigor of his arguments against utilitarianism, however, some critics have contended that Rawls's own theory displays some of the very same features that he criticizes in the utilitarian position. For example, Robert Nozick

---

[15] *Philosophy & Public Affairs* 14 (1985): 223–51, at 251n. See also PL, 176–7n.

[16] See for example PL 134–5. See also 'Justice as Fairness: Political not Metaphysical', 248–9.

holds that there is a tension between Rawls's assertion that the difference principle 'represents, in effect, an agreement to regard the distribution of natural talents as a common asset and to share in the benefits of this distribution' (TJ 101) and his charge that classical utilitarianism does not take seriously the distinction between persons. Nozick suggests that Rawls can avoid this tension only by placing an implausible degree of weight on the distinction between persons and their talents.[17] Michael Sandel, following up on Nozick's point, argues that Rawls has a 'theory of the person' according to which talents are merely 'contingently-given and wholly inessential attributes' rather than 'essential *constituents*' of the self.[18] For this reason, Sandel argues, Rawls does not see the distinctness of *persons* as violated by the idea of treating the distribution of talents as a common asset. However, Sandel believes that the underlying theory of the person suffers from 'incoherence'[19] and cannot, therefore, provide Rawls with a satisfactory response to the charge that he too is guilty of neglecting the distinctness of persons.

Sandel maintains that 'the only way out of the difficulties Nozick raises' would be to argue that what underlies the difference principle is an 'intersubjective' conception of the person, according to which 'the relevant description of the self may embrace more than a single empirically-individuated human being'.[20] This would enable Rawls to say that other people's benefiting from my natural talents need not violate the distinctness of persons, not because my talents aren't really part of me but rather because those people may not, in the relevant sense, be distinct from me. Of course, to say this would be to concede that Rawls takes the conventional distinctions among 'empirically-individuated human beings' even less seriously than does utilitarianism. Indeed, one of the broad morals of Sandel's analysis is supposed to be that the difference principle is a sufficiently communitarian notion of justice that it requires a thoroughly communitarian conception of the self.

However, I believe that Sandel's analysis raises the metaphysical stakes unnecessarily and that the tension between Rawls's principles and his criticism of utilitarianism can be dissolved without appealing to either of the two theories of the person that Sandel invokes. Classical utilitarianism identifies the good life for an individual as a life of happiness or satisfaction. However, it directs us to arrange social and political institutions in such a way as to maximize the aggregate satisfaction or good, even if this means that some individuals' ability to have good lives—in utilitarian terms—will be seriously compromised, and even though there is no sentient being who experiences the aggregate satisfaction or whose good is identified with that aggregate. In this sense, classical utilitarianism gives what it regards as the aggregate good priority over what it regards as the goods of distinct individuals. For Rawls,

---

[17] *Anarchy, State, and Utopia*, 228.
[18] *Liberalism and the Limits of Justice* (Cambridge University Press, 1982), 78.
[19] *Liberalism and the Limits of Justice*, 79.
[20] *Liberalism and the Limits of Justice*, 80.

by contrast, the good life for an individual consists in the successful execution of a rational plan of life, and his principles of justice direct us to arrange social institutions in such a way as to protect the capacity of each individual to lead such a life. The idea that the distribution of natural talents should be regarded as a common asset is not the idea of an aggregate good that takes precedence over the goods of individual human beings. Instead, the thought is that a system that treats the distribution of talents as a collective asset under the terms of the difference principle, is actually required if each person is to have a chance of leading a good life. In short, utilitarianism gives the aggregative good precedence over the goods of distinct individuals whereas Rawls's principles do not. In this sense, utilitarianism takes the distinctions among persons less seriously than his principles do. Since there is, accordingly, no inconsistency between Rawls's principles and his criticism of utilitarianism, there is no need for him to take drastic metaphysical measures to avoid it.[21]

Nevertheless, there are some genuine commonalities between Rawls's conception of justice and utilitarianism, and these commonalities may be partly responsible for the perception that there is a tension between his endorsement of the former and his criticism of the latter. I want to call attention to three of these commonalities. The first, which I have already mentioned, is Rawls's aspiration to produce a theory that shares utilitarianism's 'systematic' and 'constructive' character. The second is his agreement with the utilitarian view that common-sense precepts of justice have only a 'derivative' (TJ 307) status and must be viewed as 'subordinate' (TJ 307) to a 'higher criterion'

---

[21] There has been extensive discussion and disagreement both about the meaning and about the merits of Rawls's claim that utilitarianism does not take seriously the distinctions among persons. This is partly because Rawls's formulation has appeared to some readers to straddle two or more of the following claims: 1) *a claim of metaphysical error*, to the effect that utilitarianism simply fails to notice that persons are ontologically distinct, 2) *a claim of moral error*, to the effect that utilitarianism tolerates unacceptable interpersonal trade-offs, and thereby fails to attach sufficient moral significance to the ontological distinctions among persons, and 3) *an explanatory claim*, to the effect that utilitarianism fails to attach sufficient moral significance to the ontological distinctions among persons because it extends to society as a whole the principle of choice for one person. For pertinent discussion, see Derek Parfit, *Reasons and Persons* (Oxford: Clarendon Press, 1984), Ch. 15; James Griffin, *Well-Being* (Oxford: Clarendon Press, 1986), 167–70; H. L. A. Hart, 'Between Utility and Rights', in *The Idea of Freedom: Essays in Honour of Isaiah Berlin*, ed. Alan Ryan (Oxford University Press, 1979), 77–98; Leslie Mulholland, 'Rights, Utilitarianism, and the Conflation of Persons', *Journal of Philosophy* 83 (1986): 323–40; Will Kymlicka, 'Rawls on Teleology and Deontology', *Philosophy & Public Affairs* 17 (1988): 173–90; Samuel Freeman, 'Utilitarianism, Deontology, and the Priority of Right'; Joseph Raz, *The Morality of Freedom* (Oxford: Clarendon Press, 1986), 271–3. I believe that Rawls is not making the first of these claims, that he is making the second, and that he is also putting forward the third as at least a partial explanation. The question posed by Nozick and Sandel, as I understand it, is whether Rawls's own principles attach any more moral weight to the distinctions among persons than does utilitarianism. My argument in the text is that they do indeed, and that their ability to do so is not conditional on Rawls's conceiving of the self either as 'unencumbered' or as 'intersubjective'.

(TJ 305). And the third is the fact that both the Rawlsian and the utilitarian accounts of distributive justice are, in a sense to be explained, holistic in character. These three points of agreement, taken together, have implications that are rather far-reaching. They help to explain why it can be tempting to think that Rawls's principles display the very faults for which he criticizes utilitarianism. And although, as I have argued, this temptation should be resisted, they help us to see that Rawls does share with utilitarianism some features that are genuinely controversial and are bound to generate some strong resistance to both views.

Rawls's desire to provide a 'constructive' conception of justice is part of his desire to avoid intuitionism. Intuitionism, as Rawls understands it, holds that there are a plurality of first principles of justice which may conflict on particular occasions. Intuitionists do not believe that there are any priority rules that can enable us to resolve such conflicts; instead, we have no choice but to rely on our intuitive judgment to strike an appropriate balance in each case. In this sense, intuitionists deny that it is possible to give a general solution to what Rawls calls 'the priority problem', that is, the problem of how to assign weight to conflicting considerations of justice. But 'the assignment of weights is an essential and not a minor part of a conception of justice', for if two people differ about the weight to be assigned to different principles 'then their conceptions of justice are different' (TJ 41). In effect, then, an intuitionist conception of justice is 'but half a conception' (TJ 41). Rawls's aim, by contrast, is to reduce our reliance on unguided intuition by formulating 'explicit principles for the priority problem' (TJ 41), that is, by identifying 'constructive' and 'recognizably ethical' (TJ 39) criteria for assigning weight to competing precepts of justice. Utilitarianism, of course, achieves this aim by identifying a single principle as the ultimate standard for adjudicating among conflicting precepts. Rawls hopes to show that it is possible for a theory to be constructive without relying on the utilitarian principle, or, indeed, on any *single* principle, as the ultimate standard. Thus he hopes to produce a solution to the priority problem that offers an alternative to the utilitarian solution but remains a constructive solution nonetheless.

The fact that Rawls agrees with utilitarianism about the desirability of identifying a clear and constructive solution to the priority problem leads more or less directly to the second point of agreement. Both views hold that common-sense precepts of justice must be subordinate to some 'higher' principle or principles. For these precepts conflict and, at the level of common sense, no reconciliation is possible, since there is no determinate way of weighing them against each other. Thus, if we are to find a constructive solution to the priority problem, we must have recourse to a 'higher principle' to adjudicate these conflicts. In theory, one or more of the common-sense precepts could themselves be 'elevated' (TJ 305) to this status, but Rawls does not believe that they are plausible candidates. 'Adopting one of them as a first principle is sure to lead to the neglect of other things that should be taken into account.

And if all or many precepts are treated as first principles, there is no gain in systematic clarity. Common sense precepts are at the wrong level of generality' (TJ 308). Of course, utilitarians believe that the principle of utility provides the requisite higher standard, whereas Rawls believes that his two principles are 'the correct higher criterion' (TJ 305). But they agree on the need for such a criterion and on the derivative and subordinate character of common-sense precepts of justice.

To illuminate the third point of agreement, we may begin by noting that Rawls calls attention to, and has considerable sympathy with, the broad institutional emphasis that is characteristic of the great writers of the utilitarian tradition. In his early essay 'Two Concepts of Rules', for example, he writes: 'It is important to remember that those whom I have called the classical utilitarians were largely interested in social institutions. They were among the leading economists and political theorists of their day, and they were not infrequently reformers interested in practical affairs.'[22] In the Preface to *A Theory of Justice*, similarly, he deplores our tendency to 'forget that the great utilitarians, Hume and Adam Smith, Bentham and Mill, were social theorists and economists of the first rank; and the moral doctrine they worked out was framed to meet the needs of their wider interests and to fit into a comprehensive scheme' (TJ vii). In Rawls's own theory, of course, institutions are made the central focus from the outset, since the basic structure of society, which comprises its major institutions, is treated as the first subject of justice.[23] This in turn leads to the idea of treating the issue of distributive shares as a matter of pure procedural justice (TJ 84–5): provided the basic structure is just, any distribution of goods that results is also just.[24] Once the problem of distributive justice is understood in this way, the principles of justice can no longer be applied to individual transactions considered in isolation (TJ 87–8). Nor can the justice of an overall allocation of goods be assessed independently of the institutions that produced it. As Rawls says: 'A distribution

[22] *Philosophical Review* 64 (1955) 3–32, at 19n.

[23] Rawls gives his most extended defence of his emphasis on the basic structure in 'The Basic Structure as Subject', which is included in PL as Lecture VII. For criticism of this emphasis, see G. A. Cohen, 'Where the Action Is: On the Site of Distributive Justice', *Philosophy & Public Affairs* 26 (1997): 3–30; Liam Murphy, 'Institutions and the Demands of Justice', *Philosophy & Public Affairs* 27 (1998): 251–91; Nozick, *Anarchy, State, and Utopia*, 204–13. For discussion of the distinctiveness of Rawls's focus on the basic structure, see Hugo Bedau, 'Social Justice and Social Institutions', *Midwest Studies in Philosophy* 3 (1978): 159–75.

[24] The proviso is essential. Only if the basic structure is regulated by Rawls's substantive conception of justice can the determination of individual shares be handled as a matter of pure procedural justice. Thus, Rawls's reliance on pure procedural justice does not mean that his theory is procedural *rather than substantive*. This is a point that he emphasizes in response to Habermas (PL 421–33), and it explains what he means when he says in the index to PL (455) that 'justice is always substantive and never purely procedural'—a remark that might otherwise seem inconsistent with the role that *Theory* assigns to 'pure procedural justice'. For relevant discussion, see Joshua Cohen, 'Pluralism and Proceduralism', *Chicago-Kent Law Review* 69 (1994): 589–618, especially fn. 44.

cannot be judged in isolation from the system of which it is the outcome or from what individuals have done in good faith in the light of established expectations. If it is asked in the abstract whether one distribution of a given stock of things to definite individuals with known desires and preferences is better than another, then there is simply no answer to this question. The conception of the two principles does not interpret the primary problem of distributive justice as one of allocative justice' (TJ 88–9).

As Rawls emphasizes, utilitarianism does not share his view that 'special first principles are required for the basic structure' (PL 262), notwithstanding its broad institutional emphasis, nor does it agree that the question of distributive shares should be treated as a matter of pure procedural justice (TJ 88–9). These are important differences between the two theories. The principle of utility, as it has come to be interpreted at least, is a comprehensive standard that is used to assess actions, institutions, and the distribution of resources within a society.[25] Rawls's concentration on the basic structure and his use of pure procedural justice to assess distributions give his theory a greater institutional focus. Yet these differences, important as they are, should not be allowed to obscure an important point of agreement, namely, that neither view is willing to assess the justice or injustice of a particular assignment of benefits in isolation from the larger distributional context. In other words, neither believes that the principles of justice can appropriately be applied to 'a single transaction viewed in isolation' (TJ 87). The justice or injustice of assigning a particular benefit to a given individual will depend, for utilitarians, on whether there is any other way of allocating it that would lead to an overall distribution with greater (total or average) utility. It will depend, for Rawls, on whether the assignment is part of an overall distribution that is produced by a basic structure conforming to his two principles. In this sense, both Rawls and the utilitarian take a *holistic* view of distributive justice: both insist that the justice of any particular assignment of benefits always depends—directly or indirectly—on the justice of the larger distribution of benefits and burdens in society.

Holism about distributive justice draws support from two convictions. The first is that all people's lives are of equal value and importance. The second is that the life prospects of individuals are so densely and variously interrelated, especially through their shared participation in social institutions and practices, that virtually any allocation of resources to one person has morally relevant implications for other people. Holists conclude that it is impossible

[25] Part of Rawls's point, when calling attention in 'Two Concepts of Rules' to the interest of the classical utilitarians in social institutions, was to emphasize that the construal of utilitarianism as supplying a comprehensive standard of appraisal represents a relatively recent development of the view: one he associates, in that essay, with Moore. In his later work, however, it is the comprehensive version of utilitarianism that he himself treats as standard, and with which he contrasts his own institutional approach to justice. See, for example, section 2 of 'The Basic Structure as Subject', where he associates the comprehensive interpretation with Sidgwick (PL 260–2).

to assess the justice of an assignment of benefits to any single individual without taking into account the larger distributive context of that assignment. In conditions of moderate scarcity, we cannot tell whether a particular person should receive a given benefit without knowing how such an allocation would fit into the broader distribution of benefits and burdens within the society. Nor, to those who find holism compelling, does the project of identifying a putatively natural, pre-social baseline distribution of advantages, and assessing the justice of all subsequent distributions solely by reference to the legitimacy of each move away from the baseline, seem either conceptually sound or ethically appropriate. Social institutions structure people's lives in fundamental ways from birth to death; there is no pre-social moment in the life of the individual. That being the case, it is not clear what could reasonably count as the 'natural' baseline or what the ethical credentials of any such baseline might plausibly be thought to be.[26] Moreover, as the size of the human population keeps growing, as the scale and complexity of modern institutions and economies keep increasing, and as an ever more sophisticated technological and communications infrastructure keeps expanding the possibilities of human interaction, the obstacles in the way of a satisfactory account of the pre-social baseline loom larger, and the pressure to take a holistic view of distributive justice grows greater.[27] In their different ways, the Rawlsian and utilitarian accounts of justice are both responsive to this pressure.[28]

Although the case for holism has considerable force, and many of our intuitions about distributive justice are indeed holistic, there are other, non-holistic ideas about justice that also have widespread intuitive support. Often, for example, we seem prepared to say that an individual deserves or has a right to some benefit, and that it is therefore just that he should get it, without inquiring into the larger distributional context. Indeed, according to one familiar and traditional view, justice consists, at least in part, in giving people what they may independently be said to deserve. In other words, there is a prior standard of desert by reference to which the justice of individual actions and institutional arrangements is to be assessed. The basis for

---

[26] See Thomas Nagel, *Equality and Partiality* (Oxford University Press, 1991), 100–2.
[27] I have discussed some related themes in 'Individual Responsibility in a Global Age', Chapter Two in this volume.
[28] For related discussion, see Thomas Pogge, 'Three Problems with Contractarian-Consequentialist Ways of Assessing Social Institutions', *Social Philosophy and Policy* 12 (1995): 241–66. Pogge writes that, in recent decades, there has been a shift from thinking about justice 'interactionally' to thinking about it 'institutionally'. By this he means that there is less emphasis on individual actions and their consequences and more emphasis on the ground rules and practices that structure our social world and supply the framework for our actions. Pogge argues that contractarianism, as exemplified by Rawls's work, and consequentialism are 'the two most prominent traditions of institutional moral analysis' and that they 'are not as distinct as is widely believed'. Indeed, he argues that, when viewed 'as guides to the assessment of social institutions, contractarianism and consequentialism are for the most part not competitors but alternate presentations of a single idea: both tend to assess alternative institutional schemes exclusively by how each would affect its individual human participants' (246).

a valid desert claim, on this view, must always be some characteristic of or fact about the deserving person. In this sense, desert as traditionally understood is *individualistic* rather then holistic. No assessment of the overall distribution of benefits and burdens in society or of the institutions that produced that distribution is normally required in order to decide whether a particular individual deserves a certain benefit. Instead, it is a constraint on the justice of distributions and institutions that they should give each individual what that individual independently deserves in virtue of the relevant facts about him or her.

As I have argued elsewhere, neither Rawls nor the utilitarian thinks about distributive justice in this way.[29] For them, the principles of distributive justice, holistically understood, are fixed without reference to any prior notion of desert, and individuals may then be said to deserve the benefits to which they are entitled according to the criteria established by just institutions. This does not mean that just institutions must give people what they independently deserve, but rather that, if just institutions have announced that they will allocate rewards in accordance with certain standards, then individuals who meet those standards can be said to deserve the advertised rewards.

In summary, then, Rawls agrees with utilitarianism about the desirability of providing a systematic account of justice that reduces the scope for intuitionistic balancing and offers a clear and constructive solution to the priority problem; about the need to subordinate common-sense precepts of justice to a higher criterion; and about the holistic character of distributive justice. Taken together, these three features of his view mean that, like the utilitarian, he is prepared to appeal to higher principle, without recourse to intuitionistic balancing, to provide a systematic justification for interpersonal trade-offs that may violate common-sense maxims of justice. In light of this aspect of Rawls's theory, the temptation to claim that he attaches no more weight than utilitarianism does to the distinctions among persons, is understandable. Although I have argued that this temptation should be resisted, it seems fair to say that the Rawlsian and utilitarian approaches to justice have some important elements in common and that these elements run counter to one deeply entrenched tendency in our moral thought.

Within contemporary political philosophy, this tendency receives what is perhaps its most forceful expression in Nozick's work, and it is noteworthy that a resistance to distributive holism appears to be part of what lies behind his objection to 'end-result principles'.[30] These principles are said to assess the justice of a given distribution or sequence of distributions, solely by seeing whether the associated distributional matrix satisfies some structural criterion, rather than by taking into account historical information about how the distribution came to pass. Significantly, Nozick classifies both the

---

[29] See 'Responsibility, Reactive Attitudes, and Liberalism in Philosophy and Politics', Chapter One in this volume.
[30] *Anarchy, State, and Utopia*, 153–5.

utilitarian and the Rawlsian principles of justice as end-result principles. (Indeed, he claims that the design of the original position guarantees that only end-result principles will be chosen.) As applied to Rawls, this characterization does not seem right, given the lexical priority of his first principle over his second principle and the fact that he treats the question of distributive shares as a matter of pure procedural justice. It is Rawls, after all, who says that a 'distribution cannot be judged in isolation from the system of which it is the outcome or from what individuals have done in good faith in the light of established expectations', and who insists that 'there is simply no answer' to the abstract question of whether one distribution is better than another. Yet both the Rawlsian and the utilitarian accounts are indeed holistic, and this may be part of what Nozick finds objectionable about them. For at least part of his complaint is that they exaggerate the significance of the overall distributional context and attach insufficient importance to local features of particular transactions.

This complaint connects up with a more general source of resistance to holism, which derives from a conviction that its effect is to validate a deplorable tendency for the lives of modern individuals to be subsumed within massive bureaucratic structures and for their interests to be subordinated to the demands of larger social aggregates and to the brute power of impersonal forces they cannot control. To accept a holistic account of justice, on this view, is to acquiesce in an erosion of the status of the individual which is one of the most striking features of modern life. Indeed, for some people, this is why Rawls's complaint that utilitarianism does not take seriously the separateness of persons has such resonance. It is ironic, therefore, that the author of that complaint not only is not opposed to holism about distributive justice but in fact is one of its strongest advocates. Nevertheless, once we recognize that, for some people, the words in which Rawls articulates his criticism may serve as a way of expressing resistance to holism, it is understandable why some who have echoed those words have not followed Rawls in seeking to devise a constructive and systematic alternative to utilitarianism. For them, constructiveness, systematicity, and holism may all be symptomatic of a failure to attach sufficient moral importance to the separateness of persons. If so, however, then their ultimate concern is not the same as his, even if it can be expressed in the same words.

This is not to say that their concern is insignificant. Some people understandably abhor many of the tendencies in modern life that create pressure to think holistically about distributive justice, and believe that our moral thought, rather than seeking to accommodate those tendencies, should serve as a source of resistance to them. Whatever the merits of this view, however, it is not one that Rawls shares. On this issue, he and the utilitarian are on the same side. Rawls's objection to utilitarianism is not to its holism but rather to the particular criterion it uses for assessing the legitimacy of interpersonal trade-offs. His own theory of justice, one might say, aims not to resist the pressures toward holism but rather to tame or domesticate them: to provide a fair and humane way for a liberal, democratic society to accommodate those pressures while preserving its basic values and maintaining its commitment to the inviolability of the individual. This is something he believes that utilitarianism can never do, despite the liberal credentials of its greatest advocates. Some people may think that holism itself undermines liberal values, so that Rawls's aim is in principle unattainable. These people will inevitably conclude that his criticisms of utilitarianism do not go far enough, and that his own theory exhibits some of the same faults that they see in the utilitarian view. But, once again, these are not the same faults that *he* sees in utilitarianism, whether or not they can be expressed in the same words.

The fact that Rawls's attitude toward utilitarianism is marked not only by sharp disagreements but also by important areas of affinity may help to explain some otherwise puzzling things he says about the view in *Political Liberalism*. In that book, of course, Rawls's aims are different from his aims in *A Theory of Justice*. His primary goal is no longer to develop his two principles as an alternative to utilitarianism, but rather to explain how a just and stable liberal society can be established and sustained in circumstances marked by reasonable disagreement about fundamental moral and philosophical matters. Given his focus on this new task, utilitarianism is relegated largely to the periphery of his concern. One of the few times he has anything substantial to say about it is when he includes classical utilitarianism—'the utilitarianism of Bentham and Sidgwick, the strict classical doctrine' (PL 170)—among the views that might participate in an overlapping consensus converging on a liberal political conception of justice, the 'standard example' (PL 164) of which is justice-as-fairness. The possibility of such a consensus lies at the heart of his answer to the question of how a just and stable liberal society is possible in conditions of reasonable pluralism.

On the face of it, however, the suggestion that classical utilitarianism might participate in a consensus of this kind is startling. Rawls seems to be proposing that the putatively less plausible of the two versions of the very theory which, in *A Theory of Justice*, he had treated as his primary target of criticism, and as the primary rival for his own principles of justice, might actually join in an overlapping consensus affirming those principles. As I have argued elsewhere, it is very difficult to see how this might work.[31] For one thing, the participants in the consensus he describes are envisioned as converging not merely on the principles that constitute a political conception of justice, but also on certain fundamental ideas that are implicit in the public political culture and from which those principles are said to be derivable. The most important of these ideas is the idea of society as a fair system of co-operation. Yet Rawls had said quite explicitly in *A Theory of Justice* that classical utilitarianism does not accept that idea (TJ 33). Furthermore, the argument from the

---

[31] See 'The Appeal of Political Liberalism', Chapter Eight in this volume.

fundamental ideas to the political conception is envisioned in *Political Liberalism* as proceeding via the original position, which is said to model the relevant ideas (PL Lecture I.4). However, we know that the parties in the original position decisively reject classical utilitarianism. It is, therefore, doubly unclear how classical utilitarianism could participate in the overlapping consensus Rawls envisions; for it rejects the fundamental ideas that form the basis of the consensus, and the arguments that begin from those ideas are said to result in its own repudiation.

To be sure, Rawls does not claim that the political conception is deductively derivable from classical utilitarianism, only that the classical view might support the political conception 'as a satisfactory and perhaps the best workable approximation [to what the principle of utility would on balance require] given normal social conditions' (PL 171). Yet, as noted above, Rawls explicitly states that an overlapping consensus is 'deep' enough to include such fundamental ideas as the idea of society as a fair system of co-operation (PL 149, 158–60, 164–6), and the suggestion that classical utilitarianism might support the political conception as a 'workable approximation' does not explain what attitude the utilitarian is now supposed to have toward that idea.[32]

If this is correct, then it remains difficult to see how classical utilitarianism could be included in an overlapping consensus. Yet Rawls's willingness to treat it as a candidate for inclusion, which initially seemed startling, may appear more understandable if one keeps in mind the complexity of his attitude toward utilitarianism in *Theory*. I have argued throughout this essay that his undoubted opposition to utilitarianism, and his determination to provide an alternative to it, should not be allowed to obscure some important points of agreement. Perhaps one might even say that it is precisely because he agrees with utilitarianism about so much that Rawls is determined to provide an alternative that improves upon it in the respects in which it is deficient. While there would be no need to provide a better theory if utilitarianism did not have serious faults, the effort would hardly be worth making if it did not also have important virtues. Utilitarianism, in Rawls's view, has been the dominant systematic moral theory in the modern liberal tradition. If he did not himself agree that we need a need a clear, systematic theory to reduce our reliance on unguided intuition and provide an adequate basis for liberal, democratic institutions, he would not be so concerned to emphasize utilitarianism's deficiencies or to produce a theory that remedies those deficiencies while preserving the view's virtues.

---

[32] This is the flaw in Brian Barry's response to my earlier discussion (in 'The Appeal of Political Liberalism') of utilitarian participation in an overlapping consensus. In 'John Rawls and the Search for Stability', *Ethics* 105 (1995): 874–915, Barry argues (at 914–5n.) that, because Rawls does not hold that the political conception must be deductively derivable from within each comprehensive doctrine represented in an overlapping consensus, he should not be thought to require that the participants in such a consensus endorse anything more than the principles of justice themselves. However, this overlooks Rawls' repeated remarks about the depth of an overlapping consensus.

Up to a point, then, Rawls and the utilitarian are engaged in a common enterprise, and it is against the background of what they have in common that Rawls takes utilitarianism as his primary target of criticism in *Theory*. In *Political Liberalism*, the context of discussion has shifted. The aim now is to show how liberal institutions can achieve stability in conditions of pluralism by drawing on diverse sources of moral support. In this context, utilitarianism, with its prominent place in the traditions of liberal thought and its various more specific affinities with Rawls's own view, presents itself as a natural ally. There is still a problem, of course, given his insistence in *Theory* that neither classical nor average utilitarianism can put fundamental liberal values on a sufficiently secure footing. And the problem becomes more acute, for the reasons given above, when the overlapping consensus is conceived of as affirming not merely liberal principles in general but Rawls's theory of justice in particular. Nevertheless, the impulse to treat some form of utilitarianism as a candidate for inclusion in the consensus, when considered in the context of Rawls's aims in *Political Liberalism* and his sympathy for certain aspects of the utilitarian doctrine, no longer seems mysterious.[33] Whether or not the tensions between that impulse and his forceful objections to utilitarianism can be satisfactorily resolved, they provide a salutary reminder of the complexity of Rawls's attitude toward modern moral philosophy's 'predominant systematic theory'. At the same time, it is a measure of Rawls's achievement that utilitarianism's predominant status has been open to serious question ever since *A Theory of Justice* set forth his powerful alternative vision.

[33] It is worth noting that, in his earlier paper 'The Idea of an Overlapping Consensus' (*Oxford Journal of Legal Studies* 7 [1987]: 1–26), Rawls himself had denied (12) that the utilitarianism of Bentham and Sidgwick could belong to an overlapping consensus, but he had suggested that perhaps some form of 'indirect utilitarianism' might be able to do so. The latter suggestion seems more plausible, although still not entirely unproblematic.

10

Justice and Desert in Liberal Theory*

Introduction

Contemporary liberal theory appears to attach relatively little importance to the concept of desert. John Rawls's *A Theory of Justice*[1] is exemplary in this respect. Rawls explicitly argues that desert has only a derivative role to play in an adequate account of distributive justice, and he is frequently interpreted as advocating a purely institutional theory of desert, according to which people's deserts are in general to be identified with their legitimate institutional expectations. If a just institution has announced that it will attach rewards or penalties to behaviour of a certain kind, then according to a purely institutional theory, people who engage in such behaviour may be said to deserve the rewards or penalties in question. But claims of desert are always dependent in this way on a prior conception of justice and on the expectations actually established by just institutions. There is no independent principle of desert that provides a normative standard for the design of social institutions themselves. There is, according to a purely institutional theory, no legitimate form of 'preinstitutional desert'.

Although Rawls certainly insists on the derivative role of desert in relation to distributive justice, the ascription to him of a general theory of desert of the kind just described is difficult to reconcile with his stated views about the purposes of the criminal law, and with his explicit suggestion that desert has a more substantial role to play in relation to retributive justice. Indeed, even where distributive justice is concerned, I believe that it is misleading to describe Rawls as defending a purely institutional account. Yet the tendency of many readers to discount or downplay Rawls's remarks about the differences between distributive and retributive justice does not result from simple misreading. Instead, Rawls himself seems to encourage this tendency, for he makes statements about the relation between desert and distributive justice

* Originally published in the *California Law Review* 88 (2000): 965–90. Copyright © California Law Review, Inc. Reprinted by permission.
[1] John Rawls, *A Theory of Justice* (1971).

that seem generalizable to the case of retributive justice as well. In other words, the logic of Rawls's argument threatens to carry him beyond the position that he explicitly advocates. Thus, if he is taken to endorse a purely institutional view of desert in the context of distributive justice, the apparent generalizability of his argument from the distributive to the retributive case makes it easy to construe him as committed to a general theory according to which desert is always to be identified with legitimate institutional expectations.[2] Since such a theory appears to represent a radically revisionist position, which clashes sharply with our ordinary understanding of desert, this in turn contributes to the widespread perception that egalitarian liberals like Rawls are committed to wholesale scepticism about the moral importance of desert.[3]

---

[2] Indeed, I interpreted him in much this way in 'Responsibility, Reactive Attitudes, and Liberalism in Philosophy and Politics', Chapter One in this volume.

[3] There are many writers who ascribe this kind of scepticism to Rawls. For example, Michael Sandel says it is Rawls's view that, 'strictly speaking, no one can be said to deserve anything'. Michael J. Sandel, *Liberalism and the Limits of Justice* (1982), 88. George Sher interprets Rawls as arguing 'that nobody (pre-institutionally) deserves anything'. George Sher, *Desert* (1987), 20. And Alan Zaitchik finds in Rawls 'a completely general argument which alleges that *no* desert theory could be true for the simple reason that no one ever deserves anything'. Alan Zaitchik, 'On Deserving to Deserve', *Philosophy & Public Affairs* 6 (1977): 370–88, at 371. In 'Responsibility, Reactive Attitudes, and Liberalism in Philosophy and Politics' I argued that the influence of naturalism is at least partly responsible for the reluctance of many contemporary liberal theorists (and their critics) to rely on a robust notion of desert. Without wishing altogether to repudiate this diagnosis—I still think it constitutes one factor among others—I will attempt in this essay to identify a more positive rationale for liberal scepticism about distributive desert in particular.

One question that I cannot adequately deal with here concerns the role of desert in what Elizabeth Anderson calls 'luck egalitarianism', by which she means the view that 'the fundamental aim of equality is to compensate people for undeserved bad luck'. Elizabeth S. Anderson, 'What Is the Point of Equality?', *Ethics* 109 (1999): 287–337, at 288. Luck egalitarianism may appear to represent an exception to the general tendency within contemporary liberalism to treat desert as having relatively little importance. Yet, for the most part, the writers Anderson has in mind do not explicitly assign a central role to desert. Their main thesis is that material inequalities resulting from people's choices are acceptable whereas those resulting from unchosen circumstances are not. Some of these writers do at times express the negative part of this point by saying that people should be compensated for undeserved bad fortune, a formulation which is meant to pre-empt conservative objections to egalitarian redistribution by appealing to the truism that people do not deserve, for example, the circumstances of their birth. In this they follow Rawls's own discussion. Like Rawls himself, however, and *pace* Anderson's suggestion at 288–9, such writers generally avoid the positive claim that people *deserve* the good or bad outcomes that result from their choices. What they tend to say instead is that it is reasonable to hold people responsible for those outcomes. Of course, one might argue, in criticism of this position, that it makes sense to place such weight on the distinction between choices and circumstances only if one is tacitly assuming that people *do* deserve the outcomes of their choices. This would imply that luck egalitarianism is committed to assigning a more fundamental role to desert than its proponents acknowledge. The writings by liberal theorists that Anderson cites as examples of luck egalitarianism include Thomas Nagel, *Equality and Partiality* (1991); Eric Rakowski, *Equal Justice* (1991); and Ronald Dworkin, 'What is Equality? Part 2: Equality of Resources', *Philosophy & Public Affairs* 10 (1981): 283–345.

These considerations help to explain why Rawls's treatment of desert has been so controversial. They also suggest that, if liberal theories of justice are to be persuasive, both the sources and the extent of liberal scepticism about desert need to be better understood. In this essay, I want to re-examine the idea that desert plays a different role in relation to retributive justice than it does in relation to distributive justice. This is Rawls's stated position, and it comports with a very natural interpretation of the difference between the criminal law and the other parts of a legal system. Such an interpretation has been eloquently defended, for example, by Sanford Kadish, whose writings combine an unwavering opposition to attempts to purge the criminal law of notions of culpability and blameworthiness with a measured scepticism about the use of the criminal sanction to serve the purposes of broader social and economic policy.[4] Ultimately, I believe that there may be deep moral and philosophical motivations for seeking to de-emphasize desert in relation to distributive justice while retaining it as an element of our thinking about a variety of other topics, including retributive justice and the function of the criminal law. The question raised by the controversy about Rawls's treatment of desert is whether the reasons that generate liberal scepticism about the concept's distributive relevance can, in the end, be confined to the distributive context, or whether they must inevitably generalize to other areas as well.

I will proceed as follows. In Part I, I will discuss Joel Feinberg's influential essay 'Justice and Personal Desert',[5] whose publication preceded by eight years the appearance of Rawls's *A Theory of Justice*, and on which Rawls relies at several points in his discussion. Drawing on Feinberg's essay, I will explain in Part II why purely institutional theories of desert appear radically revisionary of our ordinary beliefs and why they have seemed objectionable to many people. In Part III, I will review Rawls's own treatment of desert, including his account of the differences between the role of desert in distributive justice and its role in retributive justice. I will explain why, even in the distributive case, it seems to me misleading to describe Rawls as defending a purely institutional theory. I will also outline an alternative theory, which I call the Liberal Theory, that seems to me to capture Rawls's most important claims while avoiding some of the major objections to institutional accounts. In Part IV, I will explain why, notwithstanding his explicit claims about the asymmetry between distributive and retributive justice, Rawls's view of distributive desert has appeared to be generalizable to the retributive case as well. In Part V, I will suggest a rationale for the view that desert has a less fundamental role to play in distributive justice than it does in retributive justice and, in Part VI, I will reconsider the supposed generalizability of Rawls's

---

[4] See Sanford H. Kadish, *Blame and Punishment: Essays in the Criminal Law* (1987). This essay was originally written for a conference honouring Professor Kadish.

[5] Joel Feinberg, 'Justice and Personal Desert', reprinted in *Doing and Deserving* (Joel Feinberg ed., 1970), 55–94.

conception of desert in light of this rationale. Finally, I will summarize my conclusions and take stock of their significance.

I. Feinberg on Justice and Desert

Feinberg's discussion is limited to cases of personal desert and, more specifically, to cases in which what a person deserves is some sort of treatment by others. The judgment that a person deserves something, Feinberg says, implies that there is something about the person in virtue of which he or she deserves that thing. This Feinberg refers to as the 'desert basis'.[6] The desert basis, he says, must be some characteristic of, or fact about, the deserving person, and different kinds of deserved treatment have different desert bases. Feinberg argues that there are five major classes of deserved treatment: awards of prizes; assignments of grades; rewards and punishments; praise, blame, and other informal responses; and reparation, liability, and other modes of compensation.[7] He does not include either positions of honour or economic benefits on this list, because he believes that they are ordinarily subsumed under one or more of the other five categories.

Feinberg argues that desert functions as a 'polar' concept with respect to some of these categories and as a 'nonpolar' concept with respect to others.[8] When it functions as a polar concept, one can either deserve good or deserve ill. When it functions as a non-polar concept, one can instead either deserve something or not deserve it. Prizes are said to exemplify non-polar desert. In a game or contest, the winner deserves the prize and the other contestants do not, but there is no further bad thing that the others deserve. There is no negative analogue of the prize. By contrast, rewards and punishment exemplify polar desert, since to deserve punishment is indeed to deserve ill. Rewards, Feinberg says, are conventional means of expressing such attitudes as gratitude, appreciation, and recognition of merit; punishments are conventional means of expressing resentment, disapproval, and condemnation. Feinberg refers to the attitudes thus expressed as 'responsive attitudes'.[9] He says that these attitudes 'have ostensible desert logically built in to them',[10] by which he means that they must always be experienced as a response to some desert basis—that is, as a response to something about the person who is their object. Thus, he writes, 'resentment without an ostensible desert basis is not resentment'.[11]

One of the main themes of Feinberg's essay is the difference between desert and institutional qualification or entitlement. In general, to qualify for something is to satisfy the relevant institutional rules governing its distribution. In order to deserve something, however, one must be worthy of it. Thus 'desert',

---

[6] Id. 58.   [7] See id. 62.   [8] Id.
[9] Id. 70.   [10] Id. 70–1.   [11] Id. 71.

Feinberg says, 'is a *moral* concept in the sense that it is logically prior to and independent of public institutions and their rules'.[12] Or as he says at another point, 'desert is a "natural" moral notion (that is, one which is not logically tied to institutions, practices, and rules)'.[13] The distinction between desert and qualification shows up in most of Feinberg's five categories. With respect to prizes, for example, the rules of a competitive game or contest typically specify certain 'victory conditions',[14] and the person or team that satisfies those conditions qualifies for and is entitled to the relevant prize. By contrast, the desert basis of a competitive contest 'is always preeminent possession of the skill singled out as a basis of competition'.[15] So the person who is victorious is not necessarily the person who deserves to win: 'In a contest of skill the man who deserves to win is the man who is most skilled, but (because of luck) he is not in every case the man who does win.'[16]

Despite these differences between desert and entitlement, Feinberg suggests that they may be related in the following way.[17] The basic things people deserve, he says, are the responsive attitudes that are appropriate to their conduct. However, in many cases we have established institutional mechanisms for acknowledging and expressing those attitudes. The institutions in question set forth qualifying conditions that people must satisfy in order to receive the 'modes of treatment'[18] that those institutions dispense. The content of the qualifying conditions is shaped by the aim of distributing the relevant modes of treatment in accordance with the appropriate desert bases, so far as possible. In other words, the institutional rules and procedures are set up with the aim of giving people what they deserve. Nevertheless, qualification and desert remain distinct notions that inevitably diverge in some cases. However, a well-designed institution may, on the whole, do a better job of giving people what they deserve than would a generalized practice of expressing all responsive attitudes in an *ad hoc*, non-institutionalized manner. Our actual practice does have this informal character in the case of praise and blame, which have no institutional qualifying conditions. Feinberg argues, however, that reliance on institutions to give public and conventional expression to various responsive attitudes may, in general, be a more dependable way of seeing that people get what they deserve.

A related theme that Feinberg emphasizes is the heterogeneity of desert and the variety of forms that conflicts of justice can take.[19] Desert is not a monolithic factor that, by itself, determines what is just. Claims of desert can conflict with each other and with considerations of institutional entitlement, and these are conflicts within the category of justice. So although one of the proper aims of institutions is to give people what they deserve, justice will sometimes require that people get what they are entitled to rather than what they deserve. Justice may be better served by adhering to a system of institutional entitlement even in cases where desert and entitlement conflict, than it would

---

[12] Id. 87.   [13] Id. 56.   [14] Id. 63.   [15] Id. 64.
[16] Id.   [17] See id. 82–5.   [18] Id. 82.   [19] See id. 79–80.

be by directing those who administer the relevant institutions to assign benefits and burdens on a case-by-case basis in accordance with perceived desert.

One final aspect of Feinberg's essay that is relevant for our purposes is his discussion of the relation between desert and economic income.[20] Here he provides what is, in effect, an argument about the bearing of desert on questions of distributive justice. Feinberg acknowledges that people often say such things as 'doctors are paid more than they deserve' or 'teachers are paid less than they deserve'. He thinks that there are various ways of interpreting such claims, none of which is wholly satisfactory. A large income cannot plausibly be construed as a prize in a competitive contest because there is no unique desert basis of the alleged competition. Construing extra income as a reward rather than a prize is more plausible, but then there is the question of what exactly is being rewarded. Possibilities include moral virtue, talent or ability, and contributions to economic welfare or the quality of life. However, Feinberg sees difficulties with all of these suggestions. In the end, he argues that economic income can plausibly be said to be deserved only in so far as it can be construed as compensation. Thus, those who have unusually hazardous or onerous jobs may deserve compensation in the form of extra income. In such cases, he argues, desert plays an egalitarian role, for the function of the deserved compensation is to restore an equality of net benefit. In fact, Feinberg claims, from the fact that income is deserved only in so far as it is compensation, it follows that to 'say that income ideally ought to be distributed only according to desert is to say that, in respect to all social benefits, all men should ideally be equal'.[21] This does not mean that everyone should in fact be equal, only that any considerations there may be in favour of inequality will have 'nothing to do with desert'.[22] For example, the prospect of extra income may serve as an incentive to engage in socially valuable activities and may help to create sufficient wealth that even those with smaller incomes end up with more than they would have received under a strictly egalitarian regime. If so, Feinberg suggests, this is a consideration that may in principle take priority over considerations of desert and provide a legitimate basis for economic inequality.

It is worth noting, however, that if income is deserved only in so far as it is compensation for unusually hazardous or burdensome work, then, contrary to what Feinberg claims, it does not follow that considerations of desert support an egalitarian distribution of income. What follows instead is that only people who perform unusually hazardous or burdensome work *deserve* any income at all. This, in turn, would seem to imply that the idea that income should be distributed solely according to desert is not an egalitarian idea but rather an absurd one. The same point may be put another way. If income is deserved only in so far as it is compensation for unusually hazardous or burdensome work, then it may be said that the function of deserved income

---

[20] See id. 88–94.   [21] Id. 94.   [22] Id. (emphasis removed).

is to restore the people who perform such work to their proper position in whatever distribution of benefits is treated as a normative baseline. However, considerations of desert do not, on this interpretation, dictate that the baseline itself should be an egalitarian one. Instead, they are simply silent about what the baseline should be.

II. Objections to the Purely Institutional Theory

If, as Feinberg argues, desert is normally understood as 'a *moral* concept in the sense that it is logically prior to and independent of public institutions and their rules',[23] then it is clear that a purely institutional theory, according to which people's deserts are to be identified exclusively with their legitimate institutional expectations, represents a radically revisionist position. Such a theory is subject to at least four important objections. The first and perhaps the most fundamental of these, which follows directly from the claim that desert is a moral concept in the sense Feinberg specifies, is simply that the theory collapses the distinction between judgements of merit or worth and judgments of institutional entitlement—the very distinction on whose importance Feinberg insists.

The second objection is that the institutional theory deprives the concept of desert of its critical force. The theory denies that there is any standard of desert that is independent of institutional rules and practices, and relative to which institutions may be found wanting. If an institution honours the expectations generated by its own rules and policies, there can be no basis for any claim that the institution fails to give people what they deserve. Furthermore, since the institutional theory identifies legitimate desert claims with the expectations generated by *just* institutions, the theory implies that in an unjust society nobody deserves anything. In such a society there will, by hypothesis, be no expectations generated by just institutions. Thus, even if such a society does not honour the expectations generated by its own rules and policies, it cannot be criticized for failing to give people what they deserve.

The third objection is that the institutional theory misconstrues the relationship between the concepts of justice and desert. Whereas Feinberg, in keeping with the traditional view that justice consists in giving each person his or her due,[24] insists that one of the aims of just institutions is to give people what they may independently be said to deserve, the institutional theory says that what people deserve is whatever just institutions have given them reason to expect that they will receive. The theory thus reverses the traditional order of dependence between the concept of justice and the concept of desert.

---

[23] Id. 87.   [24] See, e.g., Aristotle, *Nicomachean Ethics*, book V, ch. 3.

The fourth objection is that the institutional theory cannot accommodate the role played by judgements of desert in the expression of important inter-personal attitudes such as gratitude and resentment. As we saw,[25] Feinberg argues that such attitudes 'have ostensible desert logically built in to them',[26] by which he means that they must all be 'felt as deserved'.[27] Furthermore, judgements about what people deserve often serve to express these 'respon-sive' or 'reactive' attitudes.[28] For example, the judgement that an individual deserves to be punished for what he or she has done may serve to express our outrage or indignation about that person's deeds. However, the objec-tion runs, the institutional theory cannot accommodate the important expressive role thus played by judgments of desert, for, in the example just given, the content of the attitudes expressed is not that the individual who is the target of our outrage has good reason to expect some punishment. Instead, such attitudes rely on a standard of desert that is independent of institutional entitlements and expectations.

Many critics have regarded these objections as decisive against the purely institutional theory.[29] Whether or not one accepts this conclusion, the objec-tions help to explain why such a theory strikes most people as representing, at the very least, a radically revisionist way of understanding desert. It also helps to explain why the perception that egalitarian liberalism is committed to a purely institutional view has been an important source of opposition to the liberal position. To a large extent, that perception is based on Rawls's discussion of desert in *A Theory of Justice*.

III. Rawls on Justice and Desert

A Theory of Justice contains only two discussions of any length that are explic-itly about desert. The first of these occurs in Section 17, in the context of an explanation of the sense in which Rawls's 'difference principle'[30] is an egal-itarian principle of distributive justice, and one which 'expresses a conception

---

[25] See text accompanying notes 9–11.

[26] Feinberg, 'Justice and Personal Desert', 70–1.   [27] Id. at 71.

[28] The term 'reactive attitudes' is introduced by Peter Strawson in 'Freedom and Resentment', reprinted in *Free Will* (Gary Watson ed., 1982), 59–80, at 63.

[29] For some varying assessments of the respective merits of institutional and prein-stitutional conceptions of desert, see Geoffrey Cupit, *Justice as Fittingness* (1996); *What Do We Deserve? A Reader on Justice and Desert* (Louis P. Pojman and Owen McLeod eds., 1999); and George Sher, *Desert*.

[30] The difference principle states that social and economic inequalities are to be arranged in such a way that they are to the greatest benefit of the least advantaged members of society. The principle implies, for example, that it is just to pay higher salaries to some people than to others if and only if this serves to maximize the position of those who have least, perhaps by giving those who are better paid an incen-tive to engage in socially valuable activities. See Rawls, *A Theory of Justice*, 75–83.

of reciprocity'.[31] The entire discussion comprises just two paragraphs, and reads as follows:

There is a natural inclination to object that those better situated deserve their greater advantages whether or not they are to the benefit of others. At this point it is necessary to be clear about the notion of desert. It is perfectly true that given a just system of cooperation as a scheme of public rules and the expectations set up by it, those who, with the prospect of improving their condition, have done what the system announces that it will reward are entitled to their advantages. In this sense the more fortunate have a claim to their better situation; their claims are legitimate expectations established by social institutions, and the community is obligated to meet them. But this sense of desert presupposes the existence of the cooperative scheme; it is irrelevant to the question whether in the first place the scheme is to be designed in accordance with the difference principle or some other criterion.

Perhaps some will think that the person with greater natural endowments deserves those assets and the superior character that made their development possible. Because he is more worthy in this sense, he deserves the greater advantages that he could achieve with them. This view, however, is surely incorrect. It seems to be one of the fixed points of our considered judgments that no one deserves his place in the distribution of native endowments, any more than one deserves one's initial starting place in society. The assertion that a man deserves the superior character that enables him to make the effort to cultivate his abilities is equally problematic; for his character depends in large part upon fortunate family and social circumstances for which he can claim no credit. The notion of desert seems not to apply to these cases. Thus the more advantaged representative man cannot say that he deserves and therefore has a right to a scheme of cooperation in which he is permitted to acquire benefits in ways that do not contribute to the welfare of others. There is no basis for his making this claim. From the standpoint of common sense, then, the difference principle appears to be acceptable both to the more advantaged and to the less advantaged individual. Of course, none of this is strictly speaking an argument for the principle, since in a contract theory arguments are made from the point of view of the original position. But these intuitive considerations help to clarify the nature of the principle and the sense in which it is egalitarian.   (Rawls, *A Theory of Justice*, 103–4)

This passage is the primary source of the impression that Rawls favours a purely institutional theory of desert. Clearly, however, he does not explicitly avow such a theory here. Instead, he purports to be offering an 'intuitive' response—as opposed to an argument from the standpoint of the parties in the hypothetical choice situation that he calls the 'original position'[32]—to one possible objection to his difference principle. The objection is that those who are relatively well-off deserve greater benefits than they would be assigned by the difference principle, which insists that any extra economic advantages enjoyed by those who are better off must benefit those who are worse off.

[31] Id. 102.

[32] The original position is a hypothetical choice situation in which rational agents who are concerned to further their own interests but who do not know their specific identities or circumstances are asked to choose principles of justice to regulate the basic structure of their society. See id. at 11–17.

In responding to this objection, Rawls makes at least four claims. The first is that, although people are entitled to whatever benefits just institutions have led them to expect, and although they may in that sense be said to deserve those benefits, it is clear that no appeal to institutional expectations can vindicate an objection to the difference principle or, indeed, to any other candidate principle of justice. The legitimacy of such expectations itself depends on a prior conception of justice. The second claim is that people cannot properly be said to deserve their natural talents or traits of character. The third claim is that, accordingly, those who are better situated cannot argue that they deserve their greater economic advantages because they deserve the personal traits that enabled them to secure those advantages. The argument fails because the premise is false.[33] The fourth claim is that, because the better situated do not deserve their personal traits, neither can they be said to deserve the establishment of institutions that would give special advantages to people who possess those traits.

It is not difficult to see how one might get the impression that Rawls is advocating an institutional theory of desert in this passage. To begin with, his statement that 'it is necessary to be clear about the notion of desert'[34] makes it seem as if the sentences that follow are meant to provide general conceptual clarification—to unpack the concept of desert. Since those sentences proceed to affirm the significance of legitimate institutional expectations, while rejecting certain kinds of non-institutional desert claims, Rawls may appear to be insisting that desert is, as a conceptual matter, to be identified exclusively with the expectations generated by just institutions. Yet it is worth emphasizing that Rawls stops short of endorsing the institutional theory or of rejecting preinstitutional desert in general. In other words, he does not say that claims of desert are legitimate only in so far as they are understood in purely institutional terms, nor does he say that there is no place at all for a preinstitutional notion of desert.

The significance of these omissions will be easier to assess after looking at Rawls's second extended discussion of desert, which occupies the whole of Section 48, entitled 'Legitimate Expectations and Moral Desert'. By this point in the book, he has completed the presentation of his two principles of justice, outlined the main arguments for the adoption of those principles by the parties in the original position, and sketched a system of institutions that satisfies the two principles. In the section that immediately precedes the discussion of desert in Section 48, Rawls takes up the question of how well his conception of justice accords with various 'common sense precepts of justice'.[35] Section 48 extends this discussion by considering the common sense tendency to suppose 'that income and wealth, and the good things in life generally, should be distributed according to moral desert'.[36] It seems clear

---

[33] This claim corresponds roughly to what Robert Nozick, in his catalogue of possible interpretations of various of Rawls's arguments, refers to as the rebuttal of 'counterargument E'. Robert Nozick, *Anarchy, State, and Utopia* (1974), 224.
[34] Rawls, *A Theory of Justice*, 103.   [35] Id. 304.   [36] Id. 310.

that by 'moral desert' Rawls means desert for which the desert basis is moral virtue or worthiness. He argues that the principle of distributing economic benefits in accordance with moral desert is not acceptable and would not be chosen in the original position. He offers several reasons in support of these claims.

The first reason is simply that 'the notion of distribution according to virtue fails to distinguish between moral desert and legitimate expectations'.[37] Ironically, this echoes one of the main objections to the institutional theory of desert. Rawls's complaint is that, in treating desert as privileged, the principle of distribution in accordance with virtue assigns desert the role properly played by legitimate expectations. The institutional theory is said by its critics to do just the opposite; in treating legitimate expectations as privileged, it assigns them the role properly played by desert. In both cases, however, the alleged effect is the same, namely, to collapse the distinction between desert and legitimate expectations.

Rawls's second reason is that the principle of distribution in accordance with moral desert is 'impracticable'.[38] He makes this point in the context of considering the common sense precept 'which seems intuitively to come closest to rewarding moral desert'—namely, the precept that recommends 'distribution according to effort, or perhaps better, conscientious effort'.[39] Rawls argues that effort is influenced by (undeserved) natural abilities, since 'the better endowed are more likely, other things being equal, to strive conscientiously'.[40] Moreover, we have no feasible method for ascertaining the extent to which a person's conscientious efforts are attributable to his or her virtuous character and the extent to which they are the result of valuable but undeserved natural abilities. For practical purposes, the two factors are impossible to disentangle, yet only the former is plausibly seen as an indicator of moral desert. Accordingly, Rawls concludes, '[t]he idea of rewarding desert is impracticable'.[41]

The third reason is that the notion of moral desert or worth itself presupposes a prior conception of justice and cannot, accordingly, provide the basis for such a conception. The 'concept of moral worth does not provide a first principle of distributive justice . . . because it cannot be introduced until after the principles of justice . . . have been acknowledged'.[42] To be morally worthy, Rawls argues, is to have a strong sense of justice; thus 'the concept of moral worth is secondary to those of right and justice, and it plays no role in the substantive definition of distributive shares'.[43] To emphasize this point, Rawls draws an analogy between the relation of justice and desert, on the one hand, and the relation of property and theft, on the other. 'For a society to organize itself with the aim of rewarding moral desert as a first principle would be like having the institution of property in order to punish thieves.'[44]

---

[37] Id. 311.   [38] Id. 312.   [39] Id.   [40] Id.
[41] Id.   [42] Id.   [43] Id. 313.   [44] Id.

Finally, Rawls argues that the parties in the original position would reject the principle of distribution in accordance with moral desert even if there were some standard for assessing desert that was independent of and prior to justice.[45] Since the parties are interested only in maximizing their own shares of primary social goods, such a principle would have little appeal for them.

After presenting these arguments, Rawls goes on to make his claim that there is an important asymmetry between distributive and retributive justice.[46] The appeal of the principle of distribution in accordance with moral desert, he suggests, may rest on a failure to appreciate this asymmetry. Citing Feinberg for support, he characterizes the asymmetry as follows. The purpose of the criminal law, he says, is to uphold natural duties, and acts that are prohibited by criminal statutes are normally wrong quite apart from their illegality. 'Thus', Rawls writes, 'a propensity to commit such acts is a mark of a bad character, and in a just society legal punishments will only fall upon those who display these faults'.[47] However, he argues, it would be a mistake to suppose that distributive justice is 'somehow the opposite'[48] of retributive justice. That is, it would be a mistake to suppose that a just distributive scheme rewards people who are morally worthy or deserving in much the same way that a just legal system punishes people of bad character who have violated their natural duties. Instead, Rawls argues, the purpose of a just distributive scheme is to establish a social framework within which people can pursue their diverse aims without producing results that are incompatible with the demands of fairness and efficiency.[49] Toward this end, such a scheme may give some people larger shares in order to 'cover the costs of training and education, to attract individuals to places and associations where they are most needed from a social point of view, and so on'.[50] However, the assignment of these shares has nothing to do with the moral worthiness of the people who receive them. Thus, to 'think of distributive and retributive justice as converses of one another is completely misleading and suggests a different justification for distributive shares than the one they in fact have'.[51]

Rawls's discussions in Sections 17 and 48 pose a variety of interpretive puzzles that I shall not attempt to address.[52] Instead, I want to identify three

---

[45] See id.   [46] See id. 315.   [47] Id.
[48] Id. 314.   [49] See id. 315.   [50] Id.   [51] Id.
[52] One puzzle concerns Rawls's understanding of the relation between 'moral desert' and desert *simpliciter*. He uses the term 'moral desert' in Section 48 but not in Section 17. The question is whether his references to desert in the earlier section should also be understood as references to moral desert—that is, to desert for which the desert basis is moral virtue or worth. If so, then Section 17 would be claiming, for example, that people do not morally deserve their natural talents. Thomas Pogge suggests that this is the correct interpretation of Rawls's argument. He says that, in general, 'Desert, for Rawls, is *moral deservingness*, a reflection of one's moral worth in virtue of which alone one can Deserve anything.' Thomas W. Pogge, *Realizing Rawls* (1989), 77. If Pogge's interpretation is correct, it exposes Rawls to the obvious objection that there are many *morally relevant* desert claims that do not have moral virtue as their desert basis. Rawls's reference to 'a familiar although nonmoral sense' of desert in *A Theory of Justice*, 314, seems intended to allow for such claims, but it confuses matters by eliding the difference between lacking a moral desert basis and lacking moral relevance.

elements that seem to me to constitute the core of Rawls's view, and the conjunction of which I will (tendentiously) refer to as the 'Liberal Theory' of desert. First, the Liberal Theory holds that an adequate account of distributive justice must affirm the validity of legitimate institutional expectations. People are entitled to the economic benefits that just institutions lead them to expect, and in so far as claims of desert are nothing more than claims of institutional entitlement they may in principle be perfectly legitimate. Second, according to the Liberal Theory, there is no legitimate notion of desert that is prior to and independent of the principles of distributive justice themselves, and by reference to which the justice of institutional arrangements is to be assessed. There is, in other words, no legitimate form of *prejusticial* desert. Distributive justice does not consist in giving people what they may independently be said to deserve. Third, however, the Liberal Theory takes a different view of retributive justice. Whereas a just distributive scheme cannot coherently seek to reward moral desert, those whom the criminal justice system legitimately punishes have normally done something that would be wrong even in the absence of a law prohibiting it. Thus, people who are justly punished are normally unworthy or undeserving, as judged by a standard that is independent of the principles of just punishment themselves. In this sense, just retributive institutions may indeed be responsive to a conceptually independent conception of desert.

In short, the Liberal Theory denies that the principles of distributive justice make reference to a prejusticial notion of desert, but it allows that there may nevertheless be a legitimate place for prejusticial desert in our thinking about retributive justice. This is the asymmetry that I want to explore. Before I do that, however, it is worth emphasizing that, even in the distributive context, the rejection of prejusticial desert and the affirmation of legitimate expectations, taken together, do not imply a purely institutional theory of desert. They do not imply that desert is legitimate *only* if it is understood institutionally, nor do they imply that there is no legitimate *preinstitutional* notion of desert. To see this, we have only to observe that it would be compatible with the Liberal Theory to maintain that people deserve whatever economic benefits justice dictates that they should receive. On this view, desert would not be prejusticial, since it would be defined in terms of justice rather than vice versa; nevertheless, it would be preinstitutional, since it would be a normative notion that was independent of actual institutions and their rules, and could be used to assess them. In other words, an unjust institution could be described as failing to give people what they deserve, even though the institution had not violated its own rules or disappointed any expectations it had generated. It seems evident, then, that, even in the context of distributive justice, the Liberal Theory need not collapse the distinction between desert and institutional entitlement, or deprive the concept of desert of its critical force, as a purely institutional theory is said to do. This means that the Liberal Theory can avoid two of the most important objections to a purely institutional view.

Since Rawls never explicitly endorses a purely institutional view in the case of distributive justice; since he clearly rejects such a view in the case of retributive justice; since the Liberal Theory captures the most important of Rawls's explicit claims about desert; and since the Liberal Theory can avoid some of the most obvious and most influential objections to a purely institutional view, it seems to me misleading to describe Rawls as defending a purely institutional view even in the distributive case. Although the supposition that he accepts an institutional view of distributive desert may not be inconsistent with anything that he says, it is at the very least an overstatement to describe him as *defending* such a view. However, my primary concern in this essay is not with the interpretation of Rawls's text. Although I believe that the Liberal Theory constitutes the core of Rawls's position, I also believe that the theory merits attention whether or not that interpretative claim is correct.

As we have just seen, the Liberal Theory avoids two of the most important objections to a purely institutional view. Yet in denying that distributive justice consists in giving people what they may independently be said to deserve—in denying that a prejudicial notion of desert is available in the distributive context—the Liberal Theory does indeed reverse the traditional order of dependence between the concepts of justice and desert, just as a purely institutional theory does. At the same time, of course, the Liberal Theory accepts the traditional order of dependence in the context of retributive justice.[53] Before suggesting a rationale for this claim of asymmetry, it will be useful to review the reasons why many people have remained unpersuaded by Rawls's own claim of asymmetry, and have felt instead that his treatment of desert and distributive justice must inevitably generalize to the retributive case as well.

---

[53] Thus, of the four objections to purely institutional theories that were described in Part II, the Liberal Theory avoids the first two and, although it does in part reverse the order of dependence between the concepts of justice and desert (which was the third objection), the rationale I will sketch for the theory, if compelling, would show that this is not in fact objectionable. An interesting question, which I cannot pursue here, is whether the Liberal Theory also avoids the fourth objection to purely institutional views, namely, that they cannot accommodate the 'responsive' or 'reactive' attitudes. As we saw, many such attitudes are said to depend on a conception of desert that is incompatible with a purely institutional account. This is said to be true particularly of the attitudes that find expression through the institution of punishment. Since the Liberal Theory does not challenge the role of prejudicial desert in retributive justice, it clearly has no difficulty accommodating those attitudes in particular. Yet, as I argued in 'Responsibility, Reactive Attitudes, and Liberalism in Philosophy and Politics', Chapter One of this volume, judgements about the proper distribution of economic advantages may also serve to express attitudes like gratitude and resentment. To the extent that is so, there remains a legitimate question about the compatibility of the Liberal Theory and the reactive attitudes.

IV. The Generalizability of Rawls's Arguments

Doubts about Rawls's claim of asymmetry can take either a positive or a negative form. On the positive side, it may seem that Rawls's treatment of desert in the distributive context has a strategic motivation that applies with equal force to the case of retributive justice. In this spirit, for example, T. M. Scanlon maintains that 'Rawls's theory of distributive justice' employs 'a general philosophical strategy'[54] that is equally applicable in both cases:

In approaching the problems of justifying both penal and economic institutions we begin with strong pretheoretical intuitions about the significance of choice: voluntary and intentional commission of a criminal act is a necessary condition of just punishment, and voluntary economic contribution can make an economic reward just and its denial unjust. One way to account for these intuitions is by appeal to a preinstitutional notion of desert: certain acts deserve punishment, certain contributions merit rewards, and institutions are just if they distribute benefits and burdens in accord with these forms of desert.

The strategy I am describing makes a point of avoiding any such appeal. The only notions of desert which it recognizes are internal to institutions and dependent upon a prior notion of justice: if institutions are just then people deserve the rewards and punishments which those institutions assign them. In the justification of institutions, the notion of desert is replaced by an independent notion of justice; in the justification of specific actions and outcomes it is replaced by the idea of legitimate (institutionally defined) expectations. (Scanlon, 'The Significance of Choice', 188)

In this passage, Scanlon does not distinguish between preinstitutional and prejusticial desert, and he appears to interpret Rawls as advocating a purely institutional theory of economic desert. For present purposes, however, the important point is that Scanlon sees the cases of distributive and retributive justice as parallel with respect to the role of desert, and that he finds it natural to construe Rawls's treatment of desert in relation to distributive justice as part of a unified philosophical strategy for dealing with both cases.

In a more critical vein, some writers have maintained that the arguments Rawls gives for his view of economic desert, if valid, apply with equal force in the case of retributive justice.[55] Recall that in Section 17 Rawls makes at least four claims: (1) that no appeal to institutional expectations, however legitimate, can vindicate an objection to the difference principle, (2) that people do not deserve their natural abilities or characters, (3) that those who are relatively affluent cannot, therefore, say that they deserve their greater economic advantages *because* they deserve the traits that enabled them to secure those advantages, and (4) that, since those who are better situated do not deserve their personal traits, neither can they claim to deserve the establishment of

---

[54] T. M. Scanlon, Jr., 'The Significance of Choice', in *The Tanner Lectures on Human Values VIII* (Sterling M. McMurrin ed., 1988), 149–216, at 188.

[55] See text accompanying notes 56–7.

institutions that would reward people who possess such traits. Now those critics who see Rawls's arguments about economic desert as generalizable to the retributive case interpret him as making a fifth and stronger claim as well. They take him to be claiming that since people never deserve their traits and abilities, it follows that they never deserve any of the benefits that those traits might enable them to secure. In effect, these writers interpret Rawls as tacitly relying on a general principle which says that a desert claim cannot be valid unless its underlying desert basis is itself deserved.

As I will indicate in Part VI, I believe that there is room to question this interpretation of Rawls. For the moment, however, the important point is that those critics who see Rawls's argument as generalizable to the retributive case do in fact interpret him in this way. Of course, the putative principle to which they see him as appealing strikes most people as implausible; most would agree with Nozick's comment that 'the foundations underlying desert' need not themselves be deserved, *'all the way down'*.[56] However, the critics argue, in so far as Rawls himself does rely on this general principle, he cannot consistently refuse to apply it to the case of retributive justice. If, according to him, the fact that one does not deserve one's superior character means that one does not deserve any of the economic advantages that such a character might enable one to secure, then surely he must also allow that, since criminals do not deserve their bad characters, neither do they deserve the punishments that those characters may lead them to incur. These considerations lead Michael Sandel to conclude that, 'given Rawls' reasons for rejecting desert-based distributive arrangements, he seems clearly committed to rejecting desert-based retributive ones as well'.[57]

Sandel also argues, correctly in my view, that Rawls's citation of Feinberg in support of his claim that there is an asymmetry between distributive and retributive justice is misleading.[58] Feinberg does claim that, where questions of desert are concerned, there is a difference of kind between the two cases, inasmuch as it is 'nonpolar desert' that is relevant to distributive justice and 'polar desert' that is relevant to retributive justice.[59] There is no suggestion, however, that these two types of desert stand in different logical relations either to institutions or to the concept of justice. Similarly, although Feinberg would agree with Rawls both that considerations of desert provide no grounds for objecting to an egalitarian distribution of benefits and that limited inequalities of the sort introduced by the difference principle can be justified on grounds that have nothing to do with desert, there is no reason to suppose that he would rest these judgements on any claim to the effect

---

[56] Nozick, *Anarchy, State, and Utopia*, 225. For additional criticism, see the writings by Sher and Zaitchik: *Desert*, and 'On Deserving to Deserve', respectively.

[57] Sandel, *Liberalism and the Limits of Justice*, 92. I endorsed Sandel's conclusion in footnote seven of 'Responsibility, Reactive Attitudes, and Liberalism in Philosophy and Politics', Chapter One of this volume.

[58] See Sandel, *Liberalism and the Limits of Justice*, 90 n.3.

[59] Feinberg, 'Justice and Personal Desert', 62.

that desert is in principle irrelevant to what counts as a just distribution. Instead, as we have seen, Feinberg believes that considerations of desert support a thoroughgoing distributive egalitarianism but that they may be outweighed by just the sorts of maximin considerations that animate the difference principle. To be sure, I have argued that Feinberg is mistaken in thinking that he has shown desert to be egalitarian in its implications.[60] But the fact remains that he takes the content of distributive justice to be fixed in part by reference to a prior notion of desert.

It is worth repeating that, when Sandel and other critics argue that Rawls's treatment of desert in the distributive case generalizes to the retributive case as well, they tend to interpret him as advocating a purely institutional view of desert in the distributive context and as offering an argument for that view which appeals to the general principle that a desert claim cannot be valid unless the underlying desert basis is itself deserved. As I indicated in Part III, I find the first of these interpretive claims misleading, and as I will argue in Part VI, I believe that there is room to doubt the second. What is more important for my purposes, however, is that neither the purely institutional view nor the putative general principle belongs to the Liberal Theory as I have described it. In the next Part, I will propose a rationale for that theory and, more specifically, for its claim that there is an asymmetry between distributive and retributive justice with respect to the role of desert. Then, in the final Part, I will ask whether the Liberal Theory is committed to an argument of the sort that the critics impute to Rawls, an argument appealing to the general principle that a valid desert claim must be supported by a desert basis that is itself deserved. If not, and if an independent rationale for the Liberal Theory is indeed available, then egalitarian liberalism may be free to claim just what Rawls says it claims—namely, that desert plays a less fundamental role in relation to distributive justice than it does in relation to retributive justice.

V. Holism, Individualism, and Desert

The Liberal Theory comprises three claims: an affirmation of legitimate expectations, a rejection of prejusticial desert in the context of distributive justice, and an acceptance of prejusticial desert in the retributive context. The first of these claims is uncontroversial. No one argues that just institutions should fail to honour the expectations to which they have given rise. It is the second and third claims, taken together, that imply that there is an asymmetry between distributive and retributive justice with respect to the role of desert. These claims are, of course, more controversial.

---

[60] See Part I, 'Feinberg on Justice and Desert'.

I want to explore a rationale for the second claim that is suggested by, though not explicitly articulated in, the work of Rawls and other egalitarian liberals.[61] It rests on a conviction that there is a fundamental difference between the justificatory bases for claims of desert and claims of distributive justice, respectively. As we saw earlier, Feinberg asserts that the basis of a valid desert claim must always be some characteristic of or fact about the deserving person. We can express this point, using terminology I have introduced elsewhere,[62] by saying that the basis for a claim of personal desert must be *individualistic*. As Feinberg notes,[63] this does not mean that the desert basis cannot consist in some fact about the relations between the subject of the desert claim and other people. The fact that an individual has performed more skillfully than others in some competitive event, for example, may indeed be the basis for a claim about what that individual deserves. Even when the desert basis consists in a relational fact, however, it must still be individualistic in the sense that the fact in question must be a fact about the subject of the claim. Although the claim that an individual deserves a certain benefit implies that he ought, *pro tanto*, to receive it, Feinberg emphasizes that not every judgement to the effect that an individual ought to receive a certain benefit has an individualistic basis. For example, the fact that giving a certain benefit to *A* will prevent something bad from happening to *B* and *C* cannot be the basis for a claim that *A* deserves the benefit, but it may nevertheless be a (non-individualistic) reason why *A* ought—either *pro tanto* or all things considered—to get it. In short, the reasons in favour of providing some benefit to a given person may be either individualistic or non-individualistic; considerations about what the person deserves are individualistic reasons.

Now I believe that it is possible to see the Liberal Theory's second claim as motivated by a conviction that, whereas desert is individualistic, distributive justice is *holistic* in the sense that the justice of any assignment of economic benefits to a particular individual always depends—directly or indirectly—on the justice of the larger distribution of benefits in society.[64] In Rawls's theory of justice, this conviction is reflected in the claim that distributive shares should be treated as a matter of pure procedural justice[65] and that provided the basic structure is just, any distribution of goods that results is also just. This means that, for Rawls, the principles of distributive justice do not apply

---

[61] See, for example the writings of Dworkin and Nagel cited in footnote 3 above.

[62] See 'Rawls and Utilitarianism', Chapter Nine in this volume.

[63] See Feinberg, 'Justice and Personal Desert', 59 n.6.

[64] This paragraph draws on my discussion of the holism of Rawls's distributive theory in 'Rawls and Utilitarianism', Chapter Nine in this volume.

[65] Pure procedural justice obtains when there is no independent criterion for a just or fair outcome, but when instead there is a just procedure, and any outcome that results from carrying out the procedure is itself just. This is contrasted with cases in which there *is* an independent criterion for what would count as a just or fair outcome; in such cases, of course, one looks for a procedure that will lead to the just outcome so understood. See Rawls, *A Theory of Justice*, 83–90.

to 'a single transaction viewed in isolation'.[66] The justice or injustice of allocating a particular economic benefit to a given individual will always depend
instead on whether that allocation is part of an overall distribution that is
produced by a basic structure conforming to Rawls's principles of distributive justice.

The case for conceiving of distributive justice in holistic terms is partly moral
and partly empirical. It derives in part from a strong sense of the equal worth
of persons and from a firm conviction that in a just society all citizens must
enjoy equal standing. It also derives from a conviction that, in the circumstances of moderate scarcity of resources that are typical of human societies,
citizens' material prospects are profoundly interconnected through their
shared and effectively unavoidable participation in a set of fundamental practices and institutions—the economy, the legal system, the political framework—
that establish and enforce the ground rules of social co-operation. People's
prospects are seen as connected in at least three ways. First, people's productive
contributions are mutually dependent in the sense that each person's capacity to contribute depends on the contributions of others.[67] Second, the
economic value of people's talents is socially determined in the sense that it
depends both on the number of people with similar talents and on the needs,
preferences, and choices of others. Third, people's expectations of material
gain are linked in the sense that virtually any decision to assign economic
benefits to one person or class has economic implications for other persons
and classes. The holist concludes that, in light of these moral and empirical
considerations, it makes no normative sense to suppose that there could be,
at the level of fundamental principle, a standard for assigning such benefits
that appealed solely to characteristics of or facts about the proposed beneficiaries. Yet that is precisely what a prejusticial conception of desert would
have to be. Accordingly, the holist denies that there is any legitimate conception of this kind that is pertinent to questions of economic benefit. Instead,
the norms of distributive justice must be thought of as specifying the contours of a fair social framework for the allocation of scarce material resources
among citizens of equal worth and standing.

Rawls sometimes suggests that his rejection of prejusticial desert is consistent with the way in which distributive justice has traditionally been understood.[68] Although I believe that this is an overstatement, there are some things
to be said in its favour. The very term 'distributive justice', as Robert Nozick
has emphasized in objecting to it,[69] appears to import a non-individualistic

---

[66] Id. 87.

[67] Thus, Elizabeth Anderson writes: 'From the point of view of justice, the attempt,
independent of moral principles, to credit specific bits of output to specific bits of input
by specific individuals represents an arbitrary cut in the causal web that in fact makes
everyone's productive contribution dependent on what everyone else is doing.'
Anderson, 'What Is the Point of Equality?', 321.

[68] See Rawls, *A Theory of Justice*, at 10–11; see also 313.

[69] See Nozick, *Anarchy, State, and Utopia*, 149–50.

perspective. And as we noted earlier, the idea that desert has a less central role to play in distributive than in retributive justice gains support from a very natural view of the distinctiveness of the criminal law. Nevertheless, it seems implausible to deny that people have ever interpreted justice as requiring economic benefits to be assigned on the basis of a prior conception of desert. What the Liberal Theory is best understood as claiming is that, as egalitarian ideas have become more securely entrenched within moral thought, and as people's participation in social institutions of ever increasing comprehensiveness and complexity has made the interdependence of their fortunes impossible to ignore, the idea that economic benefits may justly be assigned on the basis of an individualistic standard of desert has, quite simply, ceased to be tenable. The point is not that nobody has ever subscribed to this idea but rather that in our moral and social world the idea no longer makes sense, if it ever did.

Clearly there are many questions that might be raised about the force of this argument for a holistic interpretation of distributive justice. For the purposes of this essay, however, what is important to emphasize is that the considerations which have been cited in support of distributive holism do not provide comparable support for a holistic approach to retributive justice. The argument for distributive holism depends on three important assumptions. The first is that distributive justice is concerned with the proper division of social advantages—that is, with the allocation of things that people are presumed to want. The second assumption is that questions of allocation arise primarily for societies that find themselves in conditions of moderate scarcity that make it impossible for them fully to satisfy the demand for such advantages. And the third assumption is that, because goods are scarce and their allocation is heavily dependent on social institutions, any provision of advantages to some may affect the supply available for others. In short, the problem of distributive justice is seen as the problem of how to allocate scarce goods among moral equals.

By contrast, the problem of retributive justice does not concern the allocation of advantages at all, and it is not a problem posed by conditions of scarcity. To be sure, the 'supply' of punishment is not, in principle, unlimited, and so punishing some may make it more difficult to punish others. But since punishment is a burden rather than a benefit, the problem of retributive justice is not a problem of limited supply; supply can safely be assumed to exceed demand. (That is, the supply of punishment may be assumed to exceed people's demand that they themselves be punished, although—as every American politician knows—it may not exceed their demand for the punishment of others.) The problem of retributive justice is not the problem of how to allocate a limited supply of benefits among equally worthy citizens but rather the problem of how society can ever be justified in imposing the special burden of punishment on a particular human being. To put it another way, the establishment of penal institutions is a social response, not to allocative concerns, but rather to exercises of individual agency that society deems intolerable.[70] The relevant question in this case is what, if anything, might justify such a response.[71]

One traditional answer to this question, of course, appeals to a prejusticial notion of desert. Society is justified in punishing people who have done things for which they deserve to be punished. There are, of course, many possible reasons for scepticism about this 'retributivist' view of punishment and the underlying conception of desert on which it relies. The Liberal Theory, as I am interpreting it, does not offer an affirmative defence of retributivism against all these forms of scepticism. However, it agrees that wrongful conduct—that is, conduct that would be wrong even if it were not illegal—is normally a necessary condition of just punishment. And there is nothing internal to the Liberal Theory which requires rejection of the retributivist idea that wrong-doers deserve to be punished. As we have seen,[72] it is the individualism of desert that is the source of the Liberal Theory's repudiation of prejusticial

---

[70] To be sure, allocative concerns are sometimes raised about the operations of the criminal justice system, as for example when Paul Butler cites high rates of black imprisonment in an argument for racially based jury nullification. See Paul Butler, 'Racially Based Jury Nullification: Black Power in the Criminal Justice System', *Yale Law Journal* 105 (1995), 677–725. In the end, however, Butler's argument rests not on a holistic understanding of retributive justice but rather on the claims (1) that crimes committed by blacks are often an excusable response to societal racism, and (2) that the criminal justice system enforces the criminal law in a selective and discriminatory manner. It is important to note that, even on an individualist understanding of retributive justice, the inconsistent application of retributive norms may itself be unjust.

[71] In his reply to this Article, Douglas Husak interprets this as a question about society's 'complete justification for creating an institution of punishment'. Douglas Husak, 'Holistic Retributivism', *California Law Review* 88 (2000): 991–1000, at 996. He then argues, plausibly enough, that considerations of overall cost are relevant to the latter question, and that it must therefore be answered holistically rather than individualistically. But the question I am concerned with here is not the question of society's all-things-considered justification for establishing institutions of punishment. It is rather the question of whether and when society's punishment of an individual is compatible with just treatment of that individual. Husak has not shown that *this* question must be answered holistically.

Husak also proposes the following parallel between distributive and retributive justice. In both cases, considerations of desert are individualistic and provide *pro tanto* reasons why individuals should receive certain benefits or burdens. But in both cases, the all-things-considered justification for deciding actually to give them those benefits or burdens must depend on a variety of considerations—including considerations of desert but also including holistic considerations. However, this putative parallel underestimates the radicalism of the holist's rejection of distributive desert. The holist's claim, as I have construed it, is not that considerations of economic desert must be weighed in the balance with, and may be overridden by, considerations of a holistic character. The claim is rather that there *is* no prejusticial standard of desert that is relevant to questions of economic benefit. In other words, distributive justice is seen as holistic, not in the sense that holistic considerations may trump considerations of prejusticial desert, but rather in the sense that no considerations of prejusticial desert are thought to have any normative weight or standing at all. Since Husak does not wish to make a comparable claim about retributive justice, his argument does not undermine the suggestion that there is an asymmetry between the distributive and retributive cases.

[72] See text accompanying notes 64–70.

desert in the distributive context. For the reasons just discussed, however, the Liberal Theory has no quarrel with the individualism of the retributivist view—no quarrel, in other words, with its reliance on an individualistic conception of desert as the basis for just punishment. In this respect, then, the theory takes an asymmetrical attitude towards the role of desert in the distributive and retributive contexts. It is committed to denying that an adequate account of distributive justice can appeal to a prejusticial notion of desert, but it has no comparable commitment with respect to retributive justice.

VI. Must the Liberal Theory Be Generalized?

We have now identified a rationale for denying that the principles of distributive justice make reference to a prejusticial concept of desert. Unlike the 'general philosophical strategy' that Scanlon construes Rawls as employing,[73] the rationale we have identified seems not to apply to the retributive context. As we have seen,[74] however, Rawls himself has often been interpreted as advancing an argument against distributive desert that is equally applicable to retributive justice, inasmuch as it implicitly relies on a putative general principle to the effect that a valid desert claim must be supported by a desert basis that is itself deserved. This principle, if accepted, would appear to provide just as much reason to reject the idea that criminals (prejusticially) deserve punishment as it does to reject the idea that people who are talented and hard-working (prejusticially) deserve economic rewards. For criminals presumably do not deserve to have the traits that lead them to commit crimes any more than the talented deserve their talents.

I do not know whether Rawls intended to make an argument of this kind. By itself, the fact that doing so would be inconsistent with his insistence on an asymmetry between distributive and retributive justice provides at least as much reason to doubt whether such an argument should be ascribed to him as it does to discount his claim of asymmetry. Furthermore, the textual evidence in favour of such an ascription seems to me inconclusive. The passages in Section 17 that have been interpreted as advancing such an argument do not do so explicitly,[75] and I believe that it is possible to read those passages as making only the four claims mentioned earlier.[76] In other words, there is room to doubt whether Rawls is also making the fifth and stronger claim that benefits obtained through the use of undeserved traits can never themselves be deserved.

Nevertheless, it is possible that he did mean to advance such an argument. Certainly it is clear that he possesses a strong sense of the arbitrariness of

[73] See the quotation from Scanlon's 'The Significance of Choice', following note 54.
[74] See text accompanying notes 55–7.
[75] See the quotation from Rawls's *A Theory of Justice*, following note 31.
[76] See text accompanying note 33.

fortune, and one of his central themes is the unfairness of allowing the distribution of natural talents and traits—a distribution that does not itself have any normative basis—to influence people's material prospects to an extent that is incongruous with their status as moral equals. In his eagerness to undercut our tendency to treat such natural facts as morally dispositive, Rawls may perhaps have yielded to the temptation to offer an argument that was too strong for his own purposes.

For the purposes of this essay, what is important to emphasize is that the Liberal Theory, as I have interpreted it, neither explicitly advances nor implicitly relies upon such an argument. The Liberal Theory has reasons of its own for rejecting appeals to a prejusticial conception of desert in the specific context of distributive justice, and those reasons in no way depend on the idea that a valid desert claim must have a desert basis that is itself deserved. Thus, the considerations that have led commentators to conclude that Rawls's arguments about desert must inevitably generalize from the distributive to the retributive case simply do not apply to the Liberal Theory as I have interpreted it.

Conclusion

If the argument of this essay is correct, then it is possible to deny that desert has a fundamental role to play in an account of distributive justice without committing oneself to a comparable claim about retributive justice. This means that Rawls's stated conviction that there is an asymmetry between distributive and retributive justice should be taken more seriously than it sometimes has been. More generally, it suggests that egalitarian liberals like Rawls need not endorse the kind of wholesale scepticism about desert that has sometimes been attributed to them. Furthermore, to the extent that liberal scepticism about distributive desert responds to a perceived contrast between the individualism of desert and the holism of distributive justice, much of the criticism of the liberal position has been misdirected. In so far as that position relies on the rationale I have suggested, the interesting question is not whether a valid desert claim must have a desert basis that is itself deserved, but whether the case for distributive holism is compelling.[77]

---

[77] Nozick's criticism of 'end-result' principles of distributive justice in chapter 7 of *Anarchy, State, and Utopia*, 153–5, may be interpreted as in part a response to the holistic character of such principles. End-result principles, according to Nozick, assess the justice of a distribution solely by seeing whether the associated distributional matrix satisfies some structural criterion, rather than by taking into account historical information about how the distribution arose. However, a distributive theory may be holistic without counting as an end-result view in this sense. Indeed, I believe that this is true of Rawls's theory. I have discussed the point in 'Rawls and Utilitarianism', Chapter Nine in this volume.

In addition, there is the question of whether holistic and individualistic values can coherently be integrated into a unified normative scheme. This question arises with particular urgency in relation to those categories of conduct—property crimes, for example—that appear to implicate both distributive and retributive justice. But the question is also important because, like desert, many of the other values and norms that we recognize in daily life are responsive to features of individual character and conduct. Thus, it is important to ask whether one can do justice to those values while treating the overall social framework as regulated by a holistic scheme of distributive principles.

Important as they are, however, these questions lie beyond the scope of this essay. My aim here has ben simply to call attention to an insufficiently examined rationale for the idea that desert has different roles to play in relation to distributive and retributive justice.

11

Morality Through Thick and Thin: A Critical Notice of *Ethics and the Limits of Philosophy**

Over the years, Bernard Williams's subtle and imaginative ethical writings have often defined themselves in opposition to one or another of the dominant normative theories in contemporary moral philosophy. What they have not done is to put forward an alternative theory. This does not mean that Williams's contributions have been primarily negative or critical. It simply means that his positive contributions have not taken the form of theory construction. This is no accident. Williams has often perceived particular ethical theories as failing to orient themselves convincingly in relation to conspicuous features of ethical phenomena as actually experienced. In response, he has repeatedly attempted to direct our attention away from the forms of thought associated with the prevailing theories of our day, and toward important but, as he believes, neglected dimensions of ethical life. Increasingly, this has led him to challenge the dominant agenda of contemporary moral philosophy: to raise doubts, not just about the rival answers that moral philosophers give to certain standard questions, but, more importantly, about whether the standard questions themselves are really the right ones for moral philosophy to be asking. And in recent years, these doubts

* From *The Philosophical Review* 96 (1987). Copyright 1987 Cornell University. Reprinted by permission of the publisher. This essay is a critical notice of Bernard Williams's book, *Ethics and the Limits of Philosophy* (Cambridge, MA: Harvard University Press, 1985). All page references to Williams's book will be given parenthetically in the text. The essay is based on material that was presented to a seminar on Moral Theory that I taught at Berkeley in the spring semester of 1986. I am very grateful to the participants in that seminar for their extremely helpful critical comments. I have also benefited greatly from attending a seminar based on his book that Williams taught at Berkeley during the same semester, and from numerous discussions with him over the course of that term. In addition, I am indebted to Thompson Clarke, Peter Railton, Barry Stroud, and the Editors of *The Philosophical Review* for helpful comments on an earlier draft of this paper.

have been extended with increasing vigour and frequency to the idea of an 'ethical theory' itself. Williams is not convinced that there is any legitimate philosophical question that is best answered by assembling the kind of normative intellectual structure that philosophers refer to as an ethical theory.

Williams's challenge to the agenda of contemporary moral philosophy is articulated with considerable power in *Ethics and the Limits of Philosophy*, a very rich and rewarding book which contains the most extended and best developed formulation to date of his ethical views. The book's central strand of argument consists in a sustained attack on what Williams calls 'morality' or 'the morality system', by which he means a distinctive form of ethical thought that is said to be characteristic of the modern world. Within philosophy, the morality system is associated with the production of those familiar ethical theories that purport to tell us in general terms what we ought to do. However Williams emphasizes that the system is 'not an invention of philosophers' (174), and that it is not manifested only within philosophy. It is rather a feature of the modern world more generally, and it 'is the outlook, or, incoherently, part of the outlook, of almost all of us' (174).[1]

Morality, Williams tells us, is not a single substantive ethical conception. 'It embraces a range of ethical outlooks; and morality is so much with us that moral philosophy spends much of its time discussing the differences between those outlooks, rather than the difference between all of them and everything else' (174). Nevertheless, the morality system as Williams describes it has, as he acknowledges, a decidedly Kantian flavor. Its most striking feature is the ambitious use it makes of the concept of *obligation*, and the significance with which it invests that notion. Instead of treating it as a concept which simply picks out one type of ethical consideration among others, the morality system tries to reduce as many types of ethical considerations as possible to obligations. It construes judgements of obligation as practical judgements, judgements about what one ought to do in particular situations, and it assigns them special importance because, unlike non-moral judgements and unlike even other moral judgements, judgements of obligation are conceived as categorical. Since, it seems, one cannot be categorically required to do something that one cannot possibly do, the morality system is led by its practical focus to make the famous claim that *ought* implies *can*. And the allocation of blame, which is the form of hostile expression favoured by the morality system, is for similar reasons regulated by the distinction between the voluntary and the involuntary; someone who has voluntarily failed

---

[1] To avoid confusion, I try throughout this essay to follow Williams's usage of the terms 'ethics' and 'morality' and their cognates. Thus I think of 'morality' as the narrower concept and 'ethics' as the broader, with morality conceived as a distinctive form of the ethical. I do, however, treat the terms 'moral philosophy' and 'moral philosopher' as exceptions to this policy (as does Williams); these terms are to be understood in the broader sense.

to do what he was obligated to do is blameworthy, for he was categorically required to do something, he could have done it, and he didn't do it, but nobody is to be blamed for what he does involuntarily.

Williams has many criticisms to make of the morality system, and of the familiar philosophical theories that he regards as its products. He compares morality frequently and unfavourably with the ethical thought of the ancient Greeks, which he admires for its emphasis on individual character and related notions. His official claim is that 'we would be better off without' (174) morality, and that the ethical thought of the Greeks 'may have more to offer' (198) us. Although he has many very shrewd and insightful things to say about morality, and although I find many of his broad themes and emphases quite congenial, I do not think that Williams establishes either the wisdom of or the warrant for any wholesale repudiation of the 'morality system'. In this essay, I will try to explain why not. In Section I, I will discuss a distinction he draws between 'thick' ethical concepts and others, a distinction he uses to criticize contemporary ethical theories and, through them, the morality system itself. I will suggest that the distinction as he draws it is flawed, and therefore less effective against ethical theory than he takes it to be. In addition, an examination of the use Williams makes of the distinction in elaborating his own position will lead me to identify what I regard as an important instability in that position. This instability I will go on to examine in Sections II and III. In Section II, I will examine Williams's diagnosis of the urge to theorize about ethics. I will be especially concerned with the question of whether the elimination of ethical theory, given his own diagnosis of the urge that produces it, would leave Williams with enough resources to engage in the kind of social criticism that he evidently wants to engage in. I will illustrate my doubts on this score through a discussion, in Section III, of his reflections on racism, sexism, and social injustice. The conclusion of Sections II and III will be that there is in fact a conflict between Williams's repudiation of ethical theory and his desire to engage in ethical criticism of oppressive social institutions. If that is right, it raises the question of whether ethical theory should be retained, or whether ethical criticism should instead be eschewed. The answer to this question depends on the force of Williams's objections to ethical theorizing, and those objections in turn depend in part on his doubts about the objectivity of ethics. Some of my remarks in Section I bear on these topics; but I will also provide further discussion of Williams's views about objectivity in Section IV. In particular, I will examine a distinction he draws between two different kinds of objectivity that might be claimed for ethics, and an argument he gives against the legitimacy of moving from one of these to the other. I will raise doubts about that argument, and in so doing suggest that the possibilities of ethical objectivity may be greater than Williams allows. To the extent that that is so, the case against ethical theorizing is additionally weakened.

I

As I have said, Williams distinguishes between two kinds of ethical concepts. First, there are what he calls 'thick' or substantive concepts. These are relatively specific concepts (129). They are also 'world-guided': that is, their application 'is determined by what the world is like' (129). One of the things this means is that people who have acquired them will typically agree about their application to particular cases (141). Thick concepts are also 'action-guiding', in the sense that if 'a concept of this kind applies, this often provides someone with a reason for action, though that reason need not be a decisive one and may be outweighed by other reasons' (140). Examples of thick concepts are 'treachery', 'promise', 'brutality', and 'courage' (129). The thick concepts are contrasted with a second group of concepts, which we may call 'thin'. The thin concepts are 'general and abstract' (152), and they 'do not display world-guidedness' (152). Examples of thin concepts are 'good', 'right', and 'ought' (128).

Williams sees the leading contemporary ethical theories, whether deontological, contractualist, or utilitarian, as all neglecting the thick ethical concepts in favour of the thin. And he does not regard this as a matter of simple omission or incompleteness. Rather, he claims, it is due to the fact that all of these theories are products of a 'reductive enterprise' (17), a desire 'to show that one or another type of ethical consideration is basic, with other types to be explained in terms of it' (16). Fueled by this kind of reductionist motivation, ethical theory 'looks characteristically for considerations that are very general and have as little distinctive content as possible, because it is trying to systematize and because it wants to represent as many reasons as possible as applications of other reasons' (116–17). Given its reductionist aims, ethical theory cannot afford to take seriously the thick ethical concepts in all their variety; it is committed to imposing an oversimplified structure on ethical thought, and to neglecting the complexity of the ethical ideas we actually live with. In this as in much else it accurately reflects the distinctive emphases and distortions of the morality system, with its omnivorous conception of obligation.

Before examining the distinction between thick and thin concepts directly, there is one more general point that is worth mentioning. There is a tension in Williams's account between, first, the claim that the morality system dominates contemporary ethical thought outside of philosophy and not only within it, and second, the claim our actual ethical lives are richer, more variegated, 'thicker' than the morality system can acknowledge. Thus, on the one hand, he says as earlier noted that the morality system is a feature of the modern world in general and that it is not just an invention of philosophers. He also says that thick ethical concepts have 'less currency' (163) in modern society than ever before, and that 'a society that relies on very general ethical expressions is a different sort of society from one that puts greater weight on more specific ones' (128), so that, in effect, we live in the 'thinnest' social world that has ever existed. But, on the other hand, it is a recurrent theme of the book that the morality system and the ethical theories it generates fail to do justice to the richness and variety of our present-day ethical thought and experience. Now it may be said, and truly, that there is no actual inconsistency between these two sets of claims. It is open to Williams to say, and indeed he does say, roughly, that although the morality system exercises a very powerful influence on contemporary ethical life, there are also some other strands of ethical thought, and with them some thick ethical concepts, which do nevertheless still retain their hold on us. Thus, the claim may be, our ethical lives, thin as they are, are still sufficiently thick that the morality system manages to misrepresent even them.

Two worries survive this reply, however. First, there is a question about what exactly the ethical life of a contemporary individual is supposed to be like, on this picture. What is it like to have the morality system represent one part of one's ethical outlook, while having forms of thought antithetical to the morality system represent the rest of one's outlook? Williams himself says, in a remark quoted earlier, that for the morality system to constitute *part* of one's outlook is for one's outlook to be incoherent, and it does indeed seem that the cost of accepting the reply sketched above is that one must also accept a view of our own ethical lives as fundamentally incoherent. Williams may in fact be prepared to say that this is the correct understanding of our situation, but this is a very drastic claim which requires considerably more support than he provides. I will return to this point. The second worry is that there is a puzzle, which this reply does not obviously eliminate, about the suggestion that the ethical thought of the ancient Greeks may have more to offer us than does contemporary ethical thought. If the two forms of thought are indeed antithetical in the ways Williams indicates, and if this opposition is not only correlated with but also partly responsible for the dramatic differences between ancient Greek society and our own, and if moreover any set of ethical ideas can flourish only in appropriate social and historical circumstances, then it seems hard to see how the ideas of the ancient Greeks could have more to offer those living in our society than do the ideas that flourish in our society itself. Williams acknowledges that there is an apparent puzzle here, but he says it 'is not a paradox that in these very new circumstances very old philosophies may have more to offer than moderately new ones, and a historical story could be told to show why this is so' (198). But, in the first place, he doesn't actually tell the story, apart from a one-sentence sketch, and, in the second place, the puzzle is not simply about how old ideas can be helpful in new circumstances. It is about what reason there is to suppose that our individual outlooks and social world, which, *ex hypothesi*, have been shaped and are partly constituted by ethical ideas antithetical to those of the ancient Greeks, might now prove hospitable precisely to the ethical ideas of the ancient Greeks. Some might suggest that it is up to *philosophers* to effect a change in our ethical outlooks which would make this possible, to use the powers of philosophical argument to make our world more receptive to the ideas of the ancients. But this can hardly be the reply of Williams, whose book is explicitly about the limits of philosophy's ability to direct ethical thought, and who therefore writes: 'I want to say that we can think in ethics, and in all sorts of ways, . . . but that philosophy can do little to determine how we should do so' (74).

The contrast between thick and thin ethical concepts has been taken for granted in the preceding discussion, but the distinction is not in fact a clear one. Consider the following concepts, for example: justice, fairness, and impartiality, to take one cluster of notions; liberty, equality, freedom of expression, to take another; privacy, self-respect, envy, to take a third; needs, well-being, and interests, to take a fourth; and rights, autonomy, and consent, for a fifth. Are the concepts on this list thick or thin? If they are all thick, that suggests that contemporary ethical theories are far more concerned with thick concepts than Williams allows, for surely they are concerned with the concepts on this list. If on the other hand these concepts are all thin, that suggests that the class of thin concepts is much more diverse than Williams indicates, so that even if current ethical theories are preoccupied with thin concepts, this preoccupation may not involve the kind of gross oversimplification that was earlier alleged. And if some of the concepts on the list are thick while others are thin, then each of the two foregoing conclusions is supported to some extent.

In fact, however, it is impossible confidently to classify various of the concepts on the list as either thick or thin. As we have seen, Williams associates thickness both with specificity and with world-guidedness. And the thin concepts are associated both with relative generality and with lack of world-guidedness. But, to begin with, it is far from clear how we are supposed to tell whether a particular concept is world-guided or not. On the face of it, the application of every single one of the concepts on the list *appears* to be determined to at least some extent by what the world is like. As earlier noted, Williams says that one characteristic of world-guided concepts is that people who have them typically agree about their application in all but marginal cases. However, he explicitly denies that agreement is *sufficient* for world-guidedness, and he does not seem to regard *actual* agreement as strictly *necessary* either. In any case, as reflection on the list shows, both the factor of agreement or disagreement in application, and the factor of specificity or generality, are matters of degree. Moreover, these two factors may diverge. And what these considerations suggest to me is that any division of ethical concepts into the two categories of the thick and the thin is itself a considerable oversimplification. Our ethical vocabulary is very rich and diverse, and the ethical concepts we use vary along a number of dimensions, of which the dimensions of specificity or generality and agreement or disagreement in application are two. Since this is so, and since at least some of this conceptual diversity is reflected within contemporary ethical theories, the charge that such theories neglect the thick in favour of the thin is simply too crude and coarse-grained as it stands to be fully credible. In addition, the picture of our ethical lives as incoherently constructed out of two fundamentally different forms of thought may be badly misleading, for nothing that has emerged supports the idea of an incoherent bifurcation.

Williams nevertheless makes heavy use of the distinction between the thick and the thin. He associates it with another important distinction, between the unreflective and the reflective. The members of a 'hypertraditional' society, he says, may use their thick concepts unreflectively, as 'a method of finding [their] way around [their] social world' (151). And he is also prepared to say, for the kinds of broadly Wittgensteinian reasons that have been pressed by John McDowell and others, that the judgements they make using their thick concepts can both express truths and amount to a body of knowledge.[2] However, Williams says, such knowledge tends to be undermined by the kind of reflection that occurs 'when someone stands back from the practices of the society and its use of these concepts and asks whether this is the right way to go on' (146). For such 'reflection characteristically disturbs, unseats, or replaces ... traditional concepts' (148), with the result that people cease to make judgements using them. And, at the same time, the concepts that reflection itself makes use of are 'necessarily ... the most general and abstract ethical concepts such as "right"' (152). Unlike thick concepts, these thin concepts are not 'world-guided'. And unlike the 'thick judgements' that were made before reflection drove the traditional concepts from use, the abstract and general thoughts that reflection itself produces do 'not satisfy the conditions of propositional knowledge' (167). Thus, Williams concludes, 'in ethics, *reflection can destroy knowledge*' (148).

For the purposes of our discussion, two important lines of thought are suggested by this. The first begins with the observation that Williams really has two different reasons for his opposition to the enterprise of producing ethical theories that purport to tell us in general terms what we ought to do. We have already noted that he regards it as a reductionist enterprise, and as misguided for that reason. However, it should be clear by now that Williams also has an additional, independent motivation for his opposition to such theories. He does not believe that concepts like 'ought' are 'world-guided', and as the phrase 'not world-guided' itself suggests, what this means is that Williams does not think judgements using concepts like 'ought' are objective.[3] Thus, as far as he is concerned, there is no objective subject-matter for an 'ethical theory' to be about. So even if such theories were not reductionist, they would still be misguided in so far as they purported to tell us what

---

[2] The relevant writings by McDowell have been collected in his *Mind, Value, and Reality* (Cambridge, MA: Harvard University Press, 1998).

[3] The kind of objectivity that Williams has in mind when he denies that such judgements are objective will be specified in Section IV.

we ought to do. Perhaps because he has this second reason for his anti-theoretical position, Williams is not motivated seriously to pursue the question of whether there can in fact be ethical theories which tell us in general terms what we should do, but which are not reductionist; he seems simply to assume that any such theory *must* be reductionist. I believe, however, that there are at least two reasons why the idea of non-reductionist theories should be taken seriously. First, as we have already seen, the charge that the most familiar ethical theories reduce the thick ethical concepts to the thin is too coarse-grained as it stands to be credible. There may perhaps be some ethical theories that are crudely reductionist, but there are others that take quite seriously a wide range of ethical concepts of varying degrees of specificity and apparent 'world-guidedness'.[4] Second, the motivation for seeking an ethical theory need not be reductionist at all. It need not be a wish to reduce all types of ethical considerations to just one basic type. Instead, it may be a wish to understand what one ought, ethically speaking, to do, in situations where, as often happens, various relatively specific ethical considerations that apply seem to have conflicting implications for action. And while it is true that reducing the conflicting considerations to some putatively more basic type of consideration represents one strategy for answering such questions, it is Williams himself who denies (17) that reduction provides the only model for understanding how we can rationally resolve deliberative questions involving diverse considerations.

The second line of thought suggested by Williams's discussion of thickness, reflection, and objectivity, is this. Up to a point, the distinction between thick and thin may appeal to Williams partly because it may seem to provide a way of reconciling two apparently unharmonious aspects of his overall view. The first is his respect for the complexity and human importance of the ethical life, and his desire to preserve it. The second is his ethical scepticism. The first of these is manifested not only in his antireductionism, but also in his insistence, which we will examine shortly, on the possibility of serious ethical criticism of oppressive social practices and institutions. The second is manifested in his doubts about the objectivity of ethics. Now clearly there is the potential for conflict between these two aspects of his thought, and Williams sometimes seems to use the distinction between thick and thin as a vehicle for minimizing such conflict. Roughly, the richness and variety of ethical life are associated with the prevalence of thick concepts, while the lack of ethical objectivity consists in the fact that judgements that use thin ethical concepts are not objective. However the claim that reflection can destroy knowledge reveals the precariousness of this construction. Williams says that 'the urge to reflective understanding of society and our activities goes deeper and is more widely spread in modern society than it has ever been before'

---

[4] Interestingly enough, even one of the paradigmatic thick concepts cited by Williams, the concept of a *promise*, has received considerable attention in contemporary ethical theory.

(163), and he adds that '[t]here is no route back from reflectiveness' (163). These points, together with the idea that reflection tends to destroy know-ledge in ethics, seem to imply that we have less ethical knowledge all the time, and that the prospects for the survival of a recognizable ethical life are bleak. As against this, Williams suggests that some thick concepts can 'stand up to reflection' (200), so that we may not run out of ethical knowledge entirely. He also suggests that '[e]thical knowledge . . . is not necessarily the best eth-ical state' (168) anyway, and that what is more important is something he calls ethical *confidence*, which one can have without knowledge. And he tends to regard the question of how some thick concepts can manage to stand up to reflection, or of why reflection should not destroy confidence as surely as it destroys knowledge, as questions that philosophy is incompetent to answer. In part, he thinks, the answers can come only through 'reflective living' (200). And such theoretical understanding as there is to be had on these topics will likely come not from philosophy but from the social sciences, which may tell us, for example, 'what kinds of institutions, upbringing, and public dis-course help to foster' (170) confidence.

I believe that there is an instability in Williams's position that these remarks do not really come to grips with. His repudiation, on grounds of non-objectivity and misguided reductionism, of the theoretical structures produced by reflection, leaves him with ethical resources that are inadequate to the tasks of social criticism he himself wishes to engage in. One of his main themes, of course, is that there is a 'tension . . . between reflection and practice' (197). However true this may be in general, it applies with particular force to Williams himself: there is indeed a tension, to say the least, between his own reflective scepticism about the powers of ethical reflection, and his own evident crit-ical practice. In other words, Williams's scepticism about ethical theorizing has a price, in terms of his ability consistently to engage in ethical criticism, which is higher than he acknowledges or seems willing to pay. In the next two sections I shall try to make good these claims.

II

Williams says that 'the drive to theory has roots in ethical thought itself' (111). In particular, he argues, it is the strand in ethical thought that 'seeks *justificatory reasons*' (112) that leads to ethical theory. The justificatory urge involves a wish to see our ethical life as endorsable from a standpoint external to it.[5] It leads us to demand good reasons for the ethical practices we engage

---

[5] It is worth noting, in this connection, that Williams describes Aristotle as believ-ing that the ethical life of a virtuous person can be endorsed from a point of view external to that life (52). Thus in this respect Williams's repudiation of ethical theory can claim no inspiration from the Aristotelian tradition. On the contrary, this is a place where he parts company from them both.

in and the ethical distinctions we draw, and it is this demand for justifying reasons that leads us to theory: to a search for principles capable of either 'supporting' our existing practices and distinctions, or 'requiring' changes in those practices and distinctions. In this way, the justificatory urge becomes the theoretical impulse in ethics.

Williams is not optimistic about the extent to which demands for ethical justification can be met. The quest for 'linear', or foundational, justifications is straightforwardly misguided, and the possibilities of providing even less ambitiously conceived justifications are, at the very least, limited:

We may be able to show how a given practice hangs together with other practices in a way that makes social and psychological sense. But we may not be able to find anything that will meet a demand for justification made by someone standing outside those practices. We may not be able, in any real sense, to justify it even to ourselves. A practice may be so directly related to our experience that the reason it provides will simply count as stronger than any reason that might be advanced for it.   (Williams, *Ethics and the Limits of Philosophy*, 114)

It is not clear, from this passage, how much room Williams means to leave for justification in ethics, or what form he thinks it can legitimately take. As we know, he believes that 'philosophy should not try to produce ethical theory' (17), and his diagnosis of ethical theory sees it as arising out of the justificatory urge. He is thus committed to repudiating what is at least one form that that urge can take. The question that remains is what scope there may be for justification that does not take the form of ethical theorizing. It is important for Williams's position, I think, that there should be some such scope. This is so for two reasons. First, since the justificatory urge is as deep and pervasive a human phenomenon as it appears to be, it would be very awkward for a philosopher whose book is about the limits of philosophy's ability to direct ethical thought to find himself in the position of recommending a form of ethical thought supposedly purged of any justificatory ambitions or potential. Second, the idea that existing ethical practices and distinctions can *never* legitimately be subject to justificatory scrutiny embodies such an extreme conservatism that Williams could not possibly regard it as congenial. And, indeed, he insists that '[n]othing that has been said should lead us to think that traditional distinctions are beyond criticism; practices that make distinctions between different groups of people may certainly demand justification, if we are not to be content with unreflective traditions which can provide paradigms of prejudice' (115).

As I understand it, Williams's answer to the question of what form justification can legitimately take involves appeal to a form of ethical thought that seeks 'reflective social knowledge' (199). This form of thought 'asks for understanding of our motives, psychological or social insight into our ethical practices, and while that may call for some kinds of theory, ethical theory is not among them' (112). The quest for reflective social knowledge can enable us to 'carry out the kind of critique that gives ethical insight into institutions through explanations of how they work and, in particular, of how they generate belief in themselves' (199). And Williams believes that this gives us the resources to engage in the kind of ethically informed social criticism that he regards as appropriate. He writes: 'A respect for freedom and social justice and a critique of oppressive and deceitful institutions may be no easier to achieve than they have been in the past, and may well be harder, but we need not suppose that we have no ideas to give them a basis. We should not concede to abstract ethical theory its claim to provide the only intellectual surroundings for such ideas' (198).

Despite what Williams says, I doubt whether he has left himself enough resources to do the tasks of criticism that he regards as necessary. I do not believe that, if the conceptual repertoire associated with ethical theorizing is simply abandoned, the forms of thought involved in the quest for reflective social knowledge, important as they undeniably are, can by themselves provide an adequate alternative medium for such criticism. In order to explain the basis for my reservations, I want to examine some remarks Williams makes about racism and sexism, and also his exemption of justice from a doctrine he calls 'the relativism of distance'.

III

In the course of his discussion of justification, Williams considers an argument which purports to show that ethical theory is simply 'a product of the demand for rationality' (115). The argument is that the familiar forms of racial and sexual discrimination are irrational, and that their irrationality cannot be exposed without justificatory scrutiny of the reasons for the discriminatory practices: scrutiny of a kind that must inevitably invoke theory. In response, Williams considers four different examples of people engaging in discriminatory practices. One of these is said to involve no irrationality at all. This is the case of someone for whom, say, 'being a woman' is simply in itself a sufficient reason for discrimination. This person's discriminatory conduct is 'wrong, because unjust' (115), but it is not irrational. The other three cases do, Williams says, involve some irrationality, but not irrationality that consists in a failure to accept a rationally compelling theory. The first of these is the case of someone who 'inconsistently counts intelligence and reliability as supposedly sufficient grounds for hiring a man and refuses to do so when considering a woman' (115–16). The second is the case, roughly, of someone whose discriminatory practice is self-defeating because it undermines his own goals, by, say, depriving him of effective employees. The third is the case of someone who is self-deceived and does not admit or recognize that 'she's a woman' or 'he's a black' is his real reason for acting as he does. The upshot of these four examples is supposed to be that racism and sexism need not involve any irrationality at all; and where they do, the irrationality does not consist in resistance to a rationally compelling theory. Thus, Williams concludes, the argument he is examining fails to show that considerations of rationality are sufficient by themselves to drive us to ethical theory.

Even if *this* conclusion is granted, however, Williams's four examples and his discussion of them seem inadvertently to cast doubt on the possibility of saying everything he himself would want to say about the ethics of discrimination without using the conceptual resources of the morality system. Notice first that Williams's remark about discrimination being 'wrong because unjust' uses at least one thin ethical concept and sounds for all the world like a conventional judgement made from within the morality system. But what is perhaps even more revealing is the case of the self-deceived racist or sexist. This example is meant to serve Williams's purposes, not only by depicting a kind of irrationality which can be involved in discrimination and which consists in something other than resistance to a rationally compelling theory, but also by suggesting that the kind of ethical reflection that seeks insight into people's motives may actually generate a more telling critique of their practice than ethical theorizing could. Without in any way denying the importance of this kind of insight, however, it should be pointed out that there is another salient feature of the case that is much less helpful to Williams's position. It makes sense for the person in the example to conceal his real (racist or sexist) reasons from himself or others only in a world where the substantive ethical consensus is that those reasons are objectionable. There was a time, and not so long ago, when such reasons were considered perfectly respectable, and nobody had to bother deceiving anyone about having them. If that has changed, so that discriminatory motivation has now been driven socially and psychologically underground, in some quarters at least, that is because substantive ethical ideas about the rightness and wrongness of discrimination have changed: in particular, it is now widely believed to be 'wrong because unjust'. And if there is any scheme of abstract ethical thought that has had a part in effecting that change, it is surely the morality system. It is certainly not the thought of the ancient Greeks, and neither is it the alternative form of justificatory reflection that Williams recommends.

It may be wondered at this point whether Williams is really committed to a repudiation of the morality system which is so thoroughgoing as to make it illegitimate for him to use any of the concepts or substantive ideas associated with it. His objection, it may be suggested, is to the basic orientation of the morality system and to the kind of theorizing it generates, but he is not committed to rejecting its entire conceptual apparatus. In support of this suggestion it may be noted that, in addition to the remark about the wrongness of discrimination quoted above, Williams offers an account of his own of the nature of obligation (182–7), and he appears happy to talk, for example, about 'basic human rights' (192) and their violation.

However, while it is certainly true that Williams does talk in these ways, I must confess that I find it quite puzzling when he does. A view one *might* have is that ethical theory is legitimate provided it is non-reductionist, and provided that among the various ethical concepts it recognizes are certain particular concepts which were emphasized by the Greeks and others, but which have been neglected in much recent ethical thought. On such a view there would be no objection to retaining in addition some of the concepts associated with the morality system, such as the concept of human rights or the concept of wrongness, as Williams apparently wants to. The difficulty with this view is simply that it is not the one Williams argues for. His claim is not that ethical theory is valuable provided it is non-reductionist; what he says is that 'philosophy should not try to produce ethical theory' (17), and that 'reflective criticism should basically go in a direction opposite to that encouraged by ethical theory' (116). As we have seen, he seems both to assume that ethical theory is inherently reductionist, and to think that even if it weren't it would still be misguided because of its lack of an objective subject-matter.

It may be suggested that although Williams is opposed to *theorizing* about, say, rights, that does not mean he must stop talking about them altogether. However I find this suggestion mysterious. If the idea is that it is legitimate to invoke rights in ethical discourse, but illegitimate to reflect about what rights people have, or about what one ought to do when rights conflict with other ethical considerations, then it seems to me to have little to recommend it. And I do not know how else to understand it.

In fact I think there is a deep difficulty here for Williams. He claims that we would be better off without the morality system, its theories, and its relentless demands for justification. But he is also committed to specific substantive ethical positions which have been produced by the morality system and validated by its theories. And he provides no reason for thinking that those substantive ethical features of the modern world that he wants to retain can be separated from the processes of theoretical reflection that he deplores.

Another symptom of this instability in his position emerges in connection with his discussion of justice. Williams is drawn to the idea that the concept of justice may have a special status in ethical thought. The appeal to him of this idea derives, at least in part, from the fact that he is firmly committed to certain substantive ideas about justice that are characteristic of the modern world; he is therefore concerned to provide the language of justice and injustice with an especially secure place in our critical lexicon. The specific suggestion he makes is that justice may be an exception to a doctrine he calls 'the relativism of distance'. This doctrine is defined in terms of a distinction Williams draws between 'real' and 'notional' confrontations. He writes, 'a real confrontation between two divergent outlooks occurs at a given time if there is a group of people for whom each of the outlooks is a real option. A notional confrontation, by contrast, occurs when some people know about two divergent outlooks, but at least one of those outlooks does not present a real option'

(160). The relativism of distance is a doctrine that says, of a given kind of outlook, that it is only in real confrontations that the language of appraisal is correctly applied to opposing outlooks. Judgement should be suspended with respect to the outlooks of those with whom one is in only notional confrontation. Williams is generally sympathetic to the relativism of distance as a view about ethical outlooks, but he finds the suggestion that justice in particular 'transcends' (166) this form of relativism tempting.

The suggestion that justice transcends the relativism of distance, as Williams seems to intend it, amounts to the claim that we may appropriately appraise as just or unjust societies with which we are only in notional confrontation: in particular, societies that are temporally quite remote from ours.[6] But this claim itself is much weaker than Williams appears to recognize. It authorizes us to use a certain form of words in talking about temporally distant societies, but that is all it does. What it certainly does not do is to secure the possibility of truth or objectivity for the judgements we make about the justice or injustice of those societies. Nor does it secure for our judgements of justice and injustice any sort of privilege at all as compared with conflicting judgements made from the vantage point of the remote societies themselves. To see why not, we may recall first that there is an unresolved question about whether 'justice' is a thin or a thick concept as far as Williams is concerned. In any case, he believes that '[w]e have various conceptions of social justice, with different political consequences' (166). This means that people who have the concept of justice will nevertheless disagree about its application even in central cases, and to the extent that they do, that, for Williams, suggests that the concept of justice is not 'world-guided'. This implies that even if two groups of people have divergent conceptions of justice that are in *real* confrontation, and even if each group is thus straightforwardly entitled to make judgements of justice about the other, none of those judgements can be objectively correct or incorrect. For if a concept is not world-guided, that is just to say, for Williams, that substantive disagreements about its application do not admit of objective resolutions. And this explains why the suggestion that justice transcends the relativism of distance is so weak. In allowing us to appraise as just or unjust societies with which we are only in notional confrontation, it assimilates notional confrontations about justice to real confrontations. But even real confrontations about justice have no objective resolutions. So, to speak figuratively, the suggestion that justice transcends the relativism of distance allows temporally remote societies with divergent conceptions of justice to call each other names, just as societies that are

---

[6] Williams focuses exclusively on temporal remoteness because he believes that spatial remoteness is, in the conditions of the modern world, never a weighty enough factor to bring the relativism of distance into play. He writes, 'Relativism over merely spatial distance is of no interest or application in the modern world. Today all confrontations between cultures must be real confrontations, and the existence of exotic traditional societies presents quite different, and difficult, issues of whether the rest of the world can or should use power to preserve them, like endangered species; anthropological and other field workers find themselves in the role of game wardens' (163).

contemporaries do, instead of simply glaring at each other in silence across the temporal divide; but it provides no basis whatsoever for regarding one side's ideas as right or the other's as wrong. Thus to the extent that the suggestion is motivated by Williams's attachment to certain modern ideas about justice, and by his desire to provide a distinctive basis for the use of those ideas in criticism of actual social practices and institutions, it must be accounted a failure. Once again, his sympathy for an important substantive position associated with the modern ethical consciousness comes into conflict with his scepticism about the ultimate objectivity of modern ethical ideas, and his attempts to reconcile the two fall short of success.

Before leaving the subject of justice, it is worth mentioning one other strand in Williams's remarks on the topic. He cites with approval what he calls the 'critical-theory test' (221), which consists in asking whether the acceptance in a society of a conception of justice that legitimates the distribution of power in that society is or is not 'an effect of the power it was supposed to legitimate' (166). The critical-theory test, he seems to think, can be used to generate a critique of a society's ideas about justice which does not depend on the prior acceptance of any controversial ethical notions. A critique of this kind simply exposes the conception of justice prevailing in a given society as a deceitful myth whose real function is to disguise the raw exercise of power. In this way, it can be viewed as the analogue on the social level of that critique on the individual level which consists in exposing the real motivations of the deceitful racist. In the social case as in the individual case, Williams is eager to emphasize the justificatory potential of this kind of criticism, because such criticism appears not to depend on theorizing of the sort associated with the morality system, and because it therefore seems to confirm his claim that there can be reflective justificatory thought in ethics even if ethical theory is repudiated. As in the individual case, however, the difficulty with this sort of critique is not that it is an invalid or unimportant critical tool, but rather that it is not the only critical tool we ever need to use. Since, as Williams himself insists, different groups of people genuinely hold divergent conceptions of justice, occasions sometimes arise when what we most want to say about some opposing conception is, not that it is fraudulent, deceitful or insincerely held, but rather that it is wrong. Williams's own sense that this is so is one of the things that leads him to suggest that justice may transcend the relativism of distance. As I have already argued, however, that suggestion fails to provide any objective basis for adjudication among conflicting conceptions of justice, and the critical-theory test in itself is of no help at all in that regard.

IV

If it is true that there is a conflict between the repudiation of ethical theorizing and the desire to engage in ethical criticism of oppressive social institutions, then is the correct conclusion that ethical theorizing should not be repudiated, or that there is no valid basis for such criticism? Obviously, the answer to this question depends on the force of those considerations that motivate the repudiation of ethical theory. As we saw in Section I, Williams rejects ethical theory both on the ground that it is reductionist and on the ground that it has no objective subject-matter. I have already expressed reservations about the first of these considerations. As for the second, Williams's doubts about ethical objectivity are formulated, as we have seen, in a way that depends on the distinction between thick and thin ethical concepts. And since, as we have also seen, that distinction is itself flawed, the force of his doubts about objectivity is already open to question.

Even if one takes a distinction between thick and thin for granted, however, Williams's case against objectivity in ethics is far from conclusive.[7] Obviously, the whole issue of ethical objectivity is intensely controversial, and many of the considerations on each side are very familiar. Those who deny the objectivity of ethics will most likely find Williams's characteristically acute discussion highly sympathetic, but I doubt that his arguments will change many minds. One of his most original contributions to the anti-objectivist position involves a distinction he draws between two different forms of objectivity that might be claimed for ethics, and an argument based on that distinction. The first form of objectivity is modelled on the objectivity of science. Central to this model, he says, is the idea of reflective investigation producing 'convergence on a body of ethical truths which is brought about and explained by the fact that they are truths' (151–2). It is this form of objectivity that Williams thinks ethics clearly lacks, and the lack of which he means to be asserting when he claims that the thin ethical concepts are not world-guided. The second form of objectivity involves the idea that 'ethical life [has] an objective and determinate grounding in considerations about human nature' (153). Williams doubts that ethics actually has this second form of objectivity any more than it has the first, but he at least regards it as an intelligible possibility. If this form of objectivity did obtain, that would mean that 'a certain kind of life was best for human beings' (154), and that leading such a life involved having certain ethical beliefs. However, he argues, this would not imply that the first form of objectivity also obtained, for what would have been established is not the *truth* of those ethical beliefs, but only the desirability of having a 'disposition to accept' (199) them.[8] Thus, Williams concludes, there 'would be a radical difference between ethics and science, even if ethics were objective in the only way in which it intelligibly could be' (155).

---

[7] This requires the assumption, of course, that there is some characterization of the distinction between thick and thin concepts that does not make it definitional of thin concepts that they are not objective.

[8] This is related to another important claim Williams makes, which is that people's dispositions 'are the ultimate supports of ethical value' (51).

This argument against the legitimacy of a move from the second form of ethical objectivity to the first applies primarily to judgements involving those ethical concepts Williams regards as thin. For, as he says, if there were an objectively best kind of life, that fact itself would count as a very general ethical truth. It would also license the objective judgement that some thick concepts were the best ones to use. And judgements involving particular thick concepts 'are very often known to be true anyway, even when they occur, as they always have, in a life that is not grounded at the objective level' (154). With respect to all of the foregoing judgements, therefore, it is difficult to see why the 'scientific' model of objectivity would be inappropriate.

As applied to judgements involving the sorts of ethical concepts Williams regards as thin, the argument against the legitimacy of a move from the second form of objectivity to the first seems to me to rely on unduly restrictive assumptions about the possible relations between such judgements and an objective conception of the good life. The idea, I take it, is that in order for someone to live a good life, that person might have to believe, for example, that certain things were wrong, but those things would not have actually to *be* wrong. However, if there *were* an objectively correct conception of the good life for human beings, it is imaginable that any of the following *might* be a condition of living such a life:

(1) that one believe the statement, 'killing innocent people is wrong';
(2) that one never in fact kill an innocent person;
(3) that one accept and abide by a rule prohibiting the killing of innocent people.

The argument against a move from the second form of objectivity to the first seems plausible so long as one focuses only on possibilities like (1). But (2) and (3) also represent genuine possibilities. And what is interesting about (2) and (3) is that they suggest possible understandings of wrongness that would appear to make it a 'scientifically' objective notion. Thus consider:

(2') An act is wrong iff its performance would be incompatible with the agent's living a good life;
(3') An act is wrong iff its performance is prohibited by a rule it is necessary (or, perhaps, rational) to abide by if one is (or, perhaps, wants) to live a good life.

Now if there were an objectively correct conception of the good life for human beings, and if items like (2) or (3) were conditions of living such a life, then, on construals like (2') or (3'), things like killing the innocent would actually be wrong. And the best explanation of any convergence on a belief in the wrongness of killing the innocent might very well make reference to the actual wrongness of such killing. Hence a move from the second form of objectivity to the first would on these assumptions be legitimate.

I raise these possibilities not because I am in fact convinced that there is a best life for human beings, or because I am convinced that notions like wrongness should be construed on the model of (2′) or (3′). I raise them instead because, as I have indicated, Williams's distinction between the two forms of ethical objectivity, together with his argument against moving from the second to the first, constitutes one of his most original contributions to the case against ethical objectivism. The possibilities I have mentioned are just examples which are intended to show that, even if the overall framework of his discussion is taken for granted, including a distinction between thick and thin concepts, Williams's argument still leaves objectivists room for man-œuvre. It should additionally be noted, in this connection, that even if there were *no* objectively correct conception of the good life for man, but only various competing ideals, some aspects of the 'scientific' model of objectiv-ity might still be applicable. For example, even if the wrongness of killing the innocent were taken to be a matter of its incompatibility, not with the objectively best life, but rather with a certain (non-universal) ideal of the good life, the fact that such killing was indeed incompatible with that ideal might still serve to explain a convergence in belief about the wrongness of killing among those who shared the ideal. Whether this degree of objectivity would be sufficient to make ethical theorizing appropriate seems to me a wide open question.

Conclusion

Williams's description of the morality system is an excellent caricature. In saying this, of course, I am using 'caricature' not as a term of abuse, but rather in the sense most closely associated with the form of pictorial representation to which the word refers. So understood, a caricature is a representation of a subject which, by exaggerating certain actual features of the subject, man-ages to accomplish at least two things: to make the subject instantly recog-nizable, and, simultaneously, to get us to see the importance to the subject's character of the exaggerated features. Often, but not always, this is done with the intent of exposing or unmasking something less attractive in the subject than what is conveyed by more conventional representations.

It is in this sense that Williams's description of the morality system is an excellent caricature. Through exaggeration, in other words, he calls attention to some real and very important features of contemporary ethical thought, features which are often overlooked. And he does this with revelatory intent: with the aim of getting us to see modern morality in a new way, to see how much it takes for granted that is not obvious, how much it neglects that is not trivial. In all of this he is strikingly successful, and his book challenges us, as so much of Williams's work has always done, to think more deeply and more fundamentally about our ethical ideas than we are accustomed to doing, or than most moral philosophy encourages us to do. To the extent that our ethical ideas are indeed distanced from psychological and social realities, to the extent that they substitute excellences of intellectual structure for sensitivity to human complexity, we are forced to worry both about whether these defects can be remedied, and about what our tendency to overlook them says about us and our world. At the same time, even excellent caricatures do exaggerate. And if modern ethical thought, for all its faults, has helped to produce many of the features of the modern world that most deserve our support and allegiance, we would do well not to repudiate it unless we absolutely have to, or else unless we are very sure that we have something better to put in its place.

INDEX